ACTING

READINGS IN THEATRE PRACTICE

Series Editor: Simon Shepherd

VOICE
Jane Boston

SOUND
Joss Brown

CLOWN
Jon Davison

PUPPETRY
Penny Francis

COSTUME
Alison Maclaurin and Aoife Monks

PROPS
Eleanor Margolies

LIGHT
Scott Palmer

DIRECTION
Simon Shepherd

STAGE MANAGEMENT: COMMUNICATION DESIGN AS SCENOGRAPHY
Michael Smalley

Forthcoming:

TRAINING ACTORS: KEYWORDS AND CONCEPTS
John Matthews

OPEN-AIR THEATRE: CONCEPTS AND PERFORMANCE PRACTICES
Evelyn O'Malley and Cathy Turner

MAGIC: THE PERFORMANCE PRACTICES OF CONJURING ILLUSION
Nik Taylor

ACTING

KEYWORDS AND CONCEPTS

John Matthews

methuen | drama
LONDON · NEW YORK · OXFORD · NEW DELHI · SYDNEY

METHUEN DRAMA
Bloomsbury Publishing Plc, 50 Bedford Square, London, WC1B 3DP, UK
Bloomsbury Publishing Inc, 1359 Broadway, New York, NY 10018, USA
Bloomsbury Publishing Ireland, 29 Earlsfort Terrace, Dublin 2, D02 AY28, Ireland

BLOOMSBURY, METHUEN DRAMA and the Methuen Drama logo are trademarks of Bloomsbury Publishing Plc

First published in Great Britain 2026

Copyright © John Matthews, 2026

John Matthews has asserted his right under the Copyright, Designs and Patents Act, 1988, to be identified as author of this work.

For legal purposes the Acknowledgements on p. xxv constitute an extension of this copyright page.

Series design: Ben Anslow
Cover image © CasarsaGuru/iStock

All rights reserved. No part of this publication may be: i) reproduced or transmitted in any form, electronic or mechanical, including photocopying, recording or by means of any information storage or retrieval system without prior permission in writing from the publishers; or ii) used or reproduced in any way for the training, development or operation of artificial intelligence (AI) technologies, including generative AI technologies. The rights holders expressly reserve this publication from the text and data mining exception as per Article 4(3) of the Digital Single Market Directive (EU) 2019/790.

Bloomsbury Publishing Plc does not have any control over, or responsibility for, any third-party websites referred to or in this book. All internet addresses given in this book were correct at the time of going to press. The author and publisher regret any inconvenience caused if addresses have changed or sites have ceased to exist, but can accept no responsibility for any such changes.

A catalogue record for this book is available from the British Library.

A catalog record for this book is available from the Library of Congress.

ISBN: HB: 978-1-3503-8723-2
PB: 978-1-3503-8722-5
ePDF: 978-1-3503-8724-9
eBook: 978-1-3503-8725-6

Series: Readings in Theatre Practice

Typeset by Integra Software Services Pvt. Ltd
Printed and bound in Great Britain

For product safety related questions contact productsafety@bloomsbury.com.

To find out more about our authors and books visit www.bloomsbury.com and sign up for our newsletters.

For my mother and father, with love.

CONTENTS

Series Preface — viii
Preface: What is Acting? — x
How and Why to Read *Acting: Keywords and Concepts* — xxiii
Acknowledgements — xxv

1 Actor — 1

2 Character — 7

3 Body — 16

4 Play — 24

5 Movement — 30

6 Emotion — 32

7 Truth & Truthfulness — 39

8 Voice — 50

9 Actress — 56

10 Imagination — 61

11 Status — 71

12 Believeable — 77

13 Authenticity — 81

14 A Statistically Irrelevant Keyword — 85

How and Why to Write *Acting: Keywords and Concepts* — 91
The Catalogue — 110
Bibliography — 114

SERIES PREFACE

This series aims to gather together both key historical texts and contemporary ways of thinking about the material crafts and practices of theatre.

These crafts work with the physical materials of theatre – sound, objects, light, paint, fabric and – yes – physical bodies. Out of these materials the theatre event is created.

In gathering the key texts of a craft it becomes very obvious that the craft is not simply a handling of materials, however skilful. It is also a way of thinking about both the materials and their processes of handling. Work with sound and objects, for example, involves – always, at some level – concepts of what sound is and does, what an object is and does … what a body is.

For many areas of theatre practice there are the sorts of 'how to do it' books that have been published for at least a century. These range widely in quality and interest but next to none of them is able to, or wants to, position the doing in relation to the thinking about doing or the thinking about the material being used.

This series of books aims to promote both thinking about doing and thinking about materials. Its authors are specialists in their field of practice and they are charged to reflect on their specialism and its history in order, often for the first time, to model concepts and provide the tools not just for the doing but for thinking about theatre practice.

The series title 'Readings in Theatre Practice' uses the word 'reading' in the sense both of a simple understanding or interpretation and of an authoritative explication, an exegesis as it were. Thus, the books first gather together people's opinions about, their understanding of, what they think they are making. These opinions are then framed within a broader narrative which offers an explanatory overview of the practice under investigation.

So, although the books comprise many different voices, there is a dominant authorial voice organizing the material and articulating overarching arguments. By way of promoting a further level of critique and reflection, however, authors are asked to include a few lengthy sections, in the form of interviews or essays or both, in order to make space for other voices to develop their own overviews. These may sit in tension, or indeed in harmony, with the dominant narratives.

Authors are encouraged to be sceptical about normative assumptions and canonical orthodoxy. They are asked not to ignore practices and thinking that might question dominant views; they are invited to speculate as to how canons and norms come into being and what effects they have.

We hope the shape provides a dynamic tension in which the different activities of 'reading' both assist and resist each other. The details of the lived practices refuse to fit tidily into the straitjacket of a general argument, but the dominant overview also refuses to allow itself to fragment into local prejudice and anecdote. And it's that restless play between assistance and resistance that mirrors the character of the practices themselves.

At the heart of each craft is a tense relationship. On the one hand there is the basic raw material that is worked – the wood, the light, the paint, the musculature. These have their own given identity – their weight, mechanical logics, smell, particle formation, feel. In short, the texture of the stuff. And on the other hand there is theatre, wanting its effects and illusions, its distortions and impossibilities. The raw material resists the theatre as much as yields to it, the theatre both develops the material and learns from it. The stuff and the magic. This relationship is perhaps what defines the very activity of theatre itself.

It is this relationship, the thing which defines the practice of theatre, which lies at the heart of each book in this series.

Simon Shepherd

PREFACE: WHAT IS ACTING?

'Acting' is the most recognizable, accessible and culturally-valued activity in the field of drama. Everybody knows what 'acting' is and yet there is significant disagreement and debate over how it should be defined, categorized, theorized, taught, practised, researched and understood. Some have proposed or subscribed to totalizing theories and systems of acting and some have contested the very premise of such encompassing conceptualization, asserting instead the cultural, historical and stylistic specificity and idiosyncrasy of acting in any given context. Like all contested phenomena, 'acting' has many contestable origin myths. In the Western canon, foremost amongst these might be the Antique poet, singer and choral story-teller who was either the very first 'actor' in history or a rather minor bit-part in one dramatic tradition (Fletcher, 2022: 4–5). The former version, the mythic Thespis, stepped aside from the dithyrambic chorus – an ancient Greek hymn honouring the god of festivals, festivities and debauchery or bacchanalia (this god being Bacchus to the Romans or Dionysus to the Greeks) – to speak directly as the characters of the song rather than indirectly about them, as a storyteller. This version invented Character and Tragedy and provided the first properly viable commercial template for theatre yet is remembered mostly for giving his name to a largely derogatory slang word for actors – *thesps*. In the other version, Thespis as proto-luvvy is recast as something like a miscredited 'swing' – the substitute performer who goes on stage when a principal cast member is ill or unavailable (see Eyer and Smith, 2015: 3–5).

All mythic stories can be interpreted in at least two ways but the double-facedness of acting, often simplistically reduced to the Antique Greek iconography of the masks of tragedy and comedy (which Thespis may or may not have worn) is most emphatically expressed in the mythology of another ancient thesp: Polus.

There are some stories about 'acting' so central to the 'Western' acting canon that if they were not true it would be necessary to invent them, and the Polus tale is certainly one of these. This is not to say that this apocryphal tale is not true – as the Classics scholar, Leofranc Holfrod-Strevens put it, we do not have 'any reason to cast doubt on it save a puritanical *a priori* prejudice against good stories' (2005: 499) – but rather that its meaning has transcended its historical significance. The story of the antique actor playing Electra on the Athenian stage and using a prop urn containing the ashes of his own dead son to provoke real tears, in his own eyes as well as that multitude of spectating peepers is such an apposite and useful anecdote that were it not historical fact it would necessarily become instructional fiction.

Polus-as-Electra wept over beloved-son-as-Orestes. Or perhaps it was Electra-as-Polus who cried for Orestes-as-Son. Perhaps it was the pathetic ambiguity between

Polus and Electra, son and Orestes, that made the assembled audience cry along; it was certainly this ambiguity that made the audience howl with laughter when Moliere collapsed on stage in role as the eponymous *hypochondriac* (but that's another apocryphal tale altogether).

The Polus tale has been used to mean a great many things over the course of two centuries of theorizing about acting and the only thing that has dampened its potency is its ubiquity. 'Ah, not that old chestnut!', I find myself thinking each time I encounter it anew in yet another book on acting. Indeed, I tell it twice – once in this preface and again in the final chapter of this book. This is because one of the principal aims of this book is to defamiliarize knowledge about 'acting' and enable fresh perspectives on the phenomenon; while there is no requirement to read this book cover-to-cover in linear order there is a 'before' and 'after' image of acting here, and readers will need to witness the transformation in the middle.

What is almost more noteworthy than where and how the tale is told with regards to acting theory and practice is where it is *not* told, seeing as its absence might seem to some more like an omission; like a missing or stolen artefact from an important collection whose removal is made more conspicuous than its presence by a gap in the display case and the dusty outline and un-sun-bleached imprint of its shape on an otherwise faded baize. This is why it was surprising, to me, at least, to find that one of very few key voices in the 'Western' canon of acting theory *not*[1] to retell this story seems to be its most famous and quintessential voice, and the one whose personal viewpoint on acting is most strongly reinforced by the Polus myth – Konstantin Stanislavski.

Although no consistent scholarly work has been done to establish the full curriculum that a young Stanislavski would have encountered at the Lazarevsky Institute where he was schooled it seems likely that he would have studied both business and the Indo-European language roots of Russian and Armenian, which would have included study of classic Greek language texts.[2] Given his well-documented auto-didactism in the libraries and museums of Europe, coupled with his ardent interest in theatre and the arts, it seems diminishingly unlikely that Stanislavski would not have encountered the tale of Polus during his education and research. Indeed, both Benedetti ([1990] 1999: 221) and Magarshack ([1950] 2011: 336–37) place him in a Marienbad library in the summer of 1914, where his studies encompassed Riccoboni, Coquelin, Lessing, Goethe, Schiller and Diderot whose iconic work on acting theory, *Paradoxe sur le Comedien*, which would undoubtedly have been of the keenest interest to Stanislavski, is closed with a summary vivisection of the tale:

Second Speaker. You know that of old male actors used to play female parts?

First Speaker. Yes, I know.

Second Speaker. Aulus Gellius relates in his *Attic Nights* that a certain Polus, wrapped in Electra's mourning garments, instead of coming on stage with Orestes' urn, appeared holding the urn containing the ashes of his own son, whom he had just lost, and that what followed was no empty imitation, a little grief for show, but the hall echoed with cries and genuine groans.

First Speaker. And do you think that Polus at that moment spoke on stage as he would have spoken at home? No, no. That prodigious effect, which I don't doubt took place, was not due either to Euripides' lines or to the actor's delivery, but to the sight of a grieving father who was bathing in his tears his own son's urn. Perhaps that Polus was only a mediocre actor, no better than that Aesopus of whom Plutarch relates that 'when one day he was playing onstage the part of Atreus debating with himself how he may be avenged on his brother Thyestes, there happened to be a servant of his who suddenly decided to run across in front of him, and he, Aesopus, being beside himself owing to his violent emotion and his zeal to play Atreus' raging passion to the life, gave him such a blow on the head with the sceptre he was holding in his hand that he killed him on the spot...'. Call that an actor? He was a madman whom the tribune ought to have dispatched there and then to the Tarpeian rock.[...]

'But', it is said, 'an orator is worth more when he becomes warm, when he is angry.' I deny it. It is when he imitates anger. Actors make an impression on the audience, not when they are mad, but when they play madness well. In the courts, in meetings, everywhere where anyone wishes to master men's minds, he feigns now anger, now fear, now pity, to induce those various feelings in the others. What passion itself could not do, passion well imitated achieves.

Stanislavski was not given to citing sources in his written works, reserving quotations mostly for Shakespeare, Russian literature and the odd paraphrase of Ribot but under the guise of his sublimated nom de plume, Tortsov, he was an inveterate anecdotalist. *An Actor Prepares,* in particular, is riddled with Tortsovian advice reiterating Hamlet's similarly mythic guidance to the players to *not-ham-it-up-but-also-don't-undersell-it.* (I believe that Shakespeare's words were something more like, *nor-do-not-saw-the-air-too-much-with-your-hand-thus-but-use-all-gently* but, *a rose by any other name,* and all that.)

Perhaps Stanislavski simply didn't finish reading Diderot's book. This was 1914 after all and Stanislavski was fleeing Germany as war broke out. An escape by train which, according to Stanislavski and his biographer Magarshack, saw him nearly executed twice en route, once reprieved by virtue of having played for Kaiser Wilhelm and once for lack of ammunition (Magarshack, 1950: 338). This anecdote has always been meaningful context for me when teaching the Method of Physical Actions: Stanislavski's train journey metaphor is to be found in his notes on 'improvisations on *Othello*', often published with his final work, *Creating a Role,* where the through-line of action is described by Tortsov as a railway line on which our destination is both certain and unknown.[3]

Brecht, another great didact of the canon and one who also evaded German state forces – although not by means of royal favour or poor resource-management – certainly finished the book and knew the tale. His was a decidedly Diderotian take:

Preface: What is Acting?

B: [...] Gottsched immediately refers in the famous passage to Cicero, who, writing about oratory, relates the story of the Roman actor Polus, who had to play Electra mourning her brother. Since his only son had just died, he brought the latter's urn on stage, and spoke the relevant verses 'with so powerful an appropriation to himself, that his own loss forced genuine tears out of him. And there was no-one in the place who could refrain from tears.'

That must truly be described as a barbaric proceeding.

W: The actor playing Othello might just as well wound himself with the dagger, so as to afford us the pleasure of feeling pity! It would come cheaper if shortly before coming on stage he had someone hand him favourable notices for a fellow actor, for then too we should probably come into that much-relished condition in which we cannot refrain from tears.[...]

W.: Because I must know what he is grieving over. Take Polus. Perhaps his son was a scoundrel. He may grieve all the same, but why should I? (Brecht 1988 [1953]: 412–3)

It's easy to forget now that Stanislavski's theory and technical approach to acting were self-consciously radical, adopting what he understood to be leading-edge conceptions of human psychology that would differentiate his dynamic 'realist' playing style from the oft-caricatured formalism of antique rhetoric (Roach, 1993: 205–16). To return to the point I started with, were it true that Stanislavski did know the Polus tale it might have been necessary for him *to forget it* in order to establish the novelty of his early emotion-led approach to acting and its distinction from the emotion-memory experiments of the ancient actors.

Lee Strasberg certainly noticed the sympathy between Polus and Stanislavski's early theory on acting and 'affective memory', situating the story, just as Brecht did, at a crossroads of 'mere' acting and 'real' emotion:

Genuine and feigned emotion: The most famous instance of supposed acting in ancient Greece was that of the actor Polus performing in the *Electra* of Sophocles, at Athens in the 4th century BC. The plot requires Electra to carry an urn supposed to contain the ashes of Orestes and lament and bewail the fate she believed had overtaken him. Accordingly, Polus, clad in the mourning garb of Electra, took from the tomb the ashes and urn of his own son (who had recently died), embraced them as if they were those of Orestes, and rendered not the appearance or imitation of sorrow but genuine grief and unfeigned lamentation. Rather than mere acting, this was in fact real grief being expressed.[4]

If *sympathy* with ancient techniques was less useful than *antipathy* for Stanislavski then his omission of the Polus tale might be seen in context of the *strophe* and *antistrophe* of a 'Western' acting discourse in which contrary ideas have been too readily fixed into

Preface: What is Acting?

crude and largely fictitious ideological binaries. Strophe and antistrophe – the back and forth, call and response of antique drama – is, perhaps, a prototypical form for both the perceived necessity for something called 'conflict' (see 'Status') in Modern drama but also the adversarial politics, aesthetics, and ideologies of acting discourses since at least the Modern age.

Brecht, for example, appears to have had considerable respect for Stanislavski's empathetic approach to acting despite his disdain for the barbaric proceeding of emotional display[5] and his common-place characterization in discourse as Stanislavski's conceptual opposite is simplistic. Eric Bentley, back in 1964 asked whether the profession would 'soon be divided between Method actors and Brechtians' in an article seeking to establish that the two great theorists were 'commensurable' although not identical (69). Tellingly, he conceded that this probably was or would become the case both in terms of nomenclature and 'allegiance' and that some actors would 'love Stanislavski, others, Brecht' (69–70). The subtext being that, just as with the Thebans and Athenians, Montagues and Capulets or the Sharks and the Jets, woe betide they who love both.

Insofar as both Brecht and Stanislavski read Diderot, we can assume that these conceptual antagonists would each have read the Polus tale differently, and through the prism of *the paradoxe*. Denis Diderot's *paradoxe sur le Comédien* (usually translated in English as, *The Paradox of Acting*) written in the late eighteenth century although not published till after his death – which was neither by firing squad nor on a train – in the early nineteenth. After dying of coronary thrombosis in 1830 and being published posthumously, Diderot's paradoxical theory of acting cut to the very heart of the matter and lodged itself in the central nervous system of the field for the next two centuries.

ACTING =/≠ TO PRETENDING

Diderot's treatise takes the form of a dialogue in which the two speakers hold antithetical views and in which the first speaker, typically understood to be Diderot, espouses the view that acting – or rather, good or great acting – is the simultaneous display of emotion and the absence of feeling. Predictable performances, consistently effective and affective night-after-night require the actor to *not* feel and yet to appear to be feeling most intensely.

Although Diderot's views pertain to an increasingly Modern form of narrative drama where emotions and emoting have begun to root themselves in dramaturgy as both the motivation for and purpose of narrative, his observation applies beyond the proto-realist and neo-Naturalist traditions of acting. The observation that feeling and representation – inner and outer – are not directly or causally linked pertains to all acts of self-display throughout the entirety of human history and not just the history of our performances.

The Paradoxe is, of course, only one of the numerous paradoxes in the 'Western' theory canon but it is perhaps the most foundational and thus akin to the Polus tale and its contradictory interpretations. Polus embodied and Diderot best-described what might be thought of as the *a priori* paradox of acting – that meaning and feeling are not causative or even directly correlated even though each imputes the other. Or, more concretely: audiences' perceptions and actors' intentions have no stable causational relationship and neither do actors' internal states and their external representations. Yet, they appear to be and may in fact be, very well-connected.

Perhaps paradoxically, Diderot's observation provides a unifying definition of acting, then, which certainly pertains to the major Western traditions but also encompasses philosophically all activities that exhibit or contain this paradox. This definition extends out from the stage and incorporates the everyday, as well as the workplace and provides a delimitation of the scope for this book on 'acting'. The primary focus of this book on acting is the most formal and orthodox definition of the term – *that thing which is done by actors and most specifically done by them when they are in the presence of some kind of audience* – but, as is clear from the plurality of sources on the topic in the field this category of activity is not always clearly distinct or distinguishable from the broader and more expansive definition of, *that thing that we all do all the time, more or less consciously*. This is because 'that thing which is done by actors' and which is characterized by a paradoxical relationship between 'inner' and 'outer', 'intention' and 'meaning' implicates *both* actors and audience in the practice of acting so foundationally that it is hard conceptually to say definitively who is actually doing *that thing*. This is easier to understand because the ambiguity and disjuncture between actors and audiences is spanned by the concept of mimesis which (of course, paradoxically) has at least two meanings (see 'A Statistically Irrelevant Keyword').

Mimesis comes as a concept into discourse on acting from the writings of Plato and Aristotle, and what might be thought of as the mythic 'first site' of Western theatre in ancient Greece. Plato and Aristotle provide different philosophical interpretations of 'mimesis', with the former ascribing to our now more commonplace understanding, which is rooted in the idea of imitation (as in, *to mime* or *mimetic*) and the latter providing a more radical definition which is associated with the productive power of nature. As Daniel Schulze has noted, for Aristotle, 'it was evident that art did not imitate but conveyed truths (see "Truth and Truthfulness"). It did not just play on affect, as Plato had supposed, but spoke to the rational mind by conveying experiences of truth' (2017: 44). Schulze discusses the aesthetic history of the concept of mimesis and comments on the modern belief, expressed by Kant, that imitation and genius are opposites while making his central argument that, 'theatre's fakeness evolves out of the intrinsic ontological connection between lying and acting' (7).

According to Schulze, with the emergence of written forms of drama from the fifth century BC, theatre began to lose its 'status as genuine or real' (7) altogether such that, now, Plato's understanding of mimesis is predominant in Western societies and cultures. Nonetheless, acting – that thing which actors and audience do together – is defined by the concept of mimesis, which entails a very specific mode of representation, and mimesis, as Diderot has observed, is a frustratingly tricky thing.

ACTING =/≠ SUM OF PARTS

Preface: What is Acting?

Researching the ancient, contested and conceptually paradoxical phenomenon of acting requires an albeit contingent working definition of acting, even if only to exclude phenomena. The Polus tale, and its retelling by practitioners and theorists of acting, provides the basis for such a definition precisely because it reveals that 'acting' is constructed of ambiguity and on contested grounds. Also, and more importantly, the tale also reminds that in seeking to understand 'acting', even more relevant than a unifying or cogent definition of 'acting' is an awareness and analysis of the ways by which acting is defined by different individuals and schools, and that often these ways are not the means of explicit definition but rather the telling of tales about acting. Analysing which tales are told and retold, or not retold, and by whom and why, and what they might be intended to mean is the job of this book. Looking closely at the language used to tell the tales, and what specific terms are used in that language is this book's methodological preoccupation.

For any reader wanting to know more about how the research was conducted for this book I have included a chapter – 'How and Why to Write: *Acting: Keywords and Concepts*' – which explains in narrative detail what I explain briefly here: Working with a Professor of Informatics, George Sioros, I developed a computational method for statistically analysing the words and language used about 'acting' in the world's largest digitized database of literary sources on the topic – Drama Online. Supported by the computational analysis, I read the source material extensively and intensively to identify 'keywords' in acting – words that conceptually define and practically operationalize the concept. I was then able to organize the source material into miniature databases for each keyword, enabling me to produce focused but expansively referenced descriptions of the 14 keywords in acting that make up the chapters of this book. These are, of course, not the only *keywords in acting* but the analysis shows that they are key to discourse on acting insofar as, tacitly and explicitly, the ideas and ideals expressed across the thousands of sources contained by Drama Online are reliant upon them.

Simplistically, 'keywords' might be thought of as *words-that-express-key-concepts or values* but, as you will find when you read on, this does not mean that their meaning is fixed, consistent, agreed-upon or even logically coherent. They should also be understood as words that both scaffold and penetrate other related concepts and larger fields of knowledge and because of this function they can be analysed to expose philosophical, practical and ideological things about fields of knowledge – in this case, acting.

Considering that the meaning of 'acting' will be constituted in the meaning and usage of a number of terms used to describe, discuss or critique 'acting' doesn't obviate the need to have an at-least-provisional sense of what acting *is* before even starting that analysis. Starting from a commonplace understanding of 'acting' makes good sense in this context and the Polus tale provides this: although the Polus tale may have received intensifying attention from the Renaissance to the present and although revisionist retellings, such as Strasberg's, risk de-historicizing its particulars, there are a number of very commonplace components to the tale which make it a useful reference point for a working definition of 'acting' that goes a little further than *that thing which actors do for audiences*.

Preface: What is Acting?

The tale contains many seeming keywords, such as personae, narrative, plot, staging, props, speech, audiences, emotions, actors, and it appeals to key concepts of reality, fakery, meaning and truth. It is fascinating, although perhaps unsurprising given the popularity of the tale, that some of these do turn out to be keywords in acting. Some turn out to be related to keywords and some, it appears, are little more than functional words which do not say or mean anything much to acting beyond their literal use.

This book finds yet more keywords that, although not immediately apparent in the Polus myth, can be excavated from it – body, status, voice, imagination, actress and play – and presents each keyword as a separate lemmatized, dictionary-style entry with a phonetic spelling, word classification and list of its definitions and meanings.

For some readers, the list of meanings and use-cases that begin each keyword entry might be of the most practical use. This list may provide some orientation points for engaging with a keyword, either practically or when reading other accounts of acting in the field. Indeed, these lists might be sufficient for some, especially those looking for a quick and reliable sense of the meaning or use of a phrase or saying encountered in a studio, rehearsal or classroom.

Readers from this group will not need to be told that this book doesn't have to be read cover-to-cover. These readers (perhaps you are one) will notice that the book doesn't have an index because, the book is an index of sorts. While the word 'curate' has been somewhat over-used and picked up some rather negative connotations as a result, it is quite apposite for describing what each entry does here: it curates a focused set of source material that can direct readers to some key-users of a keyword. Perhaps, some authorities on that keyword too. Indeed, not all source material comes from the catalogue, as readers will be able to verify using the segmented bibliography.

I found, during my exploration of the Drama Online collection, that key-users – authors using keywords a lot, or relying on keywords as tenets in their own work, or authors of objectively important books in the field using keywords in those books – often wrote tacitly about foundational ideas and concepts. The book's segmented bibliography shows clearly which sources cited come from the computationally derived 'catalogue' and which titles come the broader 'syncretic' source base, to facilitate readers with a specific academic interest in the methodology.

Other readers will want to explore these selected bibliographies and the source materials more closely because, well, enquiring minds want to know. For these readers the body of each entry may enable them to absorb disciplinary knowledge and debates about concepts such as 'emotion', 'status' or 'truth', for example, quite quickly because they come pre-digested, as it were. Some readers in this group (I would be one of these) will want to be satisfied of the academic rigour and be able to verify for themselves that each use-case is valid in context of the field, and this group should also have an interest in the reference list for each entry.

The intentional (and often quite difficult to achieve) brevity of entries might also be welcome for readers who may find intensive rather than extensive knowledge most useful to their needs. As I state in 'How and Why to Write: *Acting: Keywords and Concepts*' for these readers I have written to the instruction, *not exhaustive; informative*.

Preface: What is Acting?

This book does not provide a fully comprehensive analysis of keywords in acting discourse (I should think that would be impossible, for now); it provides what might be thought of as a bore sample from the field. Cutting a cross section into the largest digitized database in the field enables this book to look at the accretions of meaning that have sedimented in acting discourse and allows readers to see these relatively and comparatively.

The 'use case' of this book for readers who already possess both intensive and extensive knowledge of acting – those familiar with the Polus tale and all of the practical and theoretical knowledge it connotes – might be in its capability to both verify and challenge pre-existing knowledge or show the origins of received wisdom. For these readers, who might include professional actors, actor-trainers and coaches, academics, acting students, informed amateurs or auteurs, I have developed and applied the novel methodology used to conduct the research for this book. I designed and developed this to provide a new filter for discourse (jargon, myth) in the field that would stress-test what it might mean to be informed about key concepts and ideas in acting.

Given that there would not be much value in telling a well-informed group of people things that they already know, I developed this methodology in the fine theatrical tradition of *estrangement* – to defamiliarize 'acting' for those most familiar with it. For these readers, as I write in the methodological chapter, I have written to the instruction, *not entries; incendiaries*.

Following Raymond Williams's example, I set no minimum word-count on *keyword* entries. Although I haven't managed to be quite as pithy as Williams, I have been rigorously succinct with no entry allowed to go over 5,000 words. In many entries, this limitation entails a hyper-compression of some extremely rambling debates and an extreme redaction of some sprawling histories. For the readers who will be most attuned to this compression and redaction, the provocation to conventional norms about key concepts in each entry will be most apparent and will likely delight or agitate depending on where one is standing on a particular issue when the incendiary goes off.

I don't assume any intellectual authority by adopting a challenging perspective on debates and disagreements. Methodologically and in the interest of advancing knowledge in this field, my aim is to take the sharpest tool available to each concept to cut it open as deeply as possible and to expose it to the enquiry and exploration of all readers. Exploding a familiar concept, especially one with a well-settled status and perhaps even an unproblematized set of underpinning ideological values, requires a radical estrangement.

Theatrically speaking, as the Polus tale exemplifies, nothing is more radically estranging than a shock: in the multiple interpretations and reclamations of the Polus myth in the catalogue and the field the focus is on paradox – acting/not-acting, real/fiction, emotion/meaning, dead/alive etc/etc. Never mind Artaud's influential, *The Theatre and it's Double*, the 'Polus Interpretations' represent *The Theatre and its double entendre* – the salacious dramatic irony of the simultaneous coincidence of one face of a paradox with its other that only acting can predictably achieve.

Preface: What is Acting?

ACTING =/≠ LIVING

That acting can sustain a face-off of irreconcilability between mutually exclusive positions and facts has fascinated and horrified audiences (and philosophers) from Antique history to the present. That it can sustain irreconcilability as a singularity, and without a collapse of meaning into polar positions tugs at the very structures of thought, language and society.

In the mythic acting lore, Electra cries over the ashes of her dead brother …

… while Polus laments over the ashes of his dead son …

… while a sympathetic audience morns vicariously …

….while aficionados thrill over proto-realist acting technique …

… while ….while … while …

… but, the anecdote never seems to get beyond this dramatic moment and to the next plot point. Retellings remain stuck in a reflection on this instant as if the play, the characters and theatre history never moved forward at all.

In Sophocles' *Electra*, what is instantly recognizable to contemporary audiences as the cinematic and televisual trope of the plot twist culminates in a supremely pathetic and bathetic theatrical reveal. Orestes, dressed as a pall-bearer and carrying the urn which he pretends contains his own ashes, might whip off his fake beard at this point and shout, 'only kidding, sis, it's me! I'm alive!' were it not for the sombreness of the scene and the general morbidity of Greek Tragedy. Were it not for the humanity of Polus's paternal grief the audience might even have wrought a laugh from that.

The irony of the historical scene redoubles given that Orestes is only *pretending* – only *acting* – being bereaved whereas the actor Polus is *really* playing the part. The scene is after all a double deception; unlike Polus' son, Orestes isn't dead at all and there is no cause to cry.

While sources of the catalogue, and the field, retell the Polus tale as a foundational myth – modern acting's origin story – few (in fact, none) seem reflective on the fact that despite acting's prodigious and terrifying powers it can't bring the dead back to life. Despite the awesome power of mimesis to bring non-being into being (see 'A Statistically Irrelevant Keyword'), in the final analysis, for Polus at least, acting may be little more than a trick, a twist, a reveal. A cruel joke.

Orestes knows his urn is filled with meaning and certainly not filled with human remains. It changes its meaning without changing anything material at all about itself as, for Electra, the sacred ashes return to dust and her brother comes back to life.

Polus knows his urn is filled with his son and Electra (the character he is playing) is un-bereaved at the point of the reveal but his (the actor's) grief goes on and goes seemingly deeper and more profound by virtue of the contrast. How, I wonder, did Polus overcome the emotional pivot point when the audience witnesses the reveal and perhaps even sighed a collective sigh of relief?

Although roughly contemporaneous with Sophocles, the Ancient Greek philosopher, Heraclitus probably didn't see Polus's bravura performance but his work, which pre-dates

Preface: What is Acting?

Sophocles' play also prefigures it. 'Mortals are immortals and immortals are mortals, the one living the others' death and dying the others' life', Heraclitus is purported to have said (see Laërtius). Hugely and enduringly influential for his philosophy of 'flux' (see Plutarch), Heraclitus could have coined this phrase about Polus-playing-Electra.

While Polus might be regarded as something like a secular patron saint of actors the real patron saint is the Roman actor, St Genesius, who is mentioned only once in the catalogue (Brody, 2015: 8). Unlike the reveal in the Polus story, where nothing *really* changes at all – everyone dead stays dead and everyone living must go on living – in the Genesius tale a very real life-and-death change materially occurs.

Genesius, a third-century comedic actor famed for satirizing and ridiculing the Christian religion for an appreciative Roman audience, is reported to have experienced a divine conversion on stage while pretending to receive the sacrament of baptism (see Mershman, 1990). So this story goes, he was unwavering in his faith from this point and rejected even the Emperor Diocletian's command to recant. Predictably, he was martyred by beheading and venerated by the Church perhaps as early as the fourth century and later adopted as a patron saint of actors by several guilds and organizations (see Grig, 2004).

Polus is all over the catalogue and Genesius is nowhere. Perhaps the religiosity of Genesius's story is too specific to be universally appealing. Plus, there is no record to say whether Genesius was any good as a performer – he could raise a laugh, it seems, but Polus had them weeping in the aisles.

From a contemporary neo-realist perspective, Polus is credited with some technique. He had chops, as they say. A proto-method actor, his story has had obvious relevance and resonance for practitioners for the last hundred years or so. More obviously riven with paradoxes then Genesius, or any other actor's story – except perhaps Garrick and his wig, but that is one for another day (see Roach, 1982) – it is the contradictory elements of the Polus tale that appear to make it so compelling as a cipher for acting.

Readers will note that many keywords in this book have self-contradictory use-cases and meanings. In fact, the exposing of this inclusive mutual-exclusivity in the concepts used to define and understand acting might be considered itself a key finding of the book.

Life, as Heraclitus wrote, shortly before Electra flooded the stage with tears, is change; is a river into which we cannot step twice (see Plutarch). It is in flux, it is flux, and yet it maintains its singularity while it shape-shifts, and acting concepts do this too, it seems.

Acting meets and joins with the flux and singularity of life and, conceptually speaking, all attempts to understand either – acting or life – are made from fluctuating and unstable ideas and apprehensions fixed in problematical words – keywords. The changes of these, and changes in these, could be understood as mere changes of intellectual fashion. Increasingly better, more accurate, more relevant or just different sublanguages describing at different historical moments and in different cultural contexts, the same thing. The sempeternality of change (namecheck Heraclitus here) in the understanding of key concepts in acting, though, might in itself say something about the phenomenon of acting and not only the inadequacies of language.

Preface: What is Acting?

The digital archive of Drama Online is in flux too, of course. Since beginning the computational analysis of this archive three years ago new titles have been added to Drama Online. This book is a sample of a sample of the ideas and ideals that define 'acting' for a representative group of people who might be said to know something about it. You, reader, may already be one of these people. If you are, I hope that there is something new in here that you didn't already know. Or, that there may be something in here that you knew but didn't realize that you knew, or didn't know how you knew it. Or there may be a new perspective on something you already knew, or perhaps even a new perspective for you on yourself as *somebody who knows something about acting*.

Whether the defamiliarization achieved by this book is sufficient to cause any conversions – to make any informed readers think differently about their knowledge of acting – remains to be seen. I hope this book provides some new ways to think about the existent-non-existent remains of Orestes in Polus's urn and to talk about and to do 'acting' with an informed awareness of 'character', 'truth' 'authenticity', 'believability', 'movement', 'voice', 'body', 'status', 'emotion', 'imagination', 'mimesis', 'actors' and 'actresses'. In fact, this book shows that it is not possible to do or talk about acting *without* employing knowledge contained by one or more of these keywords, even if it is only employed to negate its own mythic meaning.

Notes

1. Leofranc Holfrod-Strevens's independent research confirms my own findings, that there is no mention of the Polus myth in any of Stanislavski's writings (2005: 517).
2. See Bournoutian (1998).
3. From trans. Hapgood *Creating a Role*, London: Bloomsbury, 2014, 220–1.
4. See, Lee Strasberg, in *Encyclopaedia Britannica*, 15th edn. (Chicago: Encyclopaedia Britannica, 1992), s.v. 'Theatre, The Art of the', xxviii. 515–30 at 525; on affective memory, see ibid. 526.
5. Brecht commended Stanislavksi and especially empathy as a phase in rehearsal, to be followed, however, by social criticism. See 'Stanislawski-Studien', *Gesammelte Werke*, xvi, 841–68, esp. 843, 852–4, 866, and on 'truth' 846–7, 859–60.

References

Benedetti, J. ([1990] 1999), *Stanislavski: His Life in Art*, London: Methuen Drama.
Bentley, E. (1964), 'Are Stanislavski and Brecht Commensurable?', *The Tulane Drama Review*, 9(1): 69–76.
Bournoutian, G. (1998). *Russia and the Armenians of Transcaucasia, 1797–1889: A Documentary Record*, Costa Mesa, CA: Mazda Press.
Brecht, B. (1988), *Große kommentierte Berliner und Frankfurter Ausgabe*, Berlin: Aufbau & Frankfurt: Suhrkamp.
Brody, J. D. (2015), *The Actor's Business Plan: A Career Guide for the Acting Life*, London: Methuen Drama.

Preface: What is Acting?

Eyer, J. A. and L. F. Smith (2015), *Broadway Swings: Covering the Ensemble in Musical Theatre*, London: Methuen Drama.

Fletcher, J. (2022), *Classical Greek Tragedy*, London: Methuen Drama.

Gordon, R. (2006), *The Purpose of Playing: Modern Acting Theories in Perspective*, Ann Arbor, MI: Michigan University Press.

Grig, L. (2004), 'Portraits, Pontiffs and the Christianization of Fourth-Century Rome', *Papers of the British School at Rome*, 72: 203–30.

Holford-Strevens, L. (2005), 'Polus and His Urn: A Case Study in the Theory of Acting, c. 300 B.C.–c. A.D. 2000', *International Journal of the Classical Tradition*, 11 (4): 499–523.

Laërtius, D. (1925), *Lives of the Eminent Philosophers*, vol. 2 book 9, Cambridge, MA: Harvard University Press.

Magarshack, D. ([1950] 2011), *Stanislavsky: A Life*, London: Faber & Faber.

Mershman, F. (1990), 'Genesius', *The Catholic Encyclopedia*, vol. 6, New York: Robert Appleton Company.

Plutarch (c.46–120s AD), *On the E at Delphi*.

Roach, J. R. (1982), *The Player's Passion: Studies in the Science of Acting*, Ann Arbor, MI: The University of Michigan Press.

Roach, J. (1993), *The Player's Passion: Studies in the Science of Acting*, Ann Arbor, MI: University of Michigan Press.

Schulze, D. (2017), *Authenticity in Contemporary Theatre and Performance: Make it Real*, London: Methuen Drama.

HOW AND WHY TO READ *ACTING: KEYWORDS AND CONCEPTS*

HOW?

If

- you are looking for practical insights, start anywhere you like. Perhaps jump straight into the entry that catches your attention the most or about which you feel that you know the least. Each entry is self-contained and so you don't need to read these in order. If you're not especially interested in how the research was undertaken to produce the book, maybe don't even bother reading 'How and Why to Write *Keywords in Acting*'. Probably, reading just 'Preface: What is Acting?' and the entries will do you quite nicely.
- you're interested in *keywords* or in acting as encompassing concepts and sets of discourses, maybe read 'How and Why to Write *Keywords in Acting*' first. You might then wish to read 'Preface: What is Acting?' and the entries in linear order (they are largely in descending frequency order).
- you're a researcher or academic in the field, teacher, coach or expert, you should probably read the whole thing in the order in which it is printed.
- you're interested in a specific topic in acting – character, imagination, voice – just read that entry, if you wish. I won't mind.

WHY?

Because,

- you want to know something about a specific topic
- you want to know something about acting as a concept
- you are interested in language and discourse
- you are interested in mixed-method computational studies
- you already know something about acting, or a given topic, and want to check that what you know is well-founded
- you already know something about acting, or a given topic, and don't know how you know it
- you already know something about acting, or a given topic, and would like to know whether others agree with you

- you would like to confirm your practical and theoretical wisdom
- you would like to test your practical and theoretical wisdom
- you like books about acting
- you're a researcher in the field and you use language and concepts in your work and you would like some scholarly reference points of origin for these, and a rigorously derived set of definitions that you can employ or critique
- you are an actor and don't always feel informed or confident in using or understanding how other people use specific words about acting practice
- you would like to become an actor and you would like to be well-informed about what other people mean when they use certain words about acting
- you are a teacher, trainer, coach, director or other professional in the field and you would like to confirm whether your practical understanding of the meaning of a given term is consistent with other professionals' understanding and use of terms.
- Because.

ACKNOWLEDGEMENTS

Thank you, Faith: another book not possible without you. I love you.

Gwen and Efa: I love you too. You make everything fun and I certainly channelled you both when writing some of the more playful parts of this book.

Thank you, George, for your invaluable support for the computational research for this book. You taught me new things and helped me to pose different questions.

Thank you, Simon and Mark, for committed editorial support and for facilitating an ambitious research project underpinning this book. Thanks to Methuen Drama for providing the digital access and support necessary to execute that ambitious project.

To my friends and colleagues – too many to name – thank you for stimulating conversations and responses to this book throughout its germination and production.

CHAPTER 1
ACTOR

(*ackk-tor*)
noun
- One who acts
- A sub-genus of the species of 'performer' correlated closely with literary and narrative traditions of theatre, TV and film
- A strongly (male) gendered word for someone who acts
- An increasingly gender-neutral word for someone who acts
- A word increasingly applied to animals and other non-human beings when theorizing their behaviour as performative. This is especially prevalent in the context of twenty-first century post-human and ecological discourses and has relevance to the literary and actor-network-theory concepts of the 'actant': a causative agent or 'source of an action' (Latour, 1996).

'Acting' will, of course, be one of the most frequently used words in the catalogue (43,944 uses, if you're counting) because it was one of the words used to parse the original data set (the Drama Online holdings) and generate the catalogue. It remains noteworthy, though, that 'actor' is the second most frequently used word in the catalogue after 'play' and yet, despite its frequency there is perhaps surprisingly little to say about its meaning.

This is because of a *very* high consensus around both meaning and use across the titles analysed, and the close alignment of this consensus to the common-language definition of 'actor' as 'one who acts'. The evidence of this predominant use-case is seen in the overwhelming frequency of the use of the definitive article – *the* actor – in titles in the catalogue: *The Actor's Survival Guide* (Robbins, 2019), *The Actor's Workbook* (Clifton, 2016), *Training the Actor's Body* (McCaw, 2017), *Rethinking the Actor's Body* (McCaw, 2020), *The Actor Speaks* (Rodenburg, 2019) and *Voice and the Young Actor* (Cook, 2012), to name just a few. In nearly half of the 40,000-odd uses of the word 'actor' in the catalogue the use-case also employs the definitive article – discourse on acting is not just talking about actors, or this or that act. Discourse talks with a strongly unifying and unified sense and definition of 'the actor' as a singular individual.

This reflects the hegemonic narrative of Western theatre history – largely attributed to the enduring influence of Aristotle and Horace's treatise on Ancient Greek drama – which hold that the first 'actor' came into being *c*.534 BCE on the Athenian stage when a chorus-member performing the dithyramb (an ancient form of choral narrative song) stepped out of the group and improvised a speaking role. Myth has it that, in this seminal moment, Thespis (the 'actor' in question) created the concepts of 'role' and 'actor' simultaneously, instituting both in cultural history and instigating a multi-millennial continuum of artistic practice ongoing today (not bad going). Judith Fletcher has noted that, while historians such as Martin West and Arthur Pickard-Cambridge have contested the veracity of this narrative and established that none of the extant fragments of the Athenian dramatic festivals are attributable to Thespis (Fletcher, 2022: 4–9), the myth holds strong and the language of 'thespian' as well as the much-parodied caricature of the 'thesp' reflect a cultural understanding of the singularity of the profession and craft of acting.

Also fond of the definitive article, David Mamet frequently punctured the mystique of the thespian (arguably to inflate the mystique of the writer) and wrote in *True and False* that:

> The actor is onstage to communicate the play to the audience. That is the beginning and the end of his and her job. To do so the actor needs a strong voice, superb diction, a supple, well-proportioned body, and rudimentary understanding of the play.
>
> ([1997] 1999: 6)

While Mamet employs male and female pronouns for 'the actor' in most pre-twenty-first-century cases 'the actor' is not only singular but implicitly male.

This statement – the acting discourse has largely thought of actors as lone males – may or may not be contentious. In the broader context of a culture and society that has been widely recognized to be sexist this contention may or may not require substantiation. Substantiating subtext is by definition a fairly difficult thing to do, but I will provide two observations that I have been able to produce from the analysis of the catalogue which, I hope, well serve sufficient evidence to move forward from this point.

Stanislavski is one of the most frequently referenced source of authority on the practice of acting through the catalogue. He is directly referenced by name 3,576 times and, while Meyerhold (3,655) and Brecht (10,231) are name-checked more often, an accurate picture of Stanislavski's influence over acting discourse emerges when Stanislavskian phrases such as 'system' (2,880), 'Method' (2,139) and 'objective' (2,417) are also factored into this calculation. A phallocentrism latent in the concept of 'the actor' might be recognized in the re-publication and citation of *An Actor's Work* as, *An Actor's Work on Himself,* including in critical anthologies of Stanislavksi (e.g. Jacono, 2016: 105, Ruffini, 2017: 36; Serrano, 2017: 262). Sometimes gender-neutralized as 'Stanislavski's work upon oneself' (Camilleri, 2023: 130), my analysis finds no instances of Stanislavski's work on *herself.*

If that approach is too oblique, the second observation that can be drawn from the analysis is the relative frequency of the pronouns 'he' and 'she' in titles using the definitive article 'the actor' in the title. In Robbins (2019), 'he' is used 73 times and 'she' 49 times. In Rodenburg (2019), 'he' is used 455 times and 'she' only 249 times. In Dick McGaw's *Training the Actor's Body,* 'he' is used 700 times and 'she' only 152, while in McCaw (2020), 'he' is used 1,059 times and 'she' only 175. This result should not be over-interpreted given that this imbalance is broadly mirrored in all titles in the catalogue, including those that do not use the definitive article. For example, my book, *Anatomy of Performance Training* (Matthews, 2014) uses 'he' 134 times and 'she' only 55 times. The ratio is similar in *The Life of Training* (Matthews, 2019) at 113:41.

However, taken together, these two observations about the gendering of the definitive article can be easily understood in the context of nineteenth-and twentieth-century literary culture that predominates in the catalogue, as well as the varyingly sexist cultural contexts seen between 400 BCE and the twenty-first century, written about in the catalogue.

Vanessa Ewan and Debbie Green take an idiosyncratic approach to gendering 'the actor' and provide their readers with 'notes on gender/third person', stating:

> The actor is referred to [throughout their book] in the third person, except … when he is addressed directly [by name]. This approach allows the actor the space to connect personally, but deliberately also remains open as an invitation to other practitioners to share in exploring the work. This book is gendered throughout as 'he' for consistency, but speaks equally to both the male and female actor.
>
> (2015: xiv)

Gendering 'the actor' as 'he' is consistent with the catalogue, although Ewan and Green are rather more explicit about this than the catalogue is in general. There is (much) more to be discussed around the gendering of 'the actor' in the catalogue (see Chapter 9: Actress), but here I want also to note a statistically small but conceptually relevant base of literature in the catalogue that equates the concept of 'actor' to non-human actors. Most commonly, this involves animals but it also includes objects and entities, such as corporations.

This equation of 'actor' with non-human subjects varies in magnitude from a largely metaphorical comparison of two un-alike things – humans and non-humans – to a co-identification of complete identicality between human-actor and animal-actor. The continuum of this equation in the catalogue's literature correlates closely with the continuum of *meaning* and *use-case of the concept* of 'acting'. Narrower definitions of the term as a descriptor for what happens on theatre stages align more closely with an anthropocentric definition of 'actor', and more expansive and inclusive definitions of 'acting' arise within Performance Studies from the 1980s onwards. The latter aligns strongly with a de-anthropomorphized account of the 'actor' as a causal agent or 'actant'.

This theme also comes up in practically instructive titles on 'animal study' as a technique in physical character-building, such as Vanessa Ewan and Debbie Green's *Actor Movement: Expression of the Physical Being* (2015). Here, 'actor' is a highly anthropocentric concept and provides a dividing line between humans, with 'complicated persona' and animals with 'uncomplicated identity' (127). With perhaps moot zoological authority, the authors assert that there 'is no possibility of confusion in deciphering what makes a cat a cat and what makes a horse a horse, and so on', because 'the animal's morphology is an unalterable fact' (127). This account of 'actor' as a human category is implicitly built upon a propositional fact about the life of the mind, and a strand of philosophical thinking that uses evidence and reason to afford humans a higher level of agency than animals (see Matthews, 2019: 25–8, 51).

Interestingly, accounts of 'animal study', such as Ewan and Green's tend to emphasize the spontaneity of animal behaviour as a counter-indicator of 'acting', in the narrow sense defined above. 'Unlike humans, animals live in the present tense', they write, but an 'actor can take animal work into anthropomorphic character development' (2015: 128).

Jackie Snow, in *Movement Training for Actors* (2012), also enforces this conceptual differentiation between animals (who don't *act*) and actors who can co-opt animal behaviour *as acting*. Snow observes a:

> total lack of self-consciousness that animals have. It is really good for an actor to not be worrying about what people think of the way they look, and to have a complete lack of self-consciousness. Studying animals in this way is particularly freeing, because animals will do everything in public that we humans would do in private.
>
> (123–4)

Snow uses this distinction to connect 'animal work' with a much-prized actorly concept of *being-in-the-moment* and *acting-as-if-for-the-first-time* and appearing to be (or even being) unpremeditated in one's actions on stage (see Chapter 6: Emotion for further discussion of this in context of a paradox of control). Snow describes a performative exercise in which students show their 'animal study' to an audience and asserts that, 'students should be in the moment and not have anything in particular planned or choreographed for the audience' (129). Students might 'plan and semichoreograph their animal' but 'the lesson is not for the students to be able to repeat something exactly but for it to appear to be done for the first time' (128).

The key association in such accounts with regard to the concepts underpinning 'actor' is between human 'nature' and 'spontaneity'. This association critiques the association between 'self' and 'culture' in the practice of acting and assigns value to spontaneous and therefore 'natural' behaviour. Curiously, despite using animal behaviour as an exemplification of this association these accounts tend to strongly delineate 'actor' as a human-only concept.

Elsewhere and towards the other pole of this continuum the disambiguation between human acting and animal behaviour becomes less clear. Karen Raber in *Shakespeare and Posthumanist Theory* (2018) writes that, 'when the fundamental exceptionalist distinction between species goes, along with it goes the division … between nature (all that is non-human) and culture (all that is human-created) that seems to define modernity' (89). Raber points out the proximity of actors to animals in Elizabethan theatre, because of the physical environment of London's Bankside, which was 'full of animal sounds, smells and actions' (101–2). Holly Dugan traces the presence of trained performing-baboons on English stages of the period, pointing out that their 'monstrous hybridity' was understood in terms of their 'bodily intimacy' with humans (2013: 84–5). Raber also challenges the exclusion of animals from the concept of 'actor' on aesthetic bases, arguing that uncertainty over whether certain characters, like Bavian in *Two Noble Kinsmen*, 'were human or baboon' suggests what Dugan calls 'a stunning slippage between human and animal actors' (2013: 78). Perhaps somewhat over-stating her case, Raber contends that, 'how "human" any given individual at the theatre or on stage could claim to be was under constant erasure by the very conditions of the location itself' (2018: 102). 'The Globe was situated in the liberties of Bankside in close proximity to the bear garden with specific consequences for moments featuring animal allusions in the plays', with apes who were 'trained to perform in one location' probably showing up in the other and 'monkeys that were used to ride dogs as part of the entertainment for bear-baiting audiences' showing up 'in street performances or on theatrical stages as well' (102). 'Actors on stage were always aping', Raber writes, adopting a more metaphorical stance on her proposition for non-human actors, 'sometimes aping their betters, sometimes simply aping foolish courtly manners or aping apes with their awkward capering' (102). At an interpretative stretch, Raber suggests that 'the point of their acting', might have been 'to signal to audiences the degree to which those who were not by profession actors nonetheless performed like trained animals for their masters' (102).

Raber's post-human theorizing focuses on an evidence base for the hybridity of human/animal actors in Shakespearean theatre but there are also in the catalogue philosophical and semantic arguments for the inclusion of animals in the concept of 'actor' driven by what might be considered an ecological turn in theory in the twenty-first century, which was prompted and accompanied by an increasing awareness of humans' negative impact on the natural environment.

Dick McCaw (2020) provides an example from this in which he develops an idea of 'ecological action' (47) which unifies the behaviour of humans and animals under the conceptual catch-all of 'action'. Carl Lavery's, chapter 'How does theatre think through ecology' in *Thinking Through Theatre and Performance* (2019: 257), comments on the ecological turn as 'best understood as a way of thinking that seeks to show how human agents are always bound up with and are part of their environment'. 'At its most progressive and expansive', Lavery writes, 'ecological thinking is concerned to highlight how human beings are always already part of "nature"' (258). Lavery cultivates a form of thought experiment – 'the ecological image' – to produce a conceptual framework which, 'uses the enigma of matter to produce transversal connections and heterogeneous assemblages in which human and "more than human" actors work together to produce a new world' (264). However, this is the only use of the term 'actor' that Lavery makes here, and this limitation is also characteristic of the ecological turn wherein 'acting' is simplified to describe an elemental causal relationship between agents and within systems. Both use of the word 'actor' and the use-case towards this end of the continuum are highly limited.

In *Performer Training Reconfigured,* following Latour, Callon and Law's developments of Actor-Network-Theory (ANT), Frank Camilleri adopts 'actants' alongside 'actors' as the noun for agentic entities in systems of causation. Camilleri 'thematizes the *environmental context* as an assemblage of active "actants" that contribute to the work of performers' (2019: 91, emphasis in original) and uses the term to encompass humans and non-humans alike. Rather than encompass animals and things within 'actor', or maintain a binary between (human) actors and (non-human) things, the adoption of 'actant' signals a considered 'relational ontology' in Camilleri, and others that he cites, including Karen Barad, Don Ihde and Susan Bennet, who all apply ANT as a conceptualizing strategy conducive to the ecological turn.

Across the post-human and ecological trend in the catalogue, which arguably pays the most thoughtful and diligent attention to interrogating and defining the term 'actor', and which meditates most prominently on inclusive and progressive politics, 'animals' appear to receive more critical attention than 'women' (see Chapter 9: Actress).

References

Camilleri, F. (2019), *Performer Training Reconfigured: Post-Psychophysical Perspectives for the Twenty-First Century*, London: Methuen Drama.
Camilleri, F. (2023), *Performer Training for Actors and Athletes*, London: Methuen Drama.
Clifton, A. (2016), *The Actor's Workbook: A Practical Guide to Training, Rehearsing and Devising*, London: Methuen Drama.
Cook, R. (2012), *Voice and the Young Actor: A Workbook and Video*, London: Methuen Drama.
Dugan, H. (2013), '"To Bark with Judgment": Playing Baboon in Early Modern England', *Shakespeare Studies*, 41: 77–93.
Ewan, V. and D. Green (2015), *Actor Movement: Expression of the Physical Being: A Movement Handbook for Actors*, London: Methuen Drama.
Fletcher, J. (2022), *Classical Greek Tragedy*, London: Methuen Drama.
Jacono, V. (2016), 'Introduction: Complexity, Cognition, and the Actor's Pedagogy', in C. Falletti, G. Sofia and V. Jacono (eds), *Theatre and Cognitive Neuroscience*, 103–16, London: Methuen Drama.
Latour, B. (1990), 'Om aktor-netvaerksteroi. Nogle fa afklaringer og mere end nogle fa forviklinger', *Philosophia*, 25 (3–4): 47–64.
Lavery, C. (2019), 'How Does Theatre Think Through Ecology?', in M. Bleeker, A. Kear, J. Kelleher and H. Roms (eds), *Thinking Through Theatre and Performance*, 257–69, London: Methuen Drama.
Mamet, D. ([1997] 1999), *True and False*, London: Vintage.
Matthews, J. (2014), *Anatomy of Performance Training*, London: Methuen Drama.
Matthews, J. (2019), *The Life of Training*, London: Methuen Drama.
McCaw, D. (2017), *Training the Actor's Body: A Guide*, London: Methuen Drama.
McCaw, D. (2020), *Rethinking the Actor's Body: Dialogues with Neuroscience*, London: Methuen Drama.
Raber, K. (2018), *Shakespeare and Posthumanist Theory*, London: The Arden Shakespeare.
Robbins, J. S. (2019), *The Actor's Survival Guide: How to Make Your Way in Hollywood*, London: Methuen Drama.
Rodenburg, P. (2019), *The Actor Speaks: Voice and the Performer*, London: Methuen Drama.
Ruffini, F. (2017), 'Three Periods of Stanislavsky in Italy', in J. Pitches and S. Aquilina (eds), *Stanislavsky in the World: The System and its Transformations Across Continents*, 35–62, London: Methuen Drama.
Serrano, R. (2017), 'A Teacher's Perspective: Stanislavsky at the Escuela de Teatro de Buenos Aires in Argentina', in J. Pitches and S. Aquilina (eds), *Stanislavsky in the World: The System and its Transformations Across Continents*, 261–8, London: Methuen Drama.
Snow, J. (2012), *Movement Training for Actors*, London: Methuen Drama.

CHAPTER 2
CHARACTER

(ka-rack-tor)
noun
- A role in a drama
- The protagonist or antagonists only in a drama, and not those roles that do not influence the narrative plot
- A personhood represented in performance
- The sum of an actor's performance understood by an audience as a semic unity representing a personhood
- The sum of an actor's performance understood by an audience to be a semic unity not representing personhood
- The motivating principle in narrative drama
- The sum of a person's actions
- An adjunct to plot as the motivating principle of narrative drama
- A conceptual fulcrum point in the pivot from modernism to postmodernity in performance
- An outmoded concept for understanding representational acts on stage
- An avatar for the audience
- A means by which an individual audience member can project themselves into the staged action
- A vicarious means by which the audience member can self-reflect, empathize with others, examine their own and other socio-cultural milieus and experience emotions germane to the lives of others
- A composite of representational acts that constitute an image of a given person
- A composite of motivations and emotions that constitute the inner life of a given person
- A key concept in and the labour of acting: *constructing, building, investigating* character
- The moral basis of action
- Not the self of the actor but the self of another person represented by the self of the actor.

Rest in Peace, 'Character', beloved parent to Western dramatic literature and much cherished child of prehistoric rites and rituals. 'Character' is survived by one sibling, 'plot', and leaves a substantial inheritance that shall be preserved within the vaults of 'mimesis' (see Chapter 14), 'actor' (see Chapter 1) and 'Truth' (see Chapter 7).

'Character' died following injuries sustained in a series of mostly unrecorded incidents occurring, accordingly to Elinor Fuchs, at some point during the twentieth century, but perhaps the fatal wound occurring during a 1959 performance of *Krapp's Last Tape*. *The Death of Character* was formally pronounced in 1996 (see Fuchs, 1996) and comes nearly three decades after *The Death of the Author* (*La mort de l'auteur*, Barthes, 1967).

Coroners have been unable to accurately age 'character' and the agreed range is somewhere between 250 and 2,500 years; either born within Aristotelian theatre-philosophy or midwifed into existence by late eighteenth-century theory that revised the origin story of character-centrism backwards only as far as Shakespeare (see Schneider, 1997: 541–2). The passing of 'character' before the end of C20 announced 'the end of drama and the emerging form of a post-metaphysical theatre' (Fuchs, 1996: 90). A collection will be taken with all proceeds going to charity.

I have eulogized 'character' here with a faux obituary because a notable sub-section of the catalogue regards 'character' posthumously. The epitaph is ironic because, another subset of the catalogue regards 'character' as not just alive-and-well but the very lifeblood of acting. The dichotomization of 'character' in acting discourse is anchored in historical and philosophical poles of theatre practice in Ancient Greece and late twentieth-century Europe.

Practically, and much to the surprise and delight of twenty-first-century audiences, 'character' appears to be having a very active afterlife following its death in the late 1990s. Rebecca Schneider has suggested that 'character' may not have died at all – in fact, 'character' may have faked their own death and hid out amongst the audience until the critical heat cooled down a bit (see Schneider, 1997: 542). Schneider might be following Isaiah Berlin's famous logic – 'enough manipulation with the definition of "man", and freedom can be made to mean whatever the manipulator wishes' (Berlin, 1969: 163) – when she intimates that, with enough manipulation of the definition of 'subject', 'self' and 'identity' during twentieth-century philosophical theorizing, 'character' has been made to mean something new. Indeed, there seems to be some agreement on the point that reports of the 'death of character' may be overstated, and that a late twentieth-century demise in play-written-drama and the emergence of 'post-dramatic' theatre forms may have coincided with a recentralization of 'character' in performance events.

Eddie Paterson, writing in 2015, argued that, over the preceding three decades, 'the problem of self' has been a prominent concern in performance as it has been in society, and that this problem is 'a feature of the dramatic history of monologue' since at least Shakespeare and which 'continues to be redefined as often fragmenting, multiple personae' (2015: 155). Paterson sees monologue as a:

> response to political rhetoric and ideology because of the way in which monologue artists from the 1980s to the 2000s make visible texts, bodies and performances

that open up spaces of ambiguity and disjunction within the dominant economic and social narratives that constitute contemporary Western culture.

(156)

'Taking into account the influence of trends in global performance from the last thirty years' Paterson observes a 'privileging of monologue in postdramatic theatre' (156) because of the utility of this form in contending with problems of selfhood and identity, which have preoccupied Western culture in recent history.

Relative to the historical continuity in 'character' even through the post-dramatic period, Paterson and others, including Dowd and Rutter have also shown the increasing intensity of interest in identity and selfhood that 'character' has facilitated through performance. In Dowd and Rutter's *Handbook of Shakespeare and Early Modern Drama: Perspectives, Culture and Identity*, as in many late twentieth- and early twenty-first-century sources in the catalogue, '"identity" serves as an *important category* of analysis' (2023: 7; emphasis added) and the persistence of 'character' within prioritized discourses of identity might even be understood in the context of what Alan Read has figured as 'the recalcitrance of the domain of theatre', which he refers to ironically as 'the abandoned practice' (2013: 26). Far from abandoned in the post-dramatic moment, theatre, and more specifically, 'character', is a highly refractory concept in the catalogue.

Dead-as-a-doornail or alive-and-kicking – depending on your philosophical and aesthetic preferences – 'character' is the lifeblood of the catalogue; a top-ten frequency word and a foundational concept in acting discourse.

Despite the seemingly diametrical definitions, 'character', statistically speaking, is most often utilized without definition or qualification. So integral is the concept to acting that it passes into discourse almost subliminally in most cases, well-greased by substantial assumed knowledge and agreement between authors and readers about the meaning of the word.

Simon Palfry's assertion that 'character' is 'the most basic theatrical fact' is not an outlier in this regard. His view that, 'there are no plays without characters' (2011: 222) is moot and disputed elsewhere in the catalogue yet, the confidence with which Palfry makes his case is not unwarranted albeit somewhat ahistorical.

Sarah Grochala contests Palfry's claim by challenging its terms with another inflection of Berlinian logic. She describes a 'shift in focalization, from an objective to a subjective perspective' in postdramatic 'character'; a shift that does not change the fundamental nature of the concept of characterization as a form of representation (Grochala, 2017: 200–1). 'The dramatic mode of a play is traditionally seen as an objective form of representation', she writes, where an audience witnesses 'a set of unmediated events happening before their eyes in the present moment' (200–1). While 'different characters may offer subjective readings of events in an attempt to enable the audience to see them from their perspective, the audience always have access to the objective truth because they witnessed "what happened"' (200–1). Grochala observes that, in this mode, the audience 'often know more about events than the characters' and this allows audiences to see 'characters' as complex beings, reacting with an apprehensible internal consistency in response to events as they see them (see 'Believable'). Grochala contrasts this dramatic mode of character with the mode of the novel, which 'is seen as a subjective mode, in which a narrator offers an account of a set of events that happened in the past' (200–1). Some contemporary plays 'attempt to offer a theatrical version of the subjective mode by presenting events through the mediating gaze of a particular character' and here 'access to an objective truth is questionable, as they only have access to the events through the narrator's interpretation of them' (200–1). 'Characters' can become less complex, consistent, reliable or (in the contemporary parlance) relatable in the shift from objective to subjective modes, although even this interpretation is evidently too simplistic to account for the differing effects and affects of 'character' across performance styles.

Notable in the catalogue, Sarah Grochala offers a helpful and eclectic historical overview of differing and competing definitions of 'character' in Western theatre history (2017: 187–218) taking in major trends from antique *Poetics*, through the Renaissance, Modernism and postmodernity and terminating (quite literally) in the early twenty-first century with post-dramatic theatre. Throughout this history, and throughout the uses of 'character' across the catalogue there are abiding trends within the varying definitions.

'Character' predominantly relates to personhood as a complex and singular proposition. This is what Grochala calls 'dramatic character' (2017: 188–9). Lorna Marshall, for example, despite not being too 'keen on the word "character" [because] it is too close to the word "caricature" and can lead to the idea that a character is a simplification of a human being' (2001: 180) asserts that 'character' is about selfhood. Acting as a 'real process of embodying another human being' is a 'full transformation', she states, 'of temporarily relinquishing your own self in order to become someone else. Someone who is just as complex, contradictory and interesting as you are' (180).

The assumption that all human beings are complex and thus all 'characters' should be 'embodied' (see 'Body' and 'Play') as complex personalities is prominent in the catalogue. Even commentators such as Harriman-Smith, who advocate acting exercises that reduce singular and complicated personalities to 'types', recognizes the danger for 'character' simplification to 'go awry' (2024: 180). 'It is possible to think about a person's character in two ways', he writes, 'either with respect to their individual qualities or in terms of what type of person they are' (180). Acting should, according to Harriman-Smith 'balance' these two 'ways of thinking' just 'as actors did three hundred years ago' (180). 'Type-based thinking' easily 'tips into prejudice', he warns, or conversely 'characters eventually become so individualized that the original, more general starting point is lost', making them redundant to story-telling (180). While Harriman-Smith's view may be quite esoteric in the catalogue, which generally eschews any stereotyping of character in the practice of acting, his focus on 'how a character and an actor interact' is quite uncontentious (Harriman-Smith, 2024: 180). The central philosophical and practice conceit here is that 'characters' are just people, and so are actors. A 'character' therefore might be a mask for the actor but it should be one that fits like a second skin.

With a Classical bent, Sara Coodin writes:

> Aristotle views moral character, a person's ethos, as a life-long process of philosophical striving, in which a person's every resource is marshalled in the service of moral growth towards *eudaemonia*, variously understood as happiness, human flourishing, or simply living a beautiful life.
>
> (2010: 184)

'Aristotle's moral understanding of character', she writes, 'can be usefully applied to the critical examination' of characters (Shakespeare's in this specific case) and that, rather than viewing 'characters as verbal patterns, or as interpellated "subjects," I prefer to engage with them as if they were actual people' (184). That 'actual people' are both complex and yet consistent is a tacit assumption about 'character' across multiple sources in the catalogue, and actors' constancy in making performance choices in alignment with a fixed understanding of a 'character' is an explicit yardstick for quality in the how-to manuals and guides in the catalogue.

Even in the twentieth- and twenty-first-century post-death-of-the-character theory and practice, 'character' is mostly understood in this way, albeit that here the response to that framing is somewhat antagonistic. Grochala notes that Fuchs 'argues that the main characterizing feature of this transitional [post-dramatic] period is a crisis of character' (Grochala, 2017: 200), with the 'socio-psychological character' understood by Marshall and Harriman-Smith 'in the process of being superseded' (Grochala, 2017: 199). Susan Blattès provides four perspectives on 'new' conceptions of character: First, a 'lack of information available' about them, their life history or personal details. Second, information about 'characters' is inconsistent, 'can be questioned and is frequently contradicted' and third, it is 'often quite difficult or even impossible to decide on characters' motivations' not least because, fourthly, 'character's' actions and dialogue lack 'coherence' (Blattès, 2007: 71).

One of the chief criticisms of Blattès and Fuchs' descriptions of post-dramatic characters as 'new' is that such 'post-dramatic' traits can be evidenced in characters from across theatre history. Further, this somatizing approach to 'character' doesn't really describe anything other than a new aesthetic attitude towards 'character', and this becomes clear when considering the fact that post-dramatic theory has found no language beyond 'character' to think and speak about the people that actors (unavoidably) represent.

Another abiding trend is the juxtaposition and mutual exclusivity between an actor's 'self' and a 'character', despite much consideration of a 'Brechtian co-presence of role and self' (Pitches and Aquilina 2017: 396). This philosophical juxtaposition of 'self' and 'character' underpins the semantic and psycholinguistic language-choices that describe the actor's work. From Lorna Marshall's actor in a state of 'becoming' (2001: 180), to MacDonald's actor being 'transformed … into a character' (MacDonald, cited in Rodosthenhos, 2017: 33), or Gaitanidi's actors 'embody[ing] their roles' (Gaitanidi, cited in Pitches and Aquilina, 2017: 129). This juxtapositioning is also integral to the value placed on 'believability' (see 'Believable') in acting, which is purposely devalued in post-dramatic theatre as part of its post-modernist critique of coherence as a social principle.

Although 'character' is occasionally applied to objects and animals it is overwhelmingly used to describe human behaviour and moral values. Even where animals are discussed in terms as 'actors' their theatrical power is seen to come from their resolute non-characterization. As Amélie Mons puts it, 'theatre is the artificial place par excellence, possibly the furthest one from nature. It is thus the most inappropriate place to have animals' (2024: 100). This is because 'they disrupt any form of theatrical illusion' (101), and the illusion of a transformation from actor to character (see 'Believable' and 'Truth') is acting's original trick.

'Character' retains a connection with the concept of agency even in cases that undervalue the human person as a relevant political or aesthetic concern. Right through post-dramatic theatre, 'character' conserves an Aristotelean sense of 'action' linked with intention. Linkable to the overbearing influence of Aristotle's *Poetics* on Western theatre history, the agentic notion of 'character' can be understood in context of the 'unity of action': 'the sequence of actions imitated in the play should be single and unified, in such a way that if any of the actions were to be displaced or removed, the whole would be disjointed and disturbed' (*Poetics* 8).

The role of 'character' in Aristotle's theory of Tragedy expressed in the *Poetics* is to be a consistent agent of what might later be called the 'throughline of action'. Under the influence of Heraclitus's *ethos anthropoi daimon* (a man's character is his fate), Aristotle connected dramatic 'character' with dramatic action and theorized what would come to be known as a 'narrative arc' by way of two alterations of circumstance experienced by characters: *Anagnorisis* ('recognition'), as a change from ignorance to knowledge and *Peripeteia* ('reversal') as a change in a hero's circumstances, usually from contentment to misery.

In Aristotelian idealized tragedy, it is the qualities in dramatic characters' personal character – *hamartia* ('flaw' or 'error') – that drives anagnorisis and peripeteia (*Poetics* 11). In the catalogue, Kenneth McLeish points out that:

> Renaissance scholars, writing from a Christian perspective in which the whole human race was tainted with the guilt of original sin and in need of God's redemption, restricted Aristotle's idea of *hamartia* to mean moral failure only.
>
> (2011: 271)

Although, in *Poetics*, *hamartia*, might just as easily be 'mispronouncing a word' or 'tripping over a stone' (271).

Despite a raft of literature on character 'journeys' and the arc of a narrative, 'character' remains a largely fixed proposition in most acting theory in the catalogue, even as protagonists transform their views and circumstances over the course of a narrative. 'Characters' who 'go on a journey' don't become different 'characters' as a result even when they undergo substantial behaviour and attitude change. The dominant interpretation of 'character' in this strand of acting theory and coaching requires actors to accept character as something quite securely fixed and unchanging. 'Character' in this sense, though, may be increasingly revealed both to the self and to the audience over the course of a journey. Grochala quotes Aristotle as contending, 'once established, they [characters] should not alter', and notes that he 'criticizes playwrights whose characters develop during the action of a play' – he 'singles out Iphigenia in Euripides's *Iphigenia at Aulis* as an example of poor characterization on the grounds that: "when she pleads for her life to be spared she is not at all like her later self"'(Aristotle, in Grochala, 2017: 194).

Perhaps Aristotle's criticism here should be cast in the light of Adam Hosein's account of the moral judgements that accompany female 'characters' in drama from Shakespeare to 1990s teen movies where women are expected to 'be themselves' consistently, despite the social pressure on them to behave in morally contradictory ways (Hosein, cited in Matthews and Torevell, 2011: 35–5).

Peta Tait argues that 'Aristotle addressed controversies around theatre's depiction of emotionally charged behaviour' by 'championing the value of tragedy but criticizing comedy' (Tait, 2021: 25) and, abiding within the dominant definitions and use-case of 'character' in the catalogue is the function of 'character' as a vicarious personae for an audience's feelings, and sometimes thoughts. Prominent in the Aristotelian concepts of 'catharsis', Tait writes that theatre:

> was controversial at this [Ancient] time because of its emotionally persuasive impact on the audience. Aristotle argues that drama should depict virtuous characters and, while he comments on a range of emotions in his non-theatre writing, his surviving commentary about theatre, *Poetics*, is concerned predominantly with pity and fear. Crucially, Aristotle asserts that both characters and dramatic circumstances need to be recognizable to the audience in order to communicate these emotions.
>
> (26)

With what sounds like artistic naivety on Aristotle's part, Tait contends that Aristotle, 'argues, a bad character will not arouse the audience's pity' and that theatrical events 'should concern characters who have strong bonds with each other, and Aristotle argues that even someone who only hears the story can react with pity and fear' (27).

John Gillett strikes a decidedly cathartic, Aristotelian tone when he claims that:

> If we [actors/theatre-makers] recreate emotions through the imaginary reality of a performance then we find that suffering in performance can give the actor and audience a sense of being uplifted, because a truth about human experience is being communicated through a story, we are wiser for it and feel more connected to our fellow humans.
>
> (2014: 130)

Acting

Alongside *character-as-action* and *character-for-emotion* sits *character-for-reflective-thought*; 'character' as a mechanism for audience members to see themselves and others as social subjects and to imagine themselves and their role within society (see Grochala, 2017: 187). Several authors point to the self-reflexive nature of acting 'character' and how this is underscored by inter-textual references to the stage that invite audiences to see themselves as quite literally in the character's shoes and part of the dramatic action. From Shakespeare's *oeuvre*, for example, Sarah Dustagheer is one of multiple authors who highlights the frequent reference in his writing to 'the globe', and the connections this supports between the world of the play and the world of the audience, in The Globe playhouse. In *Troilus and Cressida*, Ulysses asks if the 'bounded waters/should lift their bosoms higher than shores/and make a sop of all this solid globe' (1.3.111–13). Dustagheer observes that these 'self-reflexive' comments come at a 'moment of heightened emotion', such as when Hamlet promises to remember the Ghost of his father ('whiles memory holds a seat / In this distracted globe' [1.5.96–7]) or when Othello talks of the 'affrighted globe' shortly after killing Desdemona (5.2.99). Celebrations of actors' capacity to balance simultaneously ego-identifying with a 'character' that they are playing, perhaps even to the point of 'losing themselves' in that identification while also delivering lines such as these, that dramaturgically recall the artificiality of their performance, are prevalent throughout the catalogue, and these map neatly onto the 'paradox' that defines acting theory (see 'Preface: What is Acting?', 'A Statistically Irrelevant Keyword' and 'How and Why to Write *Acting: Keywords and Concepts*').

References

Barthes, R. (1967), *The Death of the Author*, London: Macat International.
Berlin, I. (1969), *Four Essays on Liberty*, Oxford: Oxford University Press.
Blattès, S. (2007), 'Is the Concept of "Character" Still Relevant in Contemporary Drama?', *Contemporary Drama in English,* 14: 69–81.
Coodin, S. (2010), 'What's Virtue Ethics Got to Do With It? Shakespearean Character as Moral Character', in M. D. Bristol (ed.), *Shakespeare and Moral Agency*, London: Bloomsbury Academic.
Dowd, M. M. and T. Rutter, eds (2023), *The Arden Handbook of Shakespeare and Early Modern Drama: Perspectives On Culture, Performance and Identity*, London: The Arden Shakespeare.
Fuchs, E. (1996), *The Death of Character*, Bloomington and Indianapolis: Indiana University Press.
Gillett, J. (2014), *Acting Stanislavski: A Practical Guide to Stanislavski's Approach and Legacy*, London: Methuen Drama.
Grochala, S. (2017), *The Contemporary Political Play: Rethinking Dramaturgical Structure*, London: Methuen Drama.
Harriman-Smith, J. (2024), *What Would Garrick Do? Or, Acting Lessons from the Eighteenth Century*, London: Methuen Drama.
Marshall, L. (2001), *The Body Speaks*, London: Methuen Drama.
Matthews, J. and D. Torevell, eds (2011), *A Life of Ethics and Performance: Liverpool Hope University Studies in Ethics Book 6*, Newcastle Upon Tyne: CSP.
McLeish, K. (2011), *A Guide to Greek Theatre and Drama*, London: Methuen Drama.

Mons, A. (2024), *Spectatorship and the Real in French Contemporary Theatre*, London: Methuen Drama.
Paterson, E. (2015), *The Contemporary American Monologue: Performance and Politics,* London: Methuen Drama.
Pitches, J. and S. Aquilina eds (2017), *Stanislavsky in the World: The System and its Transformations Across Continents*, London: Methuen Drama.
Read, A. (2013), *Theatre in the Expanded Field: Seven Approaches to Performance*, London: Methuen Drama.
Rodosthenous, G., ed. (2017), *Contemporary Adaptations of Greek Tragedy: Auteurship and Directorial Visions*, London: Methuen Drama.
Schneider, R. (1997), Review of the Book: *The Death of Character: Perspectives on Theater After Modernism* in *Theatre Journal,* 49(4): 541–3.
Tait, P. (2021), *Theory for Theatre Studies: Emotion*, London: Methuen Drama.

CHAPTER 3
BODY

(bod-ee)
- A concept in theory – *the body* – utilized to discuss the socio-cultural politics of acting and performance
- The physical envelope of the actor
- The opposite of 'the mind', or more accurately, the opposite of 'thinking' in acting practice.
- A focus of identity theory and politics in performance analysis
- An abiding interest with regards training and technique
- A prominent or primary subject of late twentieth-century theorization of identity and agency
- A component of an early twenty-first century trend in theory towards ecological models of cognition and agency
- A decidedly visual proposition.

'Body' or 'bodies' appears in the titles of books and chapters in the catalogue nearly 200 times and even more frequently – nearly 12,000 times – in the body (pun intended) of the text. Books and chapters with titles including, *The Body Speaks* (Marshall, 2001), *Rethinking the Actor's Body: Dialogues with Neuroscience* (McCaw, 2000), *Early Modern Actors and Shakespeare's Theatre: Thinking with the Body* (Tribble, 2017), *Theatre, Performance and Cognition: Languages, Bodies and Ecologies* (Blair and Cook, 2016), *Affective Performance and Cognitive Science: Body, Brain and Being* (Shaugnessey, 2013), *Theatre, Performance and Cognition: Languages, Bodies and Ecologies* (Tobin, cited in Blair and Cook [eds], 2016), 'connecting with the body' (Ewan and Green, 2015), 'bodies and minds' (Raber, 2018), 'thinking with the body' (Sirotkina and Smith, 2017), 'changing your mind-body' (Connington, 2014) or my personal favourite, 'body of work' (Matthews, 2014) might be put in the excited context of 'literary criticism's "turn to the body" in the mid-1980s' which sought to 'write the human body into the history of the subject and to situate the body and its emotions materially within the natural world' (Paster, cited in Callaghan and Gossett, 2016: 177). From literary subjects to very literal bodies, theatre and acting enthusiastically swerved into this turn proliferating titles about bodies and books restating their interest in phenomenology and 'embodiment' as a 'first philosophy' of performance.

It is virtually impossible to define what is meant by 'embodiment' in the catalogue and, while it might otherwise be considered a *keyword*, it appears fewer than 500 times. Almost all these uses have a rather generalized and banal (or, one might say, inclusive) use-case for describing bodily experiences, which is usually associated for actors with the experience of performing a role. In this rather unsatisfying catch-all use-case 'embodying' becomes little more than a synonym for 'playing' – as in 'embodying a role' rather than 'playing a role' – with the distinction between the two being largely a matter of changing semantic fashions with little to ground the apparent claim to aesthetic or phenomenological difference.

Sutton and Bicknell provide a helpfully literal definition of 'embodiment' with regards performance in their edited book, *Collaborative Embodied Performance: Ecologies of Skill* (2022) by observing performance's 'bodily or "**embodied**" nature' (emphasis in original, 2). Leaning into the corner of a twenty-first-century post-human, ecological turn (see Chapters 1 and 9), Sutton and Bicknell's collection applies a largely metaphorical (ANT-inspired) definition of 'ecology' taken from Edwin Hutchins, whose early twenty-first-century 'cognitive ecology' was a language formation used to highlight 'the web of mutual dependence among the elements of an ecosystem' (Hutchins, 2010: 706). Not an ecosystem in the original botanical sense, the 'ecology' concept emergent in contemporary performance studies discourse is a useful conceptualizing strategy for appreciating the highly interdependent and interactive elements within a performative frame. One of which is 'bodies'.

Historically speaking, 'embodiment' appears to have preceded 'ecology' in the catalogue, and in acting discourse, with the former flowing into performance studies from the 1970s/1980s social theory of Pierre Bourdieu, Marcel Mauss and Michel Foucault. Most frequent in sources from the first and second decade of the twenty-first-century, 'embodiment' appears as an organizing concept of performance studies in various sub-genus from 'embodied practice' (Chow, 2019), and 'embodied knowledge' (Spatz, 2015) to 'embodied cognition' (Sofia, 2016).

It is perhaps unfortunate that Marco De Marinis's term 'New Theatrology' did not catch on, not least because as he told us in 2016, he had been calling for it 'for over 20 years' (De Marinis, 2016). De Marinis's essay, 'Body and Corporeity in the Theatre: From Semiotics to Neuroscience. A Small Multidisciplinary Glossary' is unique in making even the turbo-charged eclecticism of the entries (incendiaries) in this book look focused and academically patient: 'nowadays', wrote De Marinis in 2016:

> the affirmation that the theatrical relationship [between actors and audience] engages the body as well as the mind, muscles no less than thought … might indeed sound banal. Theatre makers have always known all this, but the point is that theatre theory and scholars have not.
>
> (62)

With stylish casual didactism (I am envious), De Marinis wrote:

> the truth is that it was only during the twentieth century that the corporal dimension of the theatrical experience, from both sides of the barricade [actor/audience], started to be fully and explicitly accepted within theatre theory. Thus, theatre scholarship started to overcome the disembodied, logo-centric and culture-studies paradigms in which it had been imprisoned since Aristotle.

(62–3)

(Aristotle, that fool!) Despite this insight on 'the truth' (a topic that fool gave some considerable attention to in *Metaphysics*), with some magnanimity, De Marinis continued:

> after all, the delay sustained by theatre studies in accepting the body and corporeity within their theoretical discourse ought to be related to the delay and the difficulties long sustained by the humanities, including semiotics, linguistics and anthropology, with regard to the same matter.
>
> (62–3)

With vividly weary repetition of 'nowadays' he continues, 'the situation has changed profoundly; one even has the impression that an excessive emphasis is being placed on body issues [in theatre]' (64). Referencing concepts including 'body-mind', 'embodiment', 'incorporated knowledge', 'embodied knowledge' and 'somatic societies', De Marinis observes that by the early twenty-first century the 'body has become a real protagonist (if not *the* protagonist) in the theoretical discourse of humanities and social science' (64).

De Marinis's fast and loose depiction of three decades of theory across at least three academic domains is captivating, not least because, although confidently under-referenced, it is indeed 'true'. Or rather, the analysis of the catalogue confirms De Marinis's insight that 'the body' has grown in importance in performance discourse from the very late twentieth century to the early twenty-first century, at least when taking sheer frequency as a measure of import.

Sutton and Tribble (2013: 27–38) critique this discursive fashion pointing out that 'some theorizing about embodiment and embodied cognition can leave the "body" seeming depressingly inert and unconnected to the external world' (31). As it has become more frequent and more important as a *keyword* in acting, 'body' has also increasingly been cast in an antagonist role as part of relational conceptualizing strategies. Just as human corporeity has dissolved as an exclusive or singular phenomenon in the ecological turn which is still underway in scholarship. The inert 'Body' has given way to 'bodies' connected to the external world in both post-human ecological thinking but also a pluralizing ethic in books such as Kirsty Johnston's *Disability Theatre and Modern Drama: Recasting Modernism* (2016).

Johnston conceptualizes the 'body' as a very straightforward and literal concept – the physical aspect of each of us – while simultaneously recognizing the profound plurality and diversity that such a simple, literal idea connotes – the uniqueness of one physical being amidst a tremendous heterogeneity of physical beings. In Johnston, 'embodiment' relates to both the simple concept of having a body and the complex and complicated reality of how the bodies interact with and in cultural discourses, sign systems, built environments, gender and identity politics. As Johnston's critique of the social model of disability suggests, to talk about an 'actor's body' is at best misleading and at worst, nonsense. An 'actor's body' is just a body, or rather, it could be anybody's body. Or, to cite

Dick McCaw, 'the actor's body doesn't exist as such, it is simply a person's body that has been trained in a certain way' (McCaw, 2017: 1).

In Johnston (2016) 'corporeity' may be a less urgent concern for acting than 'identity' and associated 'agency'. In casting, for example, the ipseity and agency of individuals, and how these relate to the physical facts of their bodies-in-the-world has become an increasingly relevant ethical and artistic consideration. In the chapter 'Critical embodiment and casting' Johnston describes 'disability performance studies and activist discourses concerning theatre casting' as a 'central concern' in the field (38). Railing against the 'impotent infancy' of a dominant casting ethics underpinned by a 'facile and fallacious belief that physical beauty equals the good', Johnston quotes the disabled actor Nabil Shaban, stating:

> with the active and self-governing involvement of people with physical and mental differences in the performing arts, there is a chance that the more truly representative visions of the world will more effectively lead the world to a greater maturity, tolerance and safekeeping.
>
> (2016: 58)

Alongside the twenty-first-century political activism of Johnston, Shaban and others, motion capture technology has undermined the factual status of physical bodies and further complicated the ethical and artistic concerns deriving from these. One way of exemplifying this is to contrast the banal definitions of 'embodiment' operative in the late twentieth and early twenty-first-century trend described by De Marinis – which might be simplified to Sutton and Bicknell's observation that the 'embodied nature' of performance might be limited to the fact that performances have bodies – with Dower and Langdale's more recent definition in *Performing for Motion Capture* (2022):

> What do we mean by 'embodied'? For the purposes of this book we have settled on this interpretation: The most complete physical, psychological and emotional transformation an actor can make, to the point that even someone who knows them would not recognize them except for their visual features.
>
> (28)

'Embodying a role', for Dower and Langdale, is, in one sense identical to, *playing a role* (*well*) in many traditions of acting where transformation from actor to character is sine qua non. Indeed, McCaw simultaneously argues that while 'an actor's body' might not be a sensical concept, 'his body, this instrument of flesh and bone, can transform itself before our eyes into an image of another human being' (2017: 1).

Gutekunst and Gillett (2014) also adopt this popular framing of acting and an actor's 'body' as a transformational proposition: 'if we consider what constitutes a good acting performance, many would agree that the following elements need to be present': 'a sense of reality and truth in the creation of circumstances and character' and 'physical and vocal embodiment of the character' (xvii). Gutekunst and Gillett even contend that these attributes might 'offer universal criteria for the art of acting through different periods and styles of theatre, from the Greeks to Brecht', while acknowledging that their 'contemporary view … is strongly affected by the predominance of a realist theatre style since the nineteenth century, followed by the realism normally demanded by film, radio and television' (xviii).

Seemingly pouring kerosene on the smouldering distinction between *playing a role* – a bare prerequisite of acting – and *embodying a role* – an element of, or universal criterion for 'good' acting – the acting affordances of motion capture seemingly offer a new white-hot version of the transformational experiences of mimesis (see Chapter 14) ever present from 'the Greeks to Brecht'.

We might imagine one such Greek, Thespis, maybe (see 'Preface: What is Acting?'), selling tragi-comic masks on the streets of ancient Athens with the same shtick with which Pascal Langdale touts motion capture's wares today:

> What if we told you that it's possible to change your physicality so totally, your movement, gesture and posture, rhythm and tempo, that someone who knew you well could not tell who you were?
>
> (2022: 27)

Calling back to performance's earlier technological pioneers in a grand narrative of acting and the body, Langdale hyperbolizes that:

> Motion capture provides the possibility of such transformation that previous generations would envy. And previous generations *would* envy such a privilege. Because the desire for physical transformation is something that has existed for as long as storytelling, even if in the West the connection between mind and body has been generally discouraged for hundreds of years.
>
> (2022: 26)

The technologies of transformation, from masks, to costume, make-up, prosthesis, lighting, staging, camera lenses, post-production suites, motion capture, CGI and virtual production have successively provided a seemingly more technically advanced and industrially convenient means of achieving 'good' acting by variously exceeding the limitation of the human 'body' as a site of transformation.

The fixity and limitation of the human 'body', and the ideologies accompanying, have remained resolutely untransformed despite this impressive history of acting technologies. Considering Johnston and Shaban's critique, motion capture presents an ambivalent potential to the politics of casting at least equal to that of these earlier technologies, proposing both new inclusive and new repressive possibilities with regard to access, agency and identity.

The fact that 'acting' always necessarily entails *a thing* and *a thing represented* – at its most essential, it is *about* the identicality of, difference and transference between these two phenomena – makes things of all actors and actors of all things. Motion capture is a new technology capable of intervening on the transition between these two positions just as the proto-theatre-technology of the mask did (and does). Like all new technologies, while it might appear to redefine the game, so to speak, it probably only plays it faster and harder.

Tilly Norwood overtakes even mocap's position at a technical (if not ethical or artistic) leading edge. Motion captured performances intensify the visual aspect of acting and spectating with an overdetermining focus on the 'body' – its proportions and movements – as integral to representation and meaning-making. Across its longer-range history in the catalogue, the term 'the body' can be seen as part of a rhetorical strategy in acting discourse to focus attention on what is appreciable to an audience's visual sense.

The auditoria architecture of playhouses produces a scopophilia that drives staging and acting conventions attuned to sightlines and blocking. This architectural norm produces a comparative blindness, or perhaps deafness, to soundlines, and the ocular dynamics of the *theatron* (space of seeing) are carried forward into cinema, television and computer games through a primarily visual screen-based interface that can intensify the voyeuristic audience experience further still. This (crudely stated) culturally-material history of acting in the West tilted acting practice and criticism towards the visual sense, and this is evident in the relative frequency of terminology related to the other senses here in the catalogue.

'Voice' appears much less frequently than 'body' in the catalogue and terms such as 'aural' or 'vocal' appear only about 2,000 times combined. 'Visual', 'vision' and 'to see' appear over 20,000 times; 'listen' and 'hear' are used around 2,000 times. Words associated with the sense of smell barely register and 'taste', though seldom used has a very particular meaning associated with aesthetic preference, of course.

The emphasis on the actor's 'body' as a repository of meaning for the visual sense reaffirms the theatron's division between doers and watchers, assigning both a passivity and heuristic responsibility to the latter. Across the commentaries and treatise on the 'body' in the catalogue the dichotomy between its fixity and transubstantiationality abides as a primarily visual concern.

Refracting the theatrical status of bodies in relation to representation's paradoxical identicality and difference between *a thing* and *a thing represented* through the lens of geopolitics, and perhaps referring to Europeans from the Greeks to Brecht, José A. Sánchez writes that, 'the European citizen prefers the image of the body, prefers that their body be an image, an image not troubled by the shadows of ugliness, pain or death' (2022: 51). With a pejorative critique of Western capitalism, Professor at Cuenca Faculty of Fine Arts, Madrid, Sánchez writes:

> European citizens are instructed to look after their bodies with a "balanced" diet, to practise physical exercise and diverse bodily techniques, to maximize hygienic precautions, consume chemical supplements and, when necessary, subject themselves to surgical interventions that correct the deviations of nature. When we take care of our bodies, what we seek in reality is to rid ourselves of the body: being

as young as possible (even at the price of relinquishing experience in many cases), avoiding pain as much as possible (even at the price of relinquishing pleasure in many cases), shunning ugliness as much as possible (even at the price of masking ourselves in many cases). The goal is to maintain oneself as long as possible in the circuit of competition and in the chain of consumption.

(50–1)

The body and the image of the body being an already-imbricated cultural phenomenon (at least in Europe, according to Sánchez) adds yet another level of complexity to the already very complex relationships entailed in representation in European theatre and performance; when 'bodies' are the *things* and also the *things represented* who can say or know what represents and what is being represented. 'In contrast', writes Sánchez, 'migrants do not have a right to an image. They are bodies. They are allowed in as long as they are bodies' (51). 'Physical labour is reserved for them', he writes, 'in which they are above all bodies' (51) and bodies without meaning. Making a political criticism of twenty-first-century European border policies that might also be read as an assessment of the historical efforts of successive technologies to turn the 'body' into a stable visual image, Sánchez writes, 'they try to hide the bodies under the images, ignore the corpses on which those images feed' (52).

References

Bicknell, K. and J. Sutton, eds, (2022). *Collaborative Embodied Performance: Ecologies of Skill*, London: Methuen Drama.
Blair, R. and A. Cook (2016), *Theatre, Performance and Cognition*, London: Bloomsbury.
Chow, B. (2019), 'How Does the Trained Body Think?', in M. Bleeker, A. Kear, J. Kelleher and H. Roms (eds), *Thinking Through Theatre and Performance*, London: Methuen Drama.
Connington, B. (2014), 'Changing Your Mind-Body', in *Physical Expression on Stage and Screen: Using the Alexander Technique to Create Unforgettable Performances*, London: Methuen Drama.
De Marinis, M. (2016), 'Body and Corporeity in the Theatre: From Semiotics to Neuroscience. A Small Multidisciplinary Glossary', in C. Falletti, G. Sofia and V. Jacono (eds), *Theatre and Cognitive Neuroscience*, 61–74, London: Methuen Drama.
Dower, J. and P. Langdale (2022), *Performing for Motion Capture: A Guide for Practitioners*, London: Methuen Drama.
Ewan, V. and D. Green (2015), *Connecting with the Body. In Actor Movement: Expression of the Physical Being: A Movement Handbook for Actors*, London: Methuen Drama.
Gutekunst, C. and J. Gillett (2014), *Voice into Acting: Integrating Voice and the Stanislavski Approach*, London: Methuen Drama.
Hutchins, E. (2010), 'Cognitive Ecology', *Topics in Cognitive Science* 2 (4): 705–15.
Johnston, K. (2016), *Disability Theatre and Modern Drama: Recasting Modernism*, London: Methuen Drama.
Langdale, P. (2022), 'The Body', in J. Dower and P. Langdale, *Performing for Motion Capture: A Guide for Practitioners*, 25–52, London: Methuen Drama.
Marshall, L. (2001), *The Body Speaks*, London: Methuen Drama.

Matthews, J. (2014), *Body of Work. In Anatomy of Performance Training*, London: Methuen Drama.

McCaw, D. (2017), *Training the Actor's Body: A Guide*, London: Methuen Drama.

McCaw, D. (2020), *Rethinking the Actor's Body: Dialogues with Neuroscience*, London: Methuen Drama.

Paster, G. K. (2016), 'Bodies and Emotions', in D. Callaghan and S. Gossett (eds), *Shakespeare in Our Time: A Shakespeare Association of America Collection*, 177–94, London: The Arden Shakespeare.

Raber, K. (2018), *Bodies and Minds. In Shakespeare and Posthumanist Theory*, London: The Arden Shakespeare.

Sánchez, J. A. (2022), *The Bodies of Others: Essays on Ethics and Representation*, London: Methuen Drama.

Shaughnessy, N. ed, (2013), *Affective Performance and Cognitive Science: Body, Brain and Being*, London: Methuen Drama.

Sirotkina, I. and R. Smith (2017), 'Thinking with the Body', in *The Sixth Sense of the Avant-Garde: Dance, Kinaesthesia and the Arts in Revolutionary Russia*, London: Methuen Drama.

Sofia, G. (2016), 'Introduction: Towards an Embodied Theatrology?', in C. Falletti, G. Sofia and V. Jacono (eds), *Theatre and Cognitive Neuroscience*, London: Methuen Drama.

Spatz, Ben (2015), *What a Body Can Do: Technique as Knowledge, Practice as Research*, London: Routledge.

Sutton, J. and K. Bicknell, eds (2022), *Collaborative Embodied Performance: Ecologies of Skill*, London: Methuen Drama.

Tribble, E. (2017), *Early Modern Actors and Shakespeare's Theatre: Thinking with the Body*, London: The Arden Shakespeare.

Tribble, E. B. and J. Sutton (2013), 'Introduction: Interdisciplinarity and Cognitive Approaches to Performance', in N. Shaughnessy (ed.), *Affective Performance and Cognitive Science: Body, Brain and Being*, 27–38, London: Methuen Drama.

CHAPTER 4
PLAY

(Pah-lay)
noun
- the text of a staged drama
- the staged production of a dramatic text

verb
- An experimental and investigative attitude indifferent to failure that actors bring to training, rehearsal and performance (to be *playful*)
- A natural human process of inquiry and self-development disproportionately present in and required of actors
- A structure for teaching actors
- The antithesis to an intellectual exploration of character and narrative
- To act (to play)
- In compound with acting – playacting – as crude or 'bad' acting without credibility and founded exclusively on imitation
- In compound with acting – playacting – as a form of meta-acting in which players act at acting a role.

'Play' is the most frequently used word in the catalogue, with over 46,000 discrete usages. The overwhelming majority of uses of the word 'play' are in noun form and relate to two very fixed meanings: a (play)text or a production. These use-cases conform closely with common-language meanings of the word.

Where 'play' is used in verb form there is greater variance in both meaning and use-case, with a very clear sixteenth- to nineteenth-century synonym function for the verb 'act', that extends to 'player' and 'actor' also. In extant writing from this period and in commentaries on the drama of this period, 'to play' and 'players' hold to a very limited definition and use-case of 'to act' and 'actors' which is restricted to participation as a performer in a piece of theatre. Although dated, again, these meanings and use-cases stay very close to common-language definitions and are easily understood with reference to Jaques' famous 'all the world's a stage' speech, in *As You Like It*, where 'all the men and women [are] merely players'. This dramaturgical metaphor, usually attributed to Shakespeare, shows how the early-modern term 'play' was used both literally and metaphorically to describe both 'acting' in the theatrical sense and in real-life. While real-life 'playing' might carry a meaning and use-case related to dissemblance, Jaques' version of this metaphor doesn't cast 'players' as inherently duplicitous in real-life. Instead, Jaques' version of the metaphor finds a correlation between the fixedness of a written drama and the fatalism of Elizabethan cosmology. Every individual's real-life experience of 'playing a part' – a phrase that emerged with the 'parts' and 'rôles' (various translations from French into sixteenth-century English and later standardized to 'roles') of sixteenth-century theatre, wherein 'players' would receive only their own lines and cues as written segments of a larger text, rolled up as paper scrolls – might be an example of what the philosopher Max Black called a 'dead metaphor': a language term which has lost the meaning of its original imagery and has become embedded in everyday language (1954–5, 1977). The 'part' aspect certainly is but the 'play' part might be a different category of Black's dead metaphor: a separate vocabulary term whose meaning is not dependent upon previous knowledge of the metaphorical context. Just as with 'falling' in love, perhaps 'playing' parts, both on stage and in real life is not metaphorical at all.

Theatre history orthodoxy has it that, for sixteenth-century audiences, 'to play' was quite literally 'to speak' and the vocal and rhetorical modality of staged dramas was foremost. This conventional understanding is supported by the observation that early Modern audiences (from *audio*, of course) spoke of going to 'hear a play', and indeed Hamlet is much-quoted as dismissing Polonius and all but one of the 'players' off the stage saying, 'follow him, friends. We'll *hear* a play to-morrow' (Act II Scene II). Making theatrical impact from the rapid repetition of 'hear', Hamlet detains the First Player briefly with a stage-whispered aside – 'Dost thou *hear* me, old friend? Can you play "The Murther of Gonzago"?' This scene, indeed much of the drama of Hamlet's revenging relationship to Polonius is derived from what is said, heard and overheard. Hamlet's decision to entrap Polonius and reveal his guilt by inserting evocative and provocative lines about patricide into the play that Polonius will hear from the players might not have seemed quite as convoluted to early Modern audiences, who were presumably already convinced of the power of 'hearing' plays. Even to contemporary audiences, the extra status of 'speaking parts' is generally accepted.

In *Doing Shakespeare,* Simon Palfrey asks the playfully dehumanizing question of actors, 'What Should we Call These Speaking Things?':

What term should be used to denote the personages in a Shakespeare play? Many have been tried: Actors, Parts, Players, Persons, Personalities, People, Men/Women, Characters, Figures, Shadows, Subjects, Agents, Subjectivities, Individuals, Types, Roles, Identities, Inwardness, Interiority.

(2011: 233)

'Roughly speaking', he writes, 'we can divide these up into four categories':

First, there are those that emphasise the debt specifically to theatre as the enabling medium: actor, part, player, role, shadow (and perhaps even 'person', which derives from the idea of impersonating). Second are those which might apply to any mode of literature and which emphasise the debt to textuality: character, figure, type. Third are those that identify a basically straightforward human equivalence with the world outside the theatre: him/her, man/woman, individual. And finally there are those that, because they are not habitually used in discussions of 'real life', tend to reinforce the argument that we cannot simply assume that we know what we are talking about when we invoke those who act and speak in a play: subject, inwardness, agent, interiority.

(233: 2011)

Categorically minded, Palfrey's list of terms used for the 'speaking things' in Shakespeare's dramas puts 'player' in the category of language associated with the 'enabling medium', pointing out that a character, role, part, person, subject, agent, man, woman, type, etc. can (perhaps, must) all be 'played'. This insight applies to real life as well as to theatre, as Jaques had already stated.

Historiographically speaking, while 'play' appears most intensively in the catalogue with reference to the English Renaissance it also has a notable prominence in discourse in titles from and about theatre in the interwar years, and post-Second World War. Of this twentieth-century period, Roger Wooster asserts that:

it was TIE [Theatre in Education] … that took the ideas of child's play, child drama and theatrical performance to create a hybrid enveloping both feeling and rational responses in a new approach and fusing teaching and theatre in educational programmes built upon the human's innate need to learn through play.

(2016: 14)

Acknowledging 'the impact of the new wave of alternative theatre of the fifties and sixties' also, as well as the political and pedagogical experiments of Freire and Boal in the development of 'applied' theatrical practices testing and exploiting the immaterial membrane between 'playing a part' and 'having' or 'being' a part, Wooster contends that TIE was quite clearly 'walking in the footsteps' of Locke, Rousseau and educationalists such as Finlay-Johnson, who argued in *The Dramatic Method of Teaching* (1911) that 'childhood should be a time for absorbing big stores of sunshine for possible future dark times' (1911: 27) and, taking 'the aesthetics inherent in the child's play' (Wooster, 2016: 21) and the views of early twentieth-century educationalist, such as Caldwell Cook (1915), TIE adopted and coopted the belief that 'the only work worth doing is really play' (Cook, 1915: 4).

This belief, which Wooster argues was absorbed into theatrical practice by TIE, can be traced across multiple later twentieth-century sources in the catalogue in acting. Sources which contain no obvious philosophical or practical connection to TIE. Ken Rea (2021), for example, defines 'playfulness' as one of the key 'qualities' that must be nurtured in 'the outstanding actor'. 'Outstanding actors', according to Rea:

must first pass through childlike playfulness, because this allows the openness that will make an audience empathize with you. To do this may often mean you risk looking silly. But in that 'silliness' is an openness that, when focused in the service of the text, engages your audience, transports them and causes them to identify with what your character is going through. This in turn releases your individuality as an actor.

(2021: xv)

Similarly, Luke Dixon, in his book, *Play-Acting* (2003) exemplifies this twentieth-century valorization of play as an innate and foundational well-spring of creativity and knowledge for actors. 'Play is the thing', he writes, and his book is filled with exercises, games, tasks and ideas motivated to 'take the performer back to a world of play, of childhood freedom of expression and of intuition' (2003: 3).

Late twentieth- and early twenty-first-century discourse on acting assigns a prelapsarian quality to 'play'. To this end, some of what is written about 'play' in the catalogue is associated with non-quotidian aesthetics and self-consciously culturally subversive ideals about acting. Eilon Morris, for example, in *Rhythm in Acting and Performance* (2017) picks up the thread of 'impulse' running through the European laboratory theatre tradition of the late twentieth century: citing a Grotowski rehearsal diary of the early 1960s, Morris quotes:

> if I had to define our theatrical quest in one sentence, with one term, I would refer to the myth about the dance of Shiva. I would say: 'We are playing at being Shiva. We are acting out Shiva' … Shiva says … I am without name, without form, and without action … I am pulse, movement, rhythm. (Shiva-Gita). The essence of the theatre we are seeking is 'pulse, rhythm and movement'.
>
> (Grotowski cited in Osiński, 1986: 50)

There is an ideological juxtaposition between the everyday content of theatrical performance and a value-based commitment to actor training practices that undo, remove or remediate the harmful effects of society and culture (lived in the everyday) on the creative and expressive potential of the human body and mind. This ideology can certainly be tracked back to and within early twentieth-century educationalist, applied and TIE projects and treatise.

Dick McCaw's *Rethinking the Actor's Body* (2020) also illustrates this trend with a chapter devoted to 'Training: From the Everyday Body to the Actor's Body' and a running theme of 'creative play' and 'multi-sensorial, playful attentiveness' describing the cultivation of 'a bodily state in which creative affordances and discoveries can be made' (76). Indeed, the association – textual and subtextual – between 'play' and 'creativity' is strong right across the catalogue.

Interestingly, Shakespeare is described as 'playful' more frequently than any other playwright in the catalogue (662 times) with nearly all these descriptions (620) occurring in titles published since 2010. This, perhaps, indicates a theme in more recent reappraisals of Shakespeare's plays, tending towards the positive late twentieth-century attitude towards play. Scholars publishing after 2010 would have received their education late in the twentieth century, in a context of positivity towards play, and so, perhaps, a proclivity towards positively interpreting Shakespeare's outputs as 'playful' amongst these generations of authors is to be expected.

There is also a revisionist sentiment here, with other playwrights and practitioners commonly considered austere or highbrow described as 'playful' in the catalogue. Brecht, according to Katalin Trencsényi is wrongly understood as 'rigid, emotionless and propagandistic' because critics 'overlook the notion of playfulness, humour and experiment that is found in the pages of *The Messingkauf Dialogues*' (2015: 121). Brecht's experimental approach to production ('in a spirit of experiment') and desire for lightness and ease of delivery ('Leichtigkeit'), as well as his reference to slapstick and clowns 'all point to a much more complex and theatrical conception than that with which he is sometimes credited' (Trencsényi, 2015: 121–2).

'Play', as a concept associated with creativity and understood as innately human in nature, is a dominant and largely uncontested virtue in twentieth- and twenty-first-century acting discourse. A quick and crude sentiment analysis of the roughly 500 uses of 'playful' or 'playfulness' in the catalogue directly related to acting practice shows only positive associations for the term. From Paul Eslam's *Acting Characters* (2011), which exhorts actors to 'experiment in rehearsal and in private with the vigour and playfulness of a young child' (179), to Jackie Snow's *Movement Training for Actors* (2012), Gillett and Gutekunst's *Voice into Acting* (2021), Bill Britten's *From Stage to Screen: A Theatre Actor's Guide to Working on Camera*, (2014) or Cass Fleming's 'Theatre of the future' (2020) 'play' and 'playfulness' are strongly associated with exploration and freedom, and are implicitly enjoyable. 'To play' in this sense is not only 'to do' – *to do the part*, or fulfil the real-life obligation or participate in the real-world process – but to do these things with a particular childlike attitude that channels the productive power of mimesis (see Chapter 14).

References

Black, M. (1954–5), 'Metaphor', in *Proceedings of the Aristotelean Society*, N.S., 273–94, London: Harrison & Son Ltd.
Black, M. (1977), 'More About Metaphor', *Dialectica* 31 (3–4): 431–57.
Britten, B. (2014), *From Stage to Screen: A Theatre Actor's Guide to Working on Camera*, London: Methuen Drama.
Cook, H. C. (1915), *The Play Way*, London: Heinemann.
Dixon, L. (2003), *Playacting*, London: Methuen.
Finlay-Johnson, H. (1911), *The Dramatic Method of Teaching*, London: Nisbet.
Fleming, C. (2020), '"Theatre of the Future": Chekhov Technique for Devised Theatre and Catalyst Direction', in C. Fleming and T. Cornford (eds), *Michael Chekhov Technique in the Twenty-First Century: New Pathways*, London: Methuen Drama.
Gillett, J. and J. Gutekunst (2021), *Voice into Acting: Integrating Voice and the Stanislavski Approach*, London: Methuen Drama.
McCaw, D. (2020), *Rethinking the Actor's Body: Dialogues with Neuroscience*, London: Methuen Drama.

Morris, E. (2017), *Rhythm in Acting and Performance: Embodied Approaches and Understandings,* London: Methuen Drama.
Osiński, Z. (1986), *Grotowski and His Laboratory,* New York: PAJ Publications.
Palfrey, S. (2011), *Doing Shakespeare,* London: Bloomsbury Arden Shakespeare.
Rea, K. (2021), *The Outstanding Actor: Seven Keys to Success,* 2nd edn, London: Methuen Drama.
Snow, J. (2012), *Movement Training for Actors,* London: Methuen Drama.
Trencsényi, K. (2015), *Dramaturgy in the Making: A User's Guide for Theatre Practitioners,* London: Methuen Drama.
Wooster, R. (2016), *Theatre in Education in Britain: Origins, Development and Influence,* London: Methuen Drama.

CHAPTER 5
MOVEMENT

(*moo-vff-ment*)
Noun
- Everything an actor does with their body
- A specific domain of acting craft and theory
- An ambit of control connecting actors' physicality to characters' 'body language'.

A word used a lot in the catalogue and yet there is little to say about it as a keyword. Used over 9,000 times there is an exceedingly strong consensus on the meaning and use-case of the word 'movement'. Based on the catalogue's sources alone, 'movement' may not exhibit some of the characteristics of keywords at all. The sheer frequency of its use indicates that it is part of an 'active vocabulary', as Williams would define it, and might be considered useful as a term for 'recording' and 'investigating' acting, and is perhaps very practical in providing 'ways not only of discussing' but 'at another level of seeing', 'central experiences' (Williams, [1976] 1985: 15) of acting. Where 'movement' is quite different to most other keywords in the catalogue is that it does not appear to present any real 'problems of meaning' (15) in acting, at least not in the catalogue's sources anyway.

Vanessa Ewan and Debbie Green, in their 'Movement Handbook for Actors' (2015) make a compound noun – actor movement. For them, 'Actor Movement is the name the authors use for the process given to the study of the physical expression of the imagination and body of an actor' (3). Although this compound noun is used inconsistently by other authors across the catalogue, with the 'actor' part being mostly silent and implicit, this working definition is broadly applicable in the multiple contexts in which 'movement' is used to define and describe something about the craft and practice of acting.

Jackie Snow uses 'Movement for Actors' (Snow, 2012: xii) to mean mostly the same thing as Actor Movement, although with perhaps a slightly more explicit focus on practice and not just 'study' of physical expression. Ewan and Green, and Snow, recognize how the acting keyword 'movement' acquires most of its currency from actor training institutions:

> Traditional Western actor training is generally broken down into Acting, Voice and Movement. Acting and Voice function easily as distinct fields of study and have been amply documented in writing by their leading practitioners. Movement, however, perhaps precisely because it is not of the written word is not as easily captured and so remains under-represented as a field of study.
>
> (Ewan and Green, 2015: 1)

The extent to which it is underrepresented in the catalogue is moot but the level to which it is under-interrogated in the catalogue and, my wider reading would suggest, in the field more generally is apparent.

This would appear to be because of the close discursive relationship between 'movement' and 'body' (see 'Body'), with the latter providing the focus for most theoretical and philosophical enquiry into acting. Ewan and Green connect 'movement' to the 'physical heritage' (2015: 1) of actors' bodies but, despite the evident influence of twentieth-century time-and-motion studies in acting theory and practice (e.g. see McCaw, 2017) the critical focus-of-attention this creates in discourse is very firmly assigned with 'body' and oddly dissociated from 'movement'.

This dissociation of 'movement' from the philosophical problematics of, and contentious debates about, 'embodiment' (see 'Body') appears to have rendered a very fixed meaning for 'movement' and given it an almost entirely functional status in discourse and as a keyword.

Highly used in practical and theoretical titles on actor training, 'movement' appears to have been able to achieve a highly stable definition, meaning-sense and set of use-cases. In a sample of actor training titles from the catalogue (Ewan & Green, 2015; Snow, 2012; Camilleri, 2019, 2023; McCaw, 2017, 2020), 'movement' is used much more frequently even than 'acting' as a descriptive term (2:1 or greater) and with no discernible contestation of its meaning or use in language, or argumentation about the phenomenon that it denotes. Of course, as I noted in the introduction, sheer or relative volume and frequency does not equate to meaning or significance. What is significant is that, with indicators of both relative and absolute frequency in the catalogue, the meaning of 'movement' doesn't move.

References

Camilleri, F. (2019), *Performer Training Reconfigured: Post-Psychophysical Perspectives for the Twenty-First Century*, London: Methuen Drama.
Camilleri, F. (2023), *Performer Training for Actors and Athletes*, London: Methuen Drama.
Ewan, V. and D. Green (2015), *Actor Movement: Expression of the Physical Being: A Movement Handbook for Actors*, London: Methuen Drama.
McCaw, D. (2017), *Training the Actor's Body: A Guide*, London: Methuen Drama.
McCaw, D. (2020), *Rethinking the Actor's Body: Dialogues with Neuroscience*, London: Methuen Drama.
Snow, J. (2012), *Movement Training for Actors*, London: Methuen Drama.
Williams, R. (1985), *Keywords a Vocabulary of Culture and Society*, New York: Oxford University Press.

CHAPTER 6
EMOTION

(imm-oh-shenn)
noun
- A largely physiological experience for an actor or audience member usually defined dichotomously with an intellectual experience. Something one *feels* rather than *thinks*
- A response to stimuli in actors and audiences
- A psychological experience for actors and audiences
- A physiological experience for actors and audience
- A sociological experience for audiences
- An exclusive individual experience
- An inclusive collective experience
- The instigator of an actor's performance choices
- The product of an actor's performance choices
- An immediate personal response
- An onto-historical concept deeply embedded in theatrical events
- An historically discontinuous concept describing distinct phenomena in each historical period
- The basis of a sympathetic magic between fictional characters and audience sensibilities
- A longer-lived experience of affect
- A shorter-lived experience of feeling or mood
- A commodity in acting
- A reason why spectators go to the theatre
- The reason why spectators go to the theatre
- The reason of theatre
- A subsidiary function of theatre events.

Occurring 3,252 times in the catalogue as a noun but nearly the same again in an adjectival form, 'emotion' might reasonably be classified as a high-frequency term in acting discourse. As the above shows, it is one of the most multifariously defined terms and, like other key concepts, it has contradictory definitions. However, this keyword is unusual to the extent that its varying and competing definitions are applied to both actors and audiences, and often deployed within foundational concepts describing and conceptualizing the relationship *between* these two groups.

There is consensus in the catalogue that emotion is important to theatrical performance. For Brad Krumholz (2023), 'emotion is generally considered to be a central component of the theatrical experience across genres, for the actor and also for the audience' (150). Despite this unanimity, there are competing ideologies about whether it describes the same thing in acting discourse as it does in audience theory. Although one of the more philosophically banal understandings of 'emotion', a largely unifying definition of the concept in acting discourse is as a not-fully-controllable personal experience usually stimulated by an existential factor. As Daniel Dresner (2018) has it, 'a strong feeling or response triggered by an event or relationship' (63). Lorna Marshall (2001) observes that many actors see 'working with emotions … as a daunting task, like approaching a jungle full of lurking animals all ready to tear you apart' (55). In this conception, 'interesting acting requires you [the actor] to control your emotions' (Dresner, 2018: 63) and this definition underpins and motivates methods, approaches, exercises and concepts that prescribe largely neo-Naturalistic stylistic tropes in performance.

This orthodoxy is prevalent throughout the more practical 'how-to' manuals in the catalogue but also within the titles providing interpretative methodologies of scholarly performance analysis, and this may be because of the origin myth of 'the paradox of acting'. Alan Read (2013) has described the ideas within Diderot's *Paradoxe sur le Comedien* as 'the first secular theory of acting' (82) while Peta Tait, in her book *Emotion: Theory for Theatre Studies* (2021) categorizes the paradox as a key 'legacy' in theatre history. Tait observes that 'the paradox' is both philosophically and evidentially credible: 'that accomplished actors do not feel the specific emotion they perform, continues to be confirmed in more recent investigations of the acting of emotion' (47). Citing several 'major studies' with 'hundreds of actors', Tait reaffirms Diderot's insight that actors 'do not experience the character's emotions as they portray them' (Konijn, 2000: 144) but rather they 'create the illusion of real emotions' from everyday life (34). Tait notes, citing another study by Eric Hetzler, that 'the actor seeks control and develops a separate awareness of the expressed emotions of the character but this is not personally or bodily felt' (Hetzler, 2007: 70). Disclosing a similar insight, multiple authors, including Lorna Marshall (2001), recognize that 'there are two common traps that performers fall into when working with emotions': one in which the performer is 'trying to find signals to show the audience what they are feeling' creating a histrionic performance mostly incredible to an audience and a second where, 'the performer who is clearly feeling a great deal' acts in an 'inert' fashion, alienating audiences altogether (60–1).

Diderot's seminal treatise on acting is served up throughout the catalogue (including in my own books) as a foundational philosophical insight on the confounded relationship between audience and actor. Differently interpreted as article-of-truth, article-of-faith or crass-misunderstanding, Diderot's observation that actors may struggle to control a genuinely felt emotion to the extent required to choreograph its outward expression within the compositional requirements of narrative and staged event is riven throughout the catalogue like a seaside message in a stick of rock.

Many academic authors in the catalogue highlight the direct influence of the paradox on influential practitioners of acting craft. Marie-Christine Autant-Mathieu highlights the direct influence of this theory – and its critique and refutation in the pioneering psychology of Ribot and Binet – on Stanislavksi (2017: 69) and thereby re-embeds Diderot and the emotion-as-opposite-of-control definition in Western acting historiography. Acting's definition as a presentational activity of surfaces is latent within this philosophical and historiographical trend. Writers, such as Oliver Double, historicize 'the paradoxe' and note that Diderot's conclusion – that, although not mutually exclusive, presenting emotion is superior theatrically to feeling emotion (*if I really have to make a choice!*) – emerged later in his thinking and in response to the radical staging conventions of Théâtre Libre with 'Diderot's ideals of theatrical realism' only really being 'strictly implemented in the late nineteenth century' (Double, 2015: 10). Then, according to Oliver Double (2015), Diderot's prophetic idea of what will later be called the fourth wall:

> Whether you write or act, think no more of the audience than if it had never existed. Imagine a huge wall across the front of the stage, separating you from the audience, and behave exactly as if the curtain had never risen.
>
> (Diderot, [1758] 1918: 299)

This found form in André Antoine's scenography, where:

> The actors, no longer playing directly to the audience, are, by implication, no longer playing for it. No longer the acknowledged core of the action, the audience experiences the illusion of looking in on another real, self-centred world, of being the unseen witness of a moment of actual existence.
>
> (Chothia, 1991: 24–5)

Via the development of the fourth wall concept the mythic origin of the paradoxe and the centrality of the emotion-vs-control motif is further reinforced in the historical narrative of Western acting. In a very practical nugget of advice for actors, Stanislavski recalls Diderot's paradoxe in guidance that makes the ambivalence between surface representations and private personal experiences palpable: when acting on stage, writes Stanislavski, focus your eyes 'almost at the same angle as if you were looking at the tip of your nose' to simulate looking at an object on the fourth wall itself, rather than making the 'physiological error' of focusing on somebody in the orchestra (Stanislavski, 1980: 90). If you want to get a sense of the challenge of contemplating the mutual inclusivity of: (1) the intention to generate and control affects for audience members with; (2) the intention to stimulate an authentic emotional experience for actors, then try following Stanislavski's advice and see if you get a headache too.

Alan Read, in *Theatre in the Expanded Field: Seven Approaches to Performance*, subtly and sub-textually restates 'the paradoxe' between feeling emotion and presenting emotion via a fictional anecdote of the young Diderot with a recurrent motif of pairings: the country and the capital, the sacred and the profane, excitement and boredom, life and death, youthful adventure and the tomb, animals and humans, hope and truth, the left hand and the right, digital technology and the cave wall. Read's (2013) couplings remind readers of the complex unification of bipartite truths in paradoxes; he quotes Phillipe

Lacoue-Labarthe's somewhat tautological suggestion that 'the enunciation of a paradox [would] involve' more than 'it has the power to control' – 'a paradox of enunciation' (84). Read's slippery paradoxical wordplay explodes the space between the poles of Diderot's *paradoxe* and erodes the philosophical boundaries between concepts such as 'emotion' and 'affect', 'actor' and 'spectator'.

Multiple titles differentiate cleanly between emotion and affect – and between the stage and the auditorium experiences – and multiple titles draw connections and mutual inclusivities between these terms, spaces and subjectivities, umbrellaing these and related concepts under the conceptual parasol of 'feeling'.

According to Erin Hurley (2010), spectators 'attend the theatre to feel *more*, even if it doesn't make us feel *better*; we go to have our emotional life acknowledged and patterned', and potentially 'expanded' (77; emphasis in original). Martin Welton (2012) contends that it is the whole experience of attending live performance which creates spectator feeling because it arises from being in a designated space (ecology) with all its elements (8).

These different explanations of how feeling happens in theatrical performance point to multiple types of felt experience but also to an unstable common-ground, phenomenologically speaking – it is struggle enough to understand and contend with and locate the origins of one's own personal feelings, as an actor or a spectator; it is virtually impossible to know anything about other peoples' feelings.

'Affect' has, at times and in given genres, displaced 'emotion' and 'feeling' as theatre's central concern and this is an identifiable trend in twenty-first-century titles on 'contemporary' theatre and performance, such as Eddie Paterson's *The Contemporary American Monologue: Performance and Politics* (2015) and Marrisa Fragkou's *Ecologies of Precarity in Twenty-First Century Theatre: Politics, Affect, Responsibility* (2019). This reflects what Frank Camilleri has described as the '"affective turn" in the humanities of the early twenty-first century' (2019: 155). Paul Allain and Jean Harvie (2014) recognized that this turn 'shifted credit for meaning-making *from* features and practices which focus on semiotic systems, representation, sense-making and interpretation *onto* bodily experience, feelings and emotions' (149). Eddie Paterson (2015) refers to affect as 'a felt intensity that accompanies a change, or transition, in the body. It is neither emotion, nor does it contain subjective content' (163) and underscores the significance of 'contemporary artistic and cultural practices' that cultivate affects – as opposed to feelings or thoughts – for audiences. Following Mouffe (2013: xvii), Paterson asserts the disruptive potential of affect-directed performance events which 'constitute a crucial site of intervention for counter-hegemonic practices', 'because of the ways they can help to imagine and enhance the antagonistic dimensions of everyday life' (2015: 163).

Hans-Thies Lehmann (2006), suggests that one affect-directed performance style could be observed in the 'aesthetics of risk' exemplified in some postdramatic theatre. Here, extreme spectacles, 'which always also contain the possibility of offending or breaking taboos' (186–7) can generate audience reactions which are not straightforwardly classifiable as emotional in content. Martin Welton, in *Feeling Theatre* (2012), emphasizes environment as determinant of feeling and re-blurs the linguistic boundaries between emotion, feeling and sensation. The 'aestheticising' (5) of perceptual sensations – their enveloping within the conditions of the material world in which they arise – 'can be described as a "feel"', he writes (5). A 'feel', according to Welton, 'migrates between emotion, cognition and touch' and this is 'reflective of the extent to which thought, affect and sensation are bound together' (5).

Erin Hurley (2010) also interleaves 'feeling' and 'emotion' in theatre, arguing historically that, from Artistotle to Brecht, 'feeling runs like a red thread through the history of theatrical production' (2). For Peta Tait (2021), 'emotions and emotional feelings should be distinguished as happens in other disciplinary fields of study', and 'affect and emotional feeling can be separated out in theatrical patterns of engagement, patterns that additionally create an overarching emotional mood' (2). In Tait's conceptual hierarchy, 'emotions are cognitive ideas and impressions', 'emotional feelings are physiological experiences', and 'affect emphasizes embodied felt sensitivity to and within the surroundings while the concept of mood allows individual, social and aesthetic experiences to be linked' (2).

Circling back to the subject of actors' emotion, Tait finds herself constantly bumping into Diderot (as so many of us do). She notes that, 'a performer will be performing anger rather than feeling it, because he or she (they) cannot afford to be overcome with anger even where its expression draws on rehearsed processes involving feeling' (2021: 11). 'A spectator will recognize that angry feelings are being represented without becoming angry', she writes, 'therefore, theatrical performance suggests that: firstly, it is possible to present and recognize distinctive emotional feelings without feeling them or reciprocating with similar feeling; secondly, feeling exists within a spectrum of voluntary to involuntary responses' (11–12). For actors in particular, 'there can be variable levels of control arising with awareness of feeling – performers learn ways to manage feeling in their training' (12).

In Tait, as in Diderot, 'control' might be thought of as a hygiene factor with regards emotion and acting. Hygienically managing the complicated relationship between 'emotion' and 'control' in acting can be seen as an emerging commercial interest of the early modern English stage that was perfected as a reliably saleable and profit-making feature of twentieth-century narrative cinema. Mitigating the vagaries of emotional control on stage, the camera enabled the capture and perfect replicability of the kinds of emotional displays that reportedly wowed early modern audiences (see Roach, 1993). In theatre, meanwhile, the practical inability to perfectly manage this commodifiable feature of acting developed to crisis point in the 'affective turn' of the twenty-first century, giving rise to both the affect-fixation that negated it and a retrospective sensibility that muses, as James Harriman-Smith does, *What Would Garrick Do?* (2024). With witty nostalgia, his book 'presents eighteenth-century theatre theory and practice as a source of inspiration for contemporary theatre practitioners' (4).

Natalie Bainter also takes the early modern period as the epicentre of seismic activity on emotion and control. Writing in *Affective Performance and Cognitive Science: Body, Brain and Being* (2013), Bainter highlights the substantial insights of Joseph Roach's 'groundbreaking book', *The Player's Passion: Studies in the Science of Acting* (1993), which argues that 'the science of acting' in the seventeenth century, 'informed by humoral science and medicine, ensured that the virtuosity of an actor was determined by his perceived ability not merely to exhibit emotion, which anyone could do, but to demonstrate control over it' (93). According to Roach (1993), '[the actor's] art requires him to set his bodily instrument in expressive motion, not by freeing his actions, but by confining them in direction, purpose, and shape' (52). Bainter observes that the 'privileging of control and measure over outright display sprang from [contemporaneous] fears about the moral and health risks associated with the profession of acting, to the bodies in the audience but even more so to the body of the actor' (2013: 93). The 'unwieldiness of the actor's body' became 'the ground for his art of control' (93). Roach's historically-wide-ranging book meticulously historicizes the concepts of 'emotion', 'feeling' and 'passion', highlighting continuity and discontinuity with our contemporary understandings of these terms. Despite this, from Ancient Greek oratory case studies through Garrick and the early modern and up to the end of the twentieth century, Roach's historical record of acting generally reinforces Krumholz's assertion that 'emotion is generally considered to be a central component of the theatrical experience' (2023: 150).

References

Allain, P. and J. Harvie (2014), *The Routledge Companion to Theatre and Performance*, 2nd edn, London: Routledge.

Autant-Mathieu, M. (2017), 'Stanislavsky and French Theatre: Selected Affinities', in J. Pitches and S. Aquilina (eds), *Stanislavsky in the World: The System and its Transformations Across Continents*, 63–86, London: Methuen Drama.

Bainter, N. (2013), 'An Exercise in Shame: The Blush in a Woman Killed With Kindness', in N. Shaughnessy (ed.), *Affective Performance and Cognitive Science: Body, Brain and Being*, 91–102, London: Methuen Drama.

Camilleri, F. (2019), *Performer Training Reconfigured: Post-Psychophysical Perspectives for the Twenty-First Century*, London: Methuen Drama.

Chothia, J. (1991), *André Antoine*, Cambridge and New York: Cambridge University Press.

Diderot, D. ([1758] 1918), 'On Dramatic Poetry', in H. Clark Barrett (ed.), *European Theories of the Drama*, Cincinnati: Stewart & Kidd.

Double, O. (2015), 'Introduction: What is Popular Performance?', in A. Ainsworth, O. Double and L. Peacock (eds), *Popular Performance*, 1–30, London: Bloomsbury Academic.

Dresner, D. (2018), *A Life-coaching Approach to Screen Acting*, London: Methuen Drama.

Fragkou, M. (2019), *Ecologies of Precarity in Twenty-First Century Theatre: Politics, Affect, Responsibility*, London: Methuen Drama.

Harriman-Smith, J. (2024), *What Would Garrick Do? Or, Acting Lessons from the Eighteenth Century*, London: Methuen Drama.

Hetzler, E. (2007), 'Actors and Emotion in Performance', *Studies in Theatre and Performance*, 28 (1): 59–78.

Hurley, E. (2010), *Theatre and Feeling*, Basingstoke: Palgrave Macmillan.

Konijn, E. (2000), *Acting Emotions: Shaping Emotions on Stage*, trans. B. Leach with D. Chambers, Amsterdam: Amsterdam University Press.

Acting

Krumholz, B. (2023), *Why Do Actors Train?: Embodiment for Theatre Makers and Thinkers*, London: Methuen Drama.
Lehmann, Hans-Thies (2006), *Postdramatic Theatre*, Abingdon and London: Routledge.
Marshall, L. (2001), *The Body Speaks*, London: Methuen Drama.
Mouffe, C. (2013), *Agonistics: Thinking the World Politically*, London: Verso.
Paterson, E. (2015), *The Contemporary American Monologue: Performance and Politics*, London: Bloomsbury Methuen Drama.
Read, A. (2013), *Theatre in the Expanded Field: Seven Approaches to Performance*, London: Bloomsbury Methuen Drama.
Roach, J. (1993), *The Player's Passion: Studies in the Science of Acting*, Ann Arbor: University of Michigan Press.
Stanislavski, C. (1980), *An Actor Prepares*, London: Methuen.
Tait, P. (2021), *Theory for Theatre Studies: Emotion*, London: Methuen Drama.
Welton, M. (2012), *Feeling Theatre*, Basingstoke: Palgrave MacMillan.

CHAPTER 7
TRUTH & TRUTHFULNESS

(trooth)
noun
- a thing which both actors and audiences accept to be the purpose of their activities
- a latent, tacit or transcendent 'meaning' of a performance usually pertaining to a universal and or ahistorical interpretation of the human condition
- a synonym for 'verisimilitude' in certain traditions of performance
- a quality of seriousness in the subject matter of a play or an acting performance.

TRUTHFULNESS
(trooth-full-ness)
- a satisfying quality in an actor's performance that makes it credible to an audience
- a capacity for an actor's performance to reveal to an audience a hidden or dimly apprehended set of facts about reality or existence
- an actor's own sense of having physically or psychologically (or both) inhabited a character in such a way that they were no longer fully themselves for the duration of that inhabitation
- a mimetic style that usurps itself aesthetically to intensify audience interpretations of the significance of experience as opposed to the significatory capacity of experience.

'Of all the words actors use to reach to the heart of what they do when they are acting, "truth" is probably the most used' (Paget, 2018: 118). Not quite true of the authors of this catalogue – that would be 'play' – but Derek Paget's observation about actors-speaking-about-acting is plausibly derived from his 'Acting with Facts' research project, which saw him interview:

> British actors about the joys and terrors of pretending not only to be someone else (the actor's habitual work situation) but also someone who really existed and was still alive, or who really had existed, but was now dead.
>
> (110)

Plausible at least, then, for a sub-set of British actors performing in a sub-set of television drama.

'Truth' is a mid-frequency term in the acting catalogue, appearing over 2,000 times and with roughly 600 uses suffixed or prefixed – truthful, truthfully, truthfulness, untruth, mistruth. In adjective form, 'true' appears slightly more frequently – 2,777 times – but, adjusting for the number of times this is not used with any specific reference to acting, 'truth', in all formulations, isn't very frequently used at all, which might perhaps surprise Derek Paget (please do write in and tell us, Derek). Indeed, it appears far less frequently than this reader was expecting (truthfully).

What becomes evident through the computational analysis is that the use of 'truth' as a concept is concentrated in *certain* titles associated with *distinct* traditions and media. Nearly half of all uses of 'truth' appear in titles in conjunction with 'television' or 'tv' – in fact, nearly 4 per cent of all uses in the catalogue occur within one book – *Exploring Television Acting* (2018) – which contains Paget's comments about the ubiquity of 'truth' in acting discourse.

Over half of all uses of 'truth' are in conjunction with 'natural' or 'real', although far fewer (587) with real-*ist,* Natural-*ist* or *-ism*.

The word is used nearly 200 times in conjunction with Stanislavski – roughly the same numbers as in conjunction with Grotowski – and over 500 times in conjunction with Brecht, although most of these uses denote a political value for the term as opposed to the largely aesthetic one that Paget refers to. This stat also comes with the caveat that it has not been possible to weight these or other raw number counts relative to the overall volume of content on a topic – Brecht, in this case – within a consistent approach across the catalogue. In light of that, it may be most relevant to note that 'truth' is used hundreds of times in commentaries and theorizations of Brecht, Stanislavski and Grotowski, but fewer than fifty times in association with other practitioners, including Meisner, Adler or Strasberg and little more than 100 times with reference to Meyerhold. This findings may be interpreted as broadly in line with the relative popularity and influence of each of these figures rather than revealing anything specific about any one practitioner's relationship to 'truth', then.

'True' is used in conjunction with 'Chekhov' around 500 times, with the vast majority associated with the actor-and-trainer nephew, Michael as opposed to the playwright-uncle, Anton, and again these are highly concentrated in a small number of titles.

At the risk of over-interpreting these findings (but in the spirit of writing incendiaries and not just entries) it may be that 'truth' is *big* as a concept in a *small* number of titles. This may be one way of interpreting its significance in acting theory and practice more broadly where the concept is integral to few-but-culturally-dominant traditions and media of the twentieth century.

'The difficulty of analysing acting' according to Paget:

is that something that can seem so very *believable-as-real* (or, as an actor might say, 'true') always will be totally un-'real', un-'true' in existential terms.

(Paget, 2018: 121)

'The sense that something is "believable-as-real" is vital to all performance on screen, precisely because it is, was, and always has been "what people expect on telly"', as actress

Harriet Walter purportedly told Paget in interview (121). Despite this past and present TV audience expectation – one might accept Dame Walter as an informed commentator on what TV viewers expect – there are barely 200 uses of 'true' or 'truth' in the catalogue in titles published before the year 2000 and most uses are in titles published in the twenty-first century. Despite a very long history in acting discourse going back over 2,000 years, 'truth' might be seen as a quite modern and niche fixation in acting, perhaps because of the internal philosophical collapse of the concept during the twentieth century.

In an extremely rare-in-the-catalogue word, Derek Paget uses 'truthiness' as a concept to delve into the aesthetics and artistic politics of this collapse in TV acting. Paget uses 'truthiness' to unfold a double paradox in acting in docudrama where the *believable-as-real* representation by actors of *people-who-are-in-fact-real* redoubles the contradiction inherent in 'truth' as an acting concept.

'Truthiness' would appear to have entered common usage, and the Merriam-Webster dictionary in 2005, thanks to American comic, Stephen Colbert, who used the term to satirize then-President George W. Bush's proclivity for asserting views sufficiently strongly and earnestly to 'counter the fact that there was little or no real evidence' to back them up (Paget, 2018: 120). Following the contentious election campaign of President Donald Trump, in 2016 'post truth' was Oxford Dictionary's Word of the Year but Paget's niche reference to this niche word in his 2018 book is a good site at which to explode the meaning and utility of the term 'truth' in acting. It is in the least-common formulation of the word that the indirect relationship between 'truth' in acting and in reality, or truth-as-fact is most-clear.

A good place to set the charge on this *keyword*, then, because this highlights not only a contradiction between the meaning of 'truthfulness' in acting and the meaning of truthfulness as a language-term more broadly but also, as Daniel Schulze beautifully describes it, this shows the 'intrinsic ontological connection between lying and acting' (2017: 7). It is not merely that 'truth' has a specific meaning in acting discourse but rather that 'truth' in acting discourse is a paradoxical concept and one that binds multiple dichotomies of acting – imagination/reality, appearance/meaning, surface/depth, and even right/wrong or moral/immoral.

Schulze follows Aleida Assmann in locating 'truth' at the faultline of a 'fundamental split between seeming and being in Western culture, beginning with Plato' (Schulze, 2017: 15). The opposition of 'seeming' to 'being' – or *appearing to be* and *actually being* – is 'paralleled by that of exterior and interior' and a 'normative distinction between a real truth and a false simulation of a truth' (Assmann, 2012: 39). In acting, from antiquity to the present there have been different attitudes to the aesthetic and moral status of the 'false simulation' as well as differing degrees of appreciation of the fact that a false simulation is not the same thing as a falsehood. These debates have often coalesced at a meeting point in the concept of 'mimesis' (see Chapter 14) – a very much lower frequency word than 'truth', which has at least since Modernity attained and retained some rather more pragmatic usefulness to actors.

Paget, writing in the edited collection *Exploring Television Acting*, observes that:

> a major difficulty when trying to analyse actors' talk about their work is their frequent recourse to words academics avoid: words like "truth" ... they [actors] mostly speak in a language that academics schooled in "new theory" over more than a quarter of a century find problematical, even inimical.
>
> (2018: 117)

'Real truthfulness', for an academic is, perhaps, about as 'problematical as it gets' (Paget, 2018: 118). The 'problem' here, though, is a rather elemental one of semantics – of not comparing apples with apples, as they say.

One predominant meaning of 'truth' in acting (and often for actors, pragmatically) that surfaces in the catalogue is concerned with verisimilitude; the fidelity of a representation to that which it represents. 'Truth', in this use-case, denotes something about the aesthetic quality of the 'false simulation'; in the 'truthful' performance, the simulation is so credible and convincing and so closely simulates that which it represents that it is 'true'.

In acting studios and rehearsal rooms, stages and sets, auditoria and in criticism this might mean that it is *near-as-damn-it*. It might be *even-better-than-it* because the simulation also attains a kind of technical perfection which *it* (that which is being simulated) doesn't attain because *it* is, well, just *it*, without even trying to be *it*. The simulation by contrast obtains all the seeming qualities of *it* and the added quality of fulfilment precisely because the simulation could be *other-than-it* but through an act of will and skill brings itself into being *this* way and not *that* way. Again, antique theatre philosophy on mimesis has a comment to make here about the supremacy of human simulation over nature (see Chapter 14) because of its ability to do everything, be everything and not only to do or be what it is.

Daniel Dresner calls these *near-as-damn-it* performances 'truthful' (2018: 142). Bill Britten describes the activity of the actors producing such *near-as-damn-it* performances as 'living truthfully' (2014: 21–3), using the popularized Sanford Meisner phrase.

The phrase, 'living truthfully under imaginary circumstances', appears to have been formulated by Meisner and has certainly been popularized by proponents of his method, and so the notion of acting (or, perhaps, 'good' acting, in Meisner's terms) as 'behaviour' rather than simulation is often associated with his teachings. Gonsalves and Irish's *Shakespeare and Meisner: A Practical Guide for Actors, Directors, Students and Teachers* (2021) exemplifies this 'behavioural' emphasis in commentaries on Meisner (24–30), centralizing the 'reality of doing' via straightforward illustrations such as 'Meisner's metaphor of "pinch and ouch" – that an actor responding truthfully is like being pinched and yelling ouch' (30).

The art of 'living on stage' – of *doing*, or even, *doing for real* as opposed to *pretending to do* on stage – was being contested by Stanislavski and Vakhtangov at the Moscow Art

Theatre in the first decades of the twentieth century (see Malaev-Babel, 2019: 65–8). Inverting Stanislavski's 'to the subconscious through the conscious' (67), Vakhtangov asserted that:

> consciousness does not create anything – ever ... only the subconscious does. It has an independent ability to choose material for the creative process, bypassing the conscious mind.
>
> (Malaev-Babel, 2011: 111)

In Vakhtangov's later thoughts on Fantastical Realism it seems that the simulated/unsimulated dichotomy was being displaced in discourse by an elevation of the status of *doing* to the status of *being*. This ideology, also common in Meisner and other American traditions where 'acting' is seen as un-simulated doing within a simulated context, emphasizes the 'truthfulness' of behaviour and de-emphasizes the significance of material or existential facts.

Despite these contestations, usage of the word 'truth', 'truthfulness' or 'truthfully', occurs in the catalogue across writing on multiple traditions of acting. It seems likely that 'truthfulness' entered the acting lexicon along with the emergence of Naturalism in theatre, carrying over from literary commentaries and treatise on the genre and its pioneers, such as Ibsen, Zola and Chekhov.

Influential on Zola (as he acknowledged) and on Ibsen (which he didn't), was Denis Diderot's thinking on 'serious drama' which he expounded in a Preface to his play, *Le Fils naturel* (1757). Here the towering French thinker advises playwrights to, 'get as close to real life as you can' (Diderot, 1991a: 53) and that, if you want to be 'serious', 'the subject should be important. The plot should be simple, deal with domestic matters, and be modelled on real life' (52). Serious subjects, for Diderot, focus on the domestic life of the middle classes – 'men of letters, philosophers, shopkeepers, judges, lawyers, politicians, citizens, magistrates, tax-collectors, aristocrats, stewards' (56) – which seems decidedly un-radical today but, in its time, challenged the moral authority of classical and neo-classical drama with the concerns of 'low art'.

Given Naturalist drama's fixation with causality and antecedence in the present, and its preoccupation with *now* and the new (and the *nouveau riche*) as its subjects, it is apposite that the most emphatic and influential manifestos on truth in this genre come from two prefaces and not from within the plays that they precede. Sarah Grotchala provides a dissection of Diderot's preface and its influence in her 2017 book, *The Contemporary Political Play*. Here, she traces a dramatic history of 'seriousness' in drama from Aristotle's definition of tragedy as 'a representation of an action, which is serious' (Aristotle, 1987: 37) through Dryden, Lillo, Diderot and Naturalism to the work of the British playwright Shaw and his campaign for 'seriousness' in drama in the late nineteenth century, arguing that Shaw's model of the 'serious' play 'persists as a benchmark for British political playwriting' evident in the work of contemporary playwrights (2017: 25). This golden thread of seriousness running through Western and especially British playwriting is tightly woven with an ideological conviction in 'truth' as transcendent of its representation.

Diderot instigated the fixation with character dialogue that reflects how people express themselves in real life: '[t]he artist must find exactly what everyone would say in the same situation, so that all who hear it will immediately recognize it within themselves' (1991a: 42). For example, in moments of strong emotion, the dialogue should be 'broken into dislocated syllables, the speaker dart[ing] from one idea to another, beginning many different speeches, without finishing any' (43). The acting style should be naturalistic and, to encourage this style of performance, Diderot introduces the idea of an invisible fourth wall between the stage and the audience: 'take no more thought for the spectator than if he did not exist. Imagine, at the edge of the stage, a great wall separating you from the audience' (Diderot, 1991b: 65). The stage settings for the *genre sérieux* should be exact replicas of real-life places: a 'drawing-room exactly as it is' (45).

Diderot's *genre sérieux*, and perhaps his sense of the purpose of 'truth', has moral instruction at its heart: 'let the moral import of your play be universal and clear' (Diderot, 1991a: 52) and promote 'the love of virtue and the horror of vice' (55). He sees the *genre sérieux*'s combination of contemporary social issues and realistic dramaturgy as a highly effective strategy for achieving this:

> Can you not imagine the effect that would be created by realistic scenery and costumes, words that are in keeping with actions, simple plots, and dangers as real as those that must at some time have threatened your relatives, your friends, or yourself? An abrupt change of fortune, the fear of public humiliation, the effects of poverty, a passion that leads to moral or financial ruin, from ruin to despair, from despair to violent death – these are not uncommon occurrences.
>
> (Diderot, 1991a: 53)

Diderot thinks of the *genre sérieux* as having political efficacy because it encourages its audience to reflect on their actions and the possible consequences of them in response to the familiar situations they see represented on stage. Diderot's recognition of the power derived from intertwining 'seriousness', as a cipher for political or ideological 'truth' with scenographic verisimilitude prefigures the impact of late twentieth-century narrative cinema. However, the concept of truth and truthfulness emergent in Naturalism was concerned more with an essential *meaning* of things than with the *appearance* of things, as such, although, stylistically, only the former could give access to the latter.

The rigid stylistic association in Naturalism of the two orders of things – meaning and appearance – became less stable in the theatrical genre of realism into which Naturalism transmogrified in Europe giving rise to an oxymoronic 'style without style' (Counsel, 1996: 24) aesthetic ideal.

An unstable relationship between meaning and appearance was already present in the literary discourse during the Romantic period (late eighteenth to early nineteenth century), where English poet, Samuel Taylor Coleridge made an enduring distinction between 'imagination', as the creative faculty and 'fancy', as a capacity for trite associative aesthetic play. The word 'fancy' comes from the Middle English, *fantsy*, meaning something like 'mental image', and ultimately from the Greek *phantázein*, which comes closer to the contemporary ideas of artistic creativity, meaning 'to make visible' or 'present to the mind', and distinctions have been made between 'imagination' and 'fancy' or 'fantasy' in artistic endeavour since the Middle Ages. While Coleridge was asserting something about the status and capabilities of the artist to *get to the truth* through the artifice of things (including their own creations), Naturalists, such as Zola, were asserting a direct relationship between the *appearance* of things and their *meaning* and making a moral case for an aesthetic protocol. As the controversial Conservative philosopher, Roger Scruton has put it, 'the continuing relevance' of Coleridge's assertion 'lies in recognizing imagination as essentially truth-directed' (2017: 77). 'We can venture into the unreal with two quite different intentions', writes Scruton: to 'become lost there, or to find ourselves' (77–8). In the latter, 'the world of the unreal' – the imagined reality represented through art – can serve 'deeper epistemological purposes, to know through sympathy the varieties of human life, as life that could be ours' (78). In Coleridge, the term 'imagination' is reserved for this latter purpose and this sentiment accords most strongly with the predominant definition of 'truthfulness' in acting as that aesthetic quality which – perhaps synthetic, imitative or behavioural – accords with something natural.

Although 'truth' is most deeply embedded in the language of practice in Naturalist/realist traditions of acting, 'truthfulness' and related terms also appears in the catalogue associated with the late twentieth-century European Laboratory tradition of theatre-making. Here the verisimilitude of representation is not aesthetically essential.

Jennifer Kumiega, for example, writes that Jerzy Grotowski, 'sought through his work and research to give renewed vitality to an age-old truth: that the core of theatre is the communion between actor and spectator' (1985: xi). She describes a commonality between Grotowski's 'poor theatre' view on 'truth' and Peter Brook's condemnation of 'the English [stages] version of half-truth' that is 'so skilful that it's much harder to recognise … when you have a beautiful approximation of the truth and the style with which it's executed is admired more than anything else, then it's always harder to look for the real thing when what's offered in its place is almost it' (cited in Kumiega, 1985: 11).

From this same tradition, Włodzimierz Staniewski writes on 'truth' as a philosophical concept and not only an aesthetic precept: 'truth is something nostalgic and sentimental which doesn't exist anymore' (Staniewski and Hodge, 2004: 24). At least, this is the post-structuralist view of the philosophical concept of truth; a view that Gardzenice Theatre's Staniewski is perhaps chiding in this quote. Indeed, I've decontextualized this quote to highlight the starkness of the post-structuralist critique of truth. Staniewski's careful reproach to it is evident in the full quote: 'even if truth is something nostalgic and sentimental which doesn't exist anymore, do not kill this sentiment in your psyche, in your being'. Staniewski seems aware of the philosophical rigour of the post-structuralist argument against the validity of 'truth' as a concept, and the philosophical difficulty of countering it without positing a transcendent something (God, for example) as the basis of truth. As a result, he doesn't take this conflict head-on but instead sublimates it and appeals to the use-value of 'truth'; to its potential for good, psychologically, politically, emotionally, etc. and in relation to self and Being.

Although 'meaning' deteriorated as a centrally organizing principle of theatre events in the late twentieth and early twenty-first post-modern and post-dramatic trend in British and European theatre, where concepts such as character and narrative were disassembled, 'truth' appeared to remain a stubbornly recalcitrant component of drama. In Martin Crimp's production at The Royal Court, London, *Not One of These People* (November 2022), the famed British playwright performed in his own one-hander, which was inspired by a quest to produce a 'pandemic play' that would have no physical contact and would need no rehearsal. Devised in a format inspired by Forced Entertainment's iconic durational performance, *Speak Bitterness* (1994) – 'a long enumeration of confessions' which had made an 'indelible impression' on a younger Crimp – *Not One of These People* used Artificial Intelligence to generate 299 live-animated deep fake images of faces each ventriloquized by Crimp to deliver a succinct statement forming a part of a liturgical monologue of mostly angst-ridden non sequiturs:

> 5. I don't know what she said to you, but whatever it was it wasn't true.
>
> 6. I've never seen the sky looking so blue.
>
> 7. I'm not convinced by any of it – never have been.
>
> 8. There was a very good reason to kill him with a hammer.
>
> 9. When I went in for the assessment I said, look, are you medically qualified? They just didn't care that I couldn't breathe.
>
> 10. I was very surprised when she explained to me that I was part of the patriarchy.
>
> 11. I can't resist antique coffee pots.

Stylistically orthodox for a 1990s British playwright, Crimp's 2022 production exemplified key post-dramatic approaches to representation which come in the form of what Hans-Thies Lehmann described as '"concrete negations" of the dramatic' (2011: 34). Gad Kaynar (2014) expounds Lehmann's 'derivative observations' about a twentieth-century transition in Western theatre from a 'verbally predominant, narrative and sequentially structured poetics, to a performance-oriented aesthetics, distinguished by plot-less, character-less, deconstructed and fragmentary theatrical texts' (86). Kaynar observes that 'these texts highlight the performers' corporeal and concrete stage presence', as well as what Patrick Primavesi defines as 'the moment of the performance itself' (2011: 86).

In the post-dramatic moment, 'acting' was anathema to the performance event – what Nik Ridout called a key and negative term and 'truth', it would seem, was a quaint commodity (Matthews, 2014: 55). Against an overly binary opposition of theatre (understood as a dramatic poetics) and performance (understood as reification) some scholars, such as Alan Read (2013), preserved 'acting' in accounts of performance even as post-dramatic theatre-makers were eschewing the term, and the concept. Read describes theatre as 'the privileged mean of mimetically "passing" in the arts' (158) and he conserved some currency for the term 'acting' during this historical moment by utilizing Rancière's political philosophy to reinvoke a mimetic aesthetics as culturally material.

Despite Read's linguistic and philosophical sleight-of-hand, the unstable connection between 'acting' and 'truth' appeared to have been evermore bleakly exposed by both the 'British Brutalist' playwrights, such as Crimp, and post-dramatic performance-makers in the UK and Europe. Indeed, Crimp's *Not One Of These People* might be read as satirizing both concepts – truth and acting – by utilizing acting's mimetic means of passing self-reflexively to *not-pass* in a critique of truth that might be seen as nihilistic (if it weren't so joyfully comedic).

Despite the contestable definition of Crimp's performance as 'acting' in context of post-dramatic theorization, his application of generative Artificial Intelligence (GAN, or generative adversarial network deep learning architecture, to be precise) situates *Not One of These People* in the context of a newer trend of *Performance in the Age of the Technosphere* (2020), as Chris Salter has it. In this age, technology is no longer the subject but increasingly the 'substance and matter' of performance 'as an increasingly prominent focus on nonhuman forms … seems to take focus in galleries, theatres, and laboratories around the world' (248).

Art historian, Barbara Stafford has responded to this trend and observed a rising interest in the 'foggy undecidability' of such hybrid technological 'stuff' (in Salter, 2020: 253). 'Today' she argues, audiences are increasingly presented with experiences, 'entities,' that are 'not only without a concept but without the possibility of a concept' (Stafford, 2017: 9–10). For Stafford, this produces a 'failure of [audience] intuition' (9–10) giving rise to, 'not a soaring ascent into comprehension, but a bewildering descent, into ineffability' (9–10). Salter tentatively counters Stafford's despondent critique of audience apperception by focusing on the revelatory prospects of technospheric performance. Salter cites Jens Hauser's concept of 'microperformativity' as a reason to be cheerful about new tech. Here, performance is an 'experimental method' of exposure by which one can come to know that which was once thought to be unknowable (Hauser, 2020) via the deployment of technological instruments that can bring 'hidden signals previously unavailable to human perception to the surface' (Salter, 2020: 261). Both responses – Salter's and Stafford's – seem to over-estimate the effect of technological development on the epistemological quandary of 'truth' in performance which is so nakedly apparent in the mimetic activity of acting.

The 'basic fallacy', Hannah Arendt writes, 'taking precedence over all specific metaphysical fallacies' – is 'to interpret meaning on the model of truth' (Matthews, 2019: 6). One of the most niche usages of 'truth' in the catalogue is to be found in one of my books, *The Life of Training* (Matthews, 2019), where I employ Hannah Arendt's observations about Western philosophy to prize apart 'meaning-making' from 'truth' in a description of the experience of training to act. Arendt observes that one such specific metaphysical fallacy deriving from this basic one is to assume – as microperformativity may do – that truth equates to depth and its opposite, fakery, to surface. To presume that truth is by its nature hidden and must be revealed.

The root of this ideological prejudice is no-doubt very ancient and, philosophically speaking, likely to have been derived in Western secular thought from Judeo-Christian theological traditions. This might be, philosophically speaking, an inversion of the proper order considering the evident fact that we live in a world of appearance. 'Could it not be', Arendt asked, 'that appearances are not there for the sake of' depth (Matthews, 2019: 105)?

Crimp's use of deep fakes provides a touchstone to this prejudice and the 'basic fallacy' infiltrating acting. The term 'deep fake' draws its semantic power from an apparent juxtaposition between depth/truth and surface/fakery. 'Surface fakes' might be an unworrisome technological development because the surface is not important but *deep* fakes convey a terrible power because they erode the security of depth as a safehouse for truth.

The prominence in thought of a prejudice against appearance as a cite of truth both confounds and explains the relationship between acting and truth. More usefully, it elucidates the 'basic fallacy' by sharply indicating that 'meaning' and 'truth' have no direct connection despite the tendency in thought and in theatre to use these terms synonymously.

What performances, such as Crimp's, exemplify is that acting and meaning are inseverable, and their relationship is direct and profoundly stable despite audience hermeneutics. Performances in the Age of the Technosphere – indicatively those microperformative works – confirm Arendt's thesis that our thirst for understanding and the intellect's capacity to meet our need for knowledge is not inspired by a quest for truth but motivated by a quest for meaning. A yearning for 'truth' is almost definitively dissociated from meaning precisely because 'truth' is an article of faith and not of knowledge.

The shift in acting discourse has more recently been in the direction of 'experience' and away from 'meaning' as a conduit to truth. The immanence of experience that is strongly foregrounded in the post-dramatic and related forms of theatre, performance and art-making asserts itself as a more credible source of truth than mimesis, despite the facts that these cannot be so easily sundered and juxtaposed and, even more saliently, both experience and mimesis are vectors of meaning and not of truth.

References

Aristotle (1987), *The Poetics of Aristotle: Translation and Commentary*, Chapel Hill, NC: University of North Carolina Press.

Assmann, A. (2012), 'Authenticity – The Signature of Western Exceptionalism?', in J. Straub (ed.), *Paradoxes of Authenticity: Studies on a Critical Concept*, 33–50, Bielfeld: Transcript.

Britten, B. (2014), *The Finished Product. In From Stage to Screen: A Theatre Actor's Guide to Working on Camera*, London: Methuen Drama.

Counsel, C. (1996), *Signs of Performance: An Introduction to Twentieth Century Theatre*, London: Routledge.

Diderot, D. (1991a), 'Conversations on *The Natural Son*', in M. J. Sidnell (ed.), *Sources of Dramatic Theory: Volume 2, Voltaire to Hugo*, Cambridge: Cambridge University Press.

Diderot, D. (1991b), 'Discourse on Dramatic Poetry', in M. J. Sidnell (ed.), *Sources of Dramatic Theory: Volume 2, Voltaire to Hugo*, Cambridge: Cambridge University Press.

Dresner, D. (2018), *A Life-coaching Approach to Screen Acting*, London: Methuen Drama.

Gonsalves, A. and T. Irish (2021), *Shakespeare and Meisner: A Practical Guide for Actors, Directors, Students and Teachers*, London: The Arden Shakespeare.

Grotchala, S. (2017), *The Contemporary Political Play*, London: Methuen Drama.

Hauser, J. (2020), 'Editorial: On Microperformativity', *Performance Research* 25 (3): 170.

Kaynar, G. (2014). 'Textual Dramaturgy and Dramaturg-as-Text: Traditional versus New Dramaturgy in the Era of German Post-Dramatic Theatre', in A. Citron, S. Aronson-Lehavi and D. Zerbib (eds), *Performance Studies in Motion: International Perspectives and Practices in the Twenty-First Century*, London: Methuen Drama.

Kumiega, J. (1985), *The Theatre of Grotowski*, London: Methuen.

Lehmann, H.-T. (2011), 'Wie politisch ist Postdramatisches Theater?', in Jan Deck and Angelika Sieburg (eds), *Politisch Theater Machen. Neue Artikulationen des Politischen in den darstellenden Künsten*, Bielefeld: Transcript.

Malaev-Babel, A. (2011), *The Vakhtangov Sourcebook*, Abingdon: Routledge.

Malaev-Babel, A. (2019), 'Yevgeny Vakhtangov: The Future Head of the Russian Theatre', in A. Skinner (ed.), *Russian Theatre in Practice: The Director's Guide*, 61–78, London: Methuen Drama.

Matthews, J. (2014), *Anatomy of Performance Training*, London: Bloomsbury.

Matthews, J. (2019), *The Life of Training*, London: Bloomsbury.

Paget, D. (2018), 'Truth and "Truthiness" in Acting the Real', in T. Cantrell and C. Hogg (eds), *Exploring Television Acting*, 110–24, London: Bloomsbury Publishing.

Primavesi, P. (2011), 'Theater/Politik – Kontexte und Beziehungen', in J. Deck and A. Sieburg, (eds), *Politisch Theater Machen. Neue Artikulationen des Politischen in den darstellenden Künsten*, 49, Transcript: Bielefeld.

Read, A. (2013), *Theatre in the Expanded Field: Seven Approaches to Performance*, London: Methuen Drama.

Salter, C. (2020), 'Performance in the Age of the Technosphere', in B. Ferdman and J. Stokic (eds), *The Methuen Drama Companion to Performance Art*, London: Methuen Drama.

Schulze, D. (2017), *Authenticity in Contemporary Theatre and Performance: Make it Real*, London: Methuen Drama.

Scruton, R. (2017), *Coleridge and Contemplation*, Oxford: Oxford University Press.

Stafford, M. B. (2017), 'From Communicable Matter to Incommunicable "Stuff": Extreme Combinatorics and the Return of Ineffability', in T. D. Knepper and L. E. Kalmanson (eds), *Ineffability: An Exercise in Comparative Philosophy of Religion*, 9–27, Cham: Springer International.

Staniewski, W. and A. Hodge (2004), *Hidden Territories: The Theatre of Gardzienice*, London and New York: Routledge.

CHAPTER 8
VOICE

(Voy-sss)
noun
- Common language term describing sounds produced in the larynx, issued through the mouth as speech or song
- A distinct area of acting craft and the focus of 'voice work'
- Intimately related to the subjectivity of actor and character sometimes to the point of being synonymous for the agent
- In relation to the above, also concerned with the content as well as the activity of speech. *What* is said as well as *how* it is said
- Specific use-case in twentieth-century counter-social ideology of self-reclamation
- Specific use-case in twenty-first-century politics of self-identity.

The predominant use of the term 'voice' in the catalogue is to describe a specific field of craft concerned with an actor's vocal performance. There are many titles on the use and care of the voice and the cultivation of vocal capacity in actors with notable examples including those written by and about well-known voice teachers, such as Patsy Rodenburg and Kristen Linklater. Here 'freeing' the voice, the 'free' or 'freer' voice (e.g. Rodenburg, 2015, 2018; Streeton and Raymond, 2014; Snow, 2012) have prominence as concepts. 'Freeing' the voice might be placed in context of a broad twentieth-century interest in pre- or counter-social modes of 'primal' embodiment.

> The suggestion that society corrupts the body through learnt behaviours, which form as adaptations to social needs and pressures, appears in the thinking and writing of figures from F.M Alexander and Moshe Feldenkrais to Arthur Janov and R.D. Laing. Grotowski's concept of the 'via negativa' – a technique for recovering a more original movement lexis by eradicating the obstructions to this imposed on the body by culture – is one particularly theatrical version of a larger discourse on potential and the primal.
>
> (Matthews, 2014: 68)

Although much of the academic discourse on this trend in acting focuses on 'via negativa' and Grotowski's influence on pioneering 1970/80s theatre (e.g. see Hodge, 2000; Staniewski and Hodge, 2004) the discourse of 'freeing' can be found across a significant number of late twentieth-century practitioners that are not closely or directly associated with the European Laboratory theatre tradition. Declan Donnellan, for example, in *The Actor and the Target*, asserts that actors should be 'taught how *not* to block our natural instinct to act' (2002: 2; emphasis in original). Further afield again, Strasberg states, 'human beings, by the time they start their training with us, have already been conditioned to respond, react and express themselves in a particular way'. Musing on the role of 'impulse' in acting (see Chapter 4), in a section of his 'notes' (Cohen, 2010: 6) dedicated to the 'use of sound', Strasberg writes, 'we use sound to access basic areas of expression' (in Cohen, 2010: 11). These sounds – '"Ahhhhhh" or "Hah!" … which we don't make in life – feed the impulse into expression', he claims (11). When, 'an impulse may begin to rise within an actor … his conditioning says, "No. I shouldn't express that"'. 'In life you're trained not to react', Strasberg claims, and this 'has no value on stage' (11).

Belief in the primal connectedness of a 'free' voice and the sound it produces is strong in the voice manuals in the catalogue, which strike a notably remedial tone. Both prelapsarian and corrective, the 'Natural Voice' (Rodenburg, 2019: 3) and the Natural Breath (6) are the idealized prerequisites for actors in Rodenburg's highly influential treatise on 'voice work'. In Rodenburg, 'natural' and 'habitual' are antonyms and theirs is a Cain and Abel story that might have been written by Janov or Laing:

> The *natural voice* and its potential are what we came to the world with at birth … our first experience of natural voice was in that initial primal scream, that first chance we were given to "catch our breath". Life and our subsequent experiences should ideally enrich and broaden the natural voice, transforming it into a powerful instrument of self-expression. But life batters and restricts us in such ways that most of us settle into what I term an *habitual voice*: a voice encrusted with restrictive tendencies that only awareness and exercise can undo and counteract. The natural voice (a "free" or "centred" voice) is quite simply an unblocked voice that is unhampered by debilitating habits.
>
> (Rodenburg, 2015: 25)

It is notable in the catalogue that the term 'voice' is frequently part of a compound – 'voice work' – and used in the definitive article – 'the voice'. Both compound uses signal the centrality of 'voice' as a domain of craft and practice in acting that is helpfully understood in relation to 'movement' and 'the body' (see Chapters 3 and 5).

In twentieth-century acting discourse across the catalogue, 'voice' and 'movement' hold up the idea and ideals as the twin pillars of acting craft. Titles and traditions assign differing prominence to each pillar while many more-recent accounts emphasize their interconnectedness and co-dependence. In this more recent trend 'the voice' as a concept becomes pluralized, driven by a twenty-first-century intersectional sensibility towards identity: 'rather than the one "free" voice that Patsy Rodenburg writes about', Camilleri and others, including Tara McAllister-Viel, are 'interested in exploring the "multiple voices" that emerge from [actor] trainings situated in different sociocultural traditions' (McAllister-Viel, 2016: 440, 449; Camilleri, 2019: 66–7). Cahill and Hamel, in *Sounding Bodies: Identity, Injustice and the Voice* (2021) politicize 'the voice' and problematize 'freeing' discourse as they observe how complexly 'enmeshed in and deeply marked by overlapping systems of power, signification, and relations' (15) human noise-making is.

Indeed, by the early twenty-first century the somewhat monolithic concepts of 'the voice' and 'the body' that asserted themselves in late twentieth-century acting theory gave way in the catalogue to an interest in 'voices' and 'bodies', and multiplicitous ways of speaking and moving.

This emergent trend notwithstanding, the catalogue is strongly marked by the 'twin pillars' of 'voice' and 'movement'. While 'movement' appears more frequently (nearly 10,000 times) than 'voice' (nearly 7,000 times) the relative positions are reversed in a calculation of how many times 'voice' appears in the title of a book (nearly 200) with how many times 'movement' does (barely 100). These two terms and concepts – 'voice' and 'movement' – retain a close relationship in acting theory and practice and their coincidence in the catalogue is emblematic of an atomizing approach to 'the actor'[1] in acting discourse that can be traced back to a very early (and mythically *first*) ancient Greek treatise on acting.

Although mentioned barely 100 times in the catalogue, and almost invariably in the context of Renaissance drama's neoclassical fetish, Cicero's seminal and still-hugely-influential 'voice work' treatise, *De Oratore*, is a cornerstone of the history of acting craft. *De Oratore* is a complex political-philosophical work of the first century BC and among its many enduring and influential achievements is the codification of oratory excellence.

Although Cicero directs such excellence at the goal of antique state craft, in the Renaissance his practical didacticism on the mastery and execution of vocal performance was adopted as a quasi-guidebook for actors. In conjunction with a burgeoning and experimental literary culture of plays in Renaissance England, Cicero's high-minded claims about rhetoric and oratory elevated the cultural significance of the craft of acting based on speech, placing vocal training and performance at the heart of acting discourse and practice during this period.

Historically, we may see oratory and rhetoric as fields of antique acting craft but the reclamation of Cicero in English Renaissance drama certainly cemented 'voice work' as the work of the actor, and this can be seen prominently in the high density of Cicero references in titles about the Shakespearean stage.

Alison Findlay's *Women in Shakespeare: A Dictionary* (2014) combines gender theory and discourse-analysis methods with lexographical presentation modes to survey the values and attitudes expressed about women across Shakespeare's *oeuvre*, producing many novel insights about English society, culture and playwriting at the time. In her entries 'tongue' and 'breath' she makes some of the more idiosyncratic and engaging insights about 'voice' in the catalogue, including that both 'breath' and 'tongue' have distinctly gendered associations with regards the voice from Renaissance England to the present. Both feature prominently in the Blazon poetic tradition – a tradition dating back to the thirteenth century characterized by a poetic form that catalogues a beloved's physical features and attributes. The early modern Blazon subject is invariably chaste, obedient and silent and thus control of the voice was, as Findlay puts it, 'a critical part of a woman's self-fashioning' (2014: 398).

Findlay draws multiple examples from Shakespeare to show that, on the early modern stage (and in the mouths of male actors), 'the soft voice' is a 'symbolic mark' of female chastity and obedience (2014: 398). In one of the richest entries in her book, Findlay localizes her linguistic analysis of female voices around the motif of the tongue recounting multiple lines from numerous plays to argue that, 'such references to women's tongues make it clear that women are not naturally silent. Their tongues must be trained to serve the purposes of their masters; their action carefully self-policed by their owners' (398). Findlay's argument that, 'a woman's tongue, along with her sexual and social status, is a defining feature' is secured by her observation that the 'most fearful punishment the men of Navarre can devise to enforce the decree that "No woman shall come within a mile of my court" is not death but "on pain of losing her tongue"' (398).

In the context of the poetry and drama of courtly love (and in context of Elizabethan dental hygiene) 'sweet breath indicated healthy teeth and gums, of course and, used metaphorically, breath also meant the voice' (Findlay 2014: 59). Findlay explains that, in the mouths of Shakespeare's Elizabethan actors (all of them male, of course), 'the sweetness of female breath is sometimes used as a sign of the fragility of innocent life and the possibility of resurrection' (60). As a sonnet writer, Shakespeare toys with this totem of the Blazon tradition in one of the more famous references to a woman's breath: 'And in some perfumes is there more delight / Than in the breath that from my mistress reeks' (*Son.* 130.7–8). The word 'breath' appears nearly half as frequently as 'voice' in the catalogue (around 3,000 times) and in the twenty-first-century theorization of 'voice' both concepts are sensitized to identity characteristics such as gender, age or race.

Circling back in the catalogue, historically speaking; Patsy Rodenburg combines multi-identity characteristics in a single anecdote about an 80-year-old female 'black gospel singer' (2015: 16). While the gender and racial identity of the singer don't appear to be relevant to the moral of Rodenburg's tale, her age and long-experience is used to substantiate the assertions in 'voice work' titles that 'the voice' requires systematic and informed care to 'open' and 'free' (Rodenburg 2015: 22). On the encompassing topic of identity, Rodenburg observes that voice work, which is foundationally connected to the breath, is an experiential lightning rod to experiences of self-identity because 'exercises developed to open and free the voice can make anyone – female or male – suddenly vulnerable, angry, frightened, tender and unguarded, rather like a snail without a shell' (22). Voice work 'on this level can be intensely frank and personal. Human potential of any sort, once massaged and tapped, can be powerfully revealing', she writes (22).

In politicized accounts of 'voice' and identity in the catalogue, attention to *what* is said achieves some prominence over *how* it is said. Emphasizing the use-case of 'voice' to mean identity or at least subjectivity, authors write of 'giving voice to' subject positions and associated social, cultural and political ideals and causes.

Perhaps because of a connection between voice, identity, ipseity and subjectivity, content-centred use-cases of 'giving voice' (i.e. accounts interested in *what* is said and by whom) feature in the dramatic form of the monologue prominently. Eddie Paterson takes a unifying Cicerone sensibility to the form and function of rhetoric in her analysis of *The Contemporary American Monologue* (2015). Citing Imani Perry's assertion that, 'orality and verbal dexterity are highly appreciated skills in black American culture … charismatic black leadership of the past forty years has largely depended on the spoken word' (in Patterson 2015: 50). In a two millennia historical boomerang to Cicero's observations in *De Oratore,* Patterson highlights the 'importance of the spoken word and solo voice in African American culture' from poetry, speech-making and drama to hip-hop where 'monologic speech' is combined with 'political critique' (50).

Using 'voice' metaphorically and with reference to a (perceived and perhaps contentious) universality, the word 'voice' allows a tacit acknowledgement of the validity and dignity of all subjects and their ideals. In this linguistic trope 'voice' moves metaphorically and thus out from the literal domain of actors' 'voice work' and into related territories of practice, such as speech-writing and the even-less-literally-connected space of scenography. With reference to one 'site-specific' performance discussed in *Sites of Transformation: Applied and Socially Engaged Scenography in Rural Landscapes* (2022), Louise Ann Wilson states that, 'my use of the term "giving a voice" was literal' (165). 'Centring people and place' by casting 'real' (159) people to speak for themselves, this use-case of 'giving voice' collides the parochial and prosaic considerations of identity with a twenty-first-century inclusionary politics that has re-valued autobiographical performance. Amidst the twenty-first-century's ever-splintering sense of objective reality (see Chapter 7) in this performance form, 'speaking for oneself' has replaced 'speaking the truth' with 'speaking *my* truth' and provided this as 'a means of giving voice … through which we can understand and embody the perspectives of others' (Shaughnessy, 2012: 76). The urgency of attention to 'real' people 'giving voice' to their 'real lives' in performance practice seems to be in indirect relationship to the solidity of communities and the consensus on meaning in a globalizing 'post-truth' (see Chapter 7) world.

The catalogue documents how, from the twentieth to the twenty-first century, the philosophical facts of the simultaneous idiosyncrasy, exclusivity and universality of voices and the innateness of breath have given themselves to an increasingly politically-aware discourse on speech in acting.

Note

1   This is an approach that I have parodied in my 2014 book, *Anatomy of Performance Training.*

References

Cahill, A. J. and C. Hamel (2021), *Sounding Bodies: Identity, Injustice, and the Voice,* London: Methuen Drama.
Camilleri, F. (2019), *Performer Training Reconfigured: Post-Psychophysical Perspectives for the Twenty-First Century,* London: Methuen Drama.
Cohen, L., ed. (2010), *The Lee Strasberg Notes,* London and New York: Routledge.
Donnellan, D. (2002) *The Actor and the Target,* London: Nick Hern Books.
Findlay, A. (2014), *Women in Shakespeare: A Dictionary,* London: The Arden Shakespeare.

Hodge, A., ed. (2000), *Twentieth Century Actor Training*, New York and London: Routledge.
Matthews, J. (2014), *Antomy of Performance Training*, London: Bloomsbury.
McAllister-Viel, T. (2016), 'The Role of "Presence" in Training Actors' Voices', *Theatre, Dance and Performance Training*, 7 (3): 438–52.
Rodenburg, P. (2015), *The Right to Speak: Working with the Voice*, London: Methuen Drama.
Rodenburg, P. (2018), *The Need for Words: Voice and the Text*, London: Methuen Drama.
Rodenburg, P. (2019), *The Actor Speaks: Voice and the Performer*, London: Methuen Drama.
Shaughnessy, N. (2012), *Applying Performance: Live Art, Socially Engaged Theatre and Effective Practice*, Basingstoke: Palgrave Macmillan.
Snow, J. (2012), *Movement Training for Actors*, London: Methuen Drama.
Staniewski, W. and A. Hodge (2004), *Hidden Territories: The Theatre of Gardzienice*, New York and London: Routledge.
Streeton, J. and P. Raymond (2014), *In Singing on Stage: An Actor's Guide*, London: Methuen Drama.

CHAPTER 9
ACTRESS

(ackk-tress)
noun
- Someone female who acts
- A never-not-gendered descriptor for a sub-set of performers
- A gendered sub-genus of the species of 'performer' correlated closely with literary and narrative traditions of theatre, TV and film
- With reference to 'actor', a comparatively under-used common-language term in the catalogue. A fact that seems to be related to the history of women and female roles in English theatre history
- A word particularly associated with commentary and theorization of the early modern period
- A word whose ongoing meaning is marked by sixteenth- and seventeenth-century male sexual desire and historical interpretations of the gender politics and sex relations of the period.

Despite some efforts to 'un-gender' the term 'actor', and to use this to describe all subjects (including some non-human ones) who 'act', the relative frequencies of 'actor' and 'actress' in the catalogue probably illustrate the gender, and associated linguistic, biases of the catalogue as an artefact of a sexist culture.

'Actor' is the second most-used word in the catalogue after 'play' appearing over 40,000 times whereas 'actress' appears only just over 1,000 times (see Chapter 1). Given that both 'actor' and 'actress' were words used to parse the original library (the Drama Online holdings), this disparity is significant. 'Actor' appears almost exclusively without contextual commentary on the gendered aspect of the word (with some exceptions discussed below).

Actress is used in 950 titles of all the titles encompassed by the analysis for this book and in almost a third of the titles (280) where 'actress' is used it is explicitly politically contextualized, appearing in a sentence, paragraph or chapter alongside the word 'gender'. It appears in 170 titles specifically related to acting (the catalogue) and all these titles also include 'gender' in close conjunction with 'actress'. In the catalogue, then, 'actor' and 'actress' have marked disparities not only in terms of frequency but also in terms of their position in discourse formations and relative to other discursive concerns, such as sex, gender, agency and animals (see Chapter 1).

Historically and culturally speaking, this disparity does not seem to be a simple product of the relative number of male (actor) and female (actress) roles available in various genres and periods. Several titles in the catalogue intimate that the somewhat troubled semantics of 'actor' and 'actress' may be a product of the English stage specifically and also a product of the English language.

Luke Dixon gives a whirlwind and idiosyncratic tour of acting and gender in global theatre history in his 2003 book, *Play-Acting: A Guide to Theatre Workshops*. Finding a cross-cultural juxtaposition in the seventeenth century, Dixon notes that, at the same time Restoration England was adopting the continental European convention of women-playing-women onto a hitherto exclusively homosexual English stage, the Japanese shogunate was banning the playing of female roles by women. That 1629 shogunate decree inverted extant Kabuki gender conventions from the early Edo period, in which the shrine maiden Okuni is thought to have developed the genre with small performances of song and dance (the literal meaning of 'Kabuki') in the dry riverbed of Kyoto's Kamo river. From the male actors in Ancient Greek drama festivals to these female performers of Japan's Tokgawa period, Dixon contends that 'the performance of gender remain at the heart of theatrical practice' (167). Taking in 'cross-dressing' and the pantomime 'dame' alongside the 'singing boys' of India, Dixon's potted history is one that lingers on the concept of binary inversion.

The topics of 'Shakespeare' and 'women' come up in coincidence with some frequency in the catalogue, including in titles such as *Women and Indian Shakespeares* (2022), *Women Making Shakespeare: Text, Reception and Performance* (2014) and *Performing Shakespeare's Women: Playing Dead* (2019). The topic of 'actress' appears in these titles, often as part of a feminist critique and response to authors, such as Luke Dixon, who provides an apology that, 'Shakespeare wrote in a world that was without female actors. There was no such word in his London as "actress"' (2003: 168). Paige Martin Reynolds provides the rejoinder that:

> women have always had to confront, when it comes to Shakespeare's plays, the precondition of their preclusion. That is, since boy actors originated Shakespeare's female roles, the woman who steps onstage to say Shakespeare's words is always already pushing up against an unspoken accusation of usurpation – or a spoken one, as in Harley Granville-Barker's wistful fantasy of 'the restoring of the celibate stage' (a fantasy frequently fulfilled by modern all-male performances). Warning female performers that Shakespeare 'has left no blank spaces for her to fill with her charm', Granville-Barker cautions, 'Let the usurping actress remember that her sex is a liability, not an asset.' Noted.
>
> (2019: 9)

Disrupting this exclusionary and binarized dialogue and providing a revisionist historiography of 'actresses' as women-on-stage, Claire McManus, has followed Ann Thompson (1996) and Elizabeth Howe (1992) in shaking at the 'grip of the [myth of the] "all-male stage" on the history of early modern theatre' by identifying 'a tradition of English women's performance in the century preceding the Restoration' (McManus

2014: 221). In context of this tradition Thompson, Howe and McManus have argued that 'the Restoration actress is no longer a "first", no longer an exception to a hitherto unbroken rule [in England]' (221).

The debate notwithstanding, the early modern period appears to dominate discourse on 'actresses' in the catalogue with a particular fixation on Shakespeare and boy actors playing female characters. Marianne Novy's book, *Shakespeare and Feminist Theory* (2017) compiles a breadth of historical research on the topic drawing out key and contentious themes of female vulnerability, dissemblance and sexual attractiveness to men (Orgel, 1997: 70; Jardine [1983] 1989; Howard, 1994 in Novy, 2017: 14–17). Alongside these mainstays of discourse Novy also surfaces key contentions from twentieth-century historians such as Thomas Laquer (1990) and Janet Adelman (1999) about the status of women in the Elizabethan Galenic model of humanity, including the 'belief (related perhaps to Laqueur's suggestion that women were seen as incomplete men) that women and boys were similar' (Novy, 2017: 17). 'This belief', writes Novy, 'is part of what made the performance of women's roles by boys believable onstage' (17).

Although theatre history scholarship indicates that there is limited evidence that early modern audiences had any real interest in what many authors in the catalogue would call 'believable acting', Kathleen McLuskie has argued that boys' unbroken voices also helped to make them 'acceptable when performing as women' (Novy, 2017: 17). 'The fictions of Elizabethan drama would have been rendered nonsensical if at every appearance of a female character ... their gender was called into question', McLuskie (1989: 102) writes. Given the overwhelming imbalance between extant and contemporary accounts and theorization of Elizabethan drama (also evident in the catalogue) the apparent logic of this statement is difficult to verify. This sounds logical from a twenty-first-century perspective looking backwards but there is sufficient historical record to indicate that the sense-making done by early modern theatre audiences operated via a quite different logic to the sense-making done by audiences today. Novy argues that, 'most early modern representations of female characters on the English stage showed them as clearly female' but also that 'many plays [of the period] are theatrically self-conscious enough that there are moments that call attention to the sex of the actors' (2017: 17). Mollifying the debate, Novy concludes, 'most probably spectators differed in their interest and productions also differed in their emphasis' (17).

Whether boys-playing-women were ever credible as women, or were a cipher for women, or whether they were 'accepted' or even desired as a distinct gender category is moot. What is notable about the discourse on early modern 'actress' is the dominant framing of the topic within the ambit of male sexual desire. Alison Findley (2014) has recorded the fact that the sixteenth- and seventeenth-century word 'harlot' had a dual meaning-use, referring to both 'unchaste' women and prostitutes and 'often with the theatrical sense of a juggler, dancing-girl or actress' (175). The more specifically coded seventeenth-century term 'orange seller', used to describe sex workers who solicited in playhouses under the necessary subterfuge of selling refreshments appears to have cemented a connection between 'actress' and 'sex work' following Charles II's well-documented affair with Nell Gwyn – the 'orange-selling' daughter of a brothel-keeper and subsequent leading 'actress' of Drury Lane (see Sierz and Ghilardi, 2021: 70–4).

As Novy notes, the early modern 'association of boys with women, combined with the later history of performance and interpretation, means that the use of boy actors for female characters is too complicated to be accounted for by, or to reinforce, a simple belief in either the difference or the similarity of the sexes' (Callaghan, 2000). Indeed, the seeming-indivisibility of men (or boys) from the definition and use of 'actress', and the additional and lingering influence of sex work on the word further reinforces the over-determining influence of male sex and gender on the meaning of the term.

Away from the English stage (and to some extent, the English language), Poonam Trivedi notes that, while 'names of actresses of ancient India do not survive', 'it is well known that women had a sanctioned role as *nati* (actress) in Sanskrit theatre which flourished *c.*400BCE–1000CE' (2022: 23–4). However, according to Trivedi, 'women performers, like dancers, singers and musicians, flourished through the ages, but the identifiable "actress", enacting a scripted role, comes into being only with the emulation of Western theatre practice in India' (23).

Testing the periodization of 'actress' from a different genre perspective, Jozey Grae has dissected the male/female binary in British West End musicals and argues that, alongside male-gendered roles for 'actors' and female-gendered roles for 'actresses', 'only two canonically gender non-binary characters have ever featured in a West End and/or Broadway musical, both since 2018' (2024: 55). Grae notes that James Lovelock has drawn attention to the fact that 'musical theatre scholarship around gender and sexuality has been limited to binary categories' and has called for a 'move away from the binary of discussing "sexuality – both hetero- and homo"' and a fresh consideration of 'bisexual, asexual, transgender and gender fluid identities' (Grae, 2024: 55). Taking a Queer Theory approach to the semantic baggage of 'actress', Hannah Thuraisingam Robbins adopts the term:

> 'femme' to include all actors who are willing to play a feminine role. That may include non-binary femmes and gender fluid actors who do not identify as 'female' or 'woman' but are comfortable interpreting a role situated with feminine characteristics.
>
> (2024: 136)

Grae's writing exemplifies a small but notable body of work in the catalogue providing a continuum (as opposed to binary) model of gender and acting. This body of work is characterized by a genre focus on musical and drag performance. Edward and Farrier, for example, edited a 2020 collection called *Contemporary Drag Practices and Performers: Drag in a Changing Scene Volume 1*, that collates a range of contemporary perspectives focused on drag performances. It is notable that 'actor' appears only seven times across the contributions in this volume and in each case as a classificatory description for professionals. 'Actress' doesn't appear at all, which is perhaps to be expected in context of an art form – drag – that favours the nomenclature of 'performer' and abides with and in

Acting

the theoretical context of gender performativity (Judith Butler's seminal work in this field is cited nearly 150 times across the volume). Further computational analysis of this title shows that the noun 'acting' is used just ten times whereas the noun 'performing' is used closer to 400 times. This coincidence of 'performance' and 'gender' in discourse, traceable through performance scholarship and back to Butler's work, marks a conceptual parting between critical theory and 'acting' as a concept from the 1990s as well as a linguistic movement away from the binarized language of 'actor' and 'actress' (with all of its historical baggage) and towards a unitary semantics of 'the performer'.

References

Adelman, J. (1999), 'Making Defect Perfection: Shakespeare and the One-Sex Model', in V. Comensoli and A. Russell (eds), *Enacting Gender on the Renaissance Stage*, 23–52, Urbana, IL: University of Illinois Press.

Callaghan, D. (2000), *Shakespeare without Women: Representing Gender and Race on the Renaissance Stage*, London: Routledge.

Dixon, L. (2003), *Play-acting: A Guide to Theatre Workshops*, London: Methuen Drama.

Edward, M. and S. Farrier (2020), 'Drag: Applying Foundation and Setting the Scene', in M. Edward and S. Farrier (eds), *Contemporary Drag Practices & Performers: Drag in a Changing Scene: Volume 1*, 1–18, London: Methuen Drama.

Grae, J. (2024), "'Glitching' of Gender and Temporality in *Lift* (2013)", in C. Chandler and G. Gowland (eds), *Contemporary British Musicals: 'Out of the Darkness'*, 53–62, London: Methuen Drama.

Howard, J. E. (1994), *The Stage and Social Struggle in Early Modern England*, New York: Routledge.

Howe, E. (1992), *The First English Actresses: Women and Drama, 1660–1700*, Cambridge: Cambridge University Press.

Jardine, L. ([1983] 1989), *Still Harping on Daughters: Women and Drama in the Age of Shakespeare*, 2nd edn, New York: Columbia University Press.

Laqueur, T. (1990), *Making Sex: Body and Gender from the Greeks to Freud*, Cambridge, MA: Harvard University Press.

McLuskie, K. (1989), *Renaissance Dramatists*, Hemel Hempstead: Harvester Wheatsheaf.

Novy, M. (2017), *Shakespeare and Feminist Theory*, London: The Arden Shakespeare.

Orgel, S. (1997), *Impersonations: The Performance of Gender in Shakespeare's England*, Cambridge: Cambridge University Press.

Reynolds, P. M. (2019), *Performing Shakespeare's Women: Playing*, London: The Arden Shakespeare.

Robbins, H. T. (2024), "'Something Precious You Don't Simply Give Away': Intersections of Love and Queer Expression in *Everybody's Talking About Jamie*", in C. Chandler and G. Gowland (eds), *Contemporary British Musicals: 'Out of the Darkness'*, 125–36, London: Methuen Drama.

Sierz, A. and L. Ghilardi (2021), *The Time Traveller's Guide to British Theatre: The First Four Hundred Years*, London: Methuen Drama.

Thompson, A. (1996), 'Women/"Women" and the Stage', in H. Wilcox (ed.), *Women and Literature in Britain 1500–1700*, 100–16, Cambridge: University of Cambridge Press.

Trivedi, P. (2022), 'The "Woman's Part": Recovering the Contribution of Women to the Circulation of Shakespeare in India', in T. Buckley et al. (eds), *Women and Indian Shakespeares*, 21–42, London: The Arden Shakespeare.

CHAPTER 10
IMAGINATION

(imm-adj-in-ah-shun)
noun
- A visual image perceived with the 'mind's eye'; a full-bodied sense-perception of a fictive idea
- A trainable capability (sometimes a 'tool', or a 'muscle')
- Connected in a reciprocal causal relationship with emotion
- Linked to empathy and the other
- Associated with heightened states of attention; associated with lowered states of attention
- A creative force; sometimes (especially from the 1960s to the 1990s) implicitly juxtaposed with everyday cognition and social mores and norms.

Defining the meanings and use cases of 'imagination' in the field of acting would be easy were it not for the fact that, 'not only are the accepted views regarding imagination far from settled, it is also the case that philosophical approaches to imagination are often somewhat inapplicable to our experience of it in everyday life, to say nothing of their relevance to the practical realm of the theatre' (Krumholz, 2023: 155). Brad Krumholz is certainly right, but my analysis of the catalogue shows that there are six predominant and accepted views regarding imagination in the practical realm of acting. At least five of these (the first five in the list above) might be considered 'Stanislavskian'. This is not because Stanislavski himself appears to have had anything particularly original or unique to say about 'imagination' but rather that in the scholarly journeys of recirculation, reinterpretation, rejection and reclamation of his ideas and practices about acting across the domain of the catalogue, 'imagination' is a key nodal point.

Daniel Dresner's (2018) account of imagination is orthodox in context of the 'how to' acting manuals in the catalogue. For Dresner, the imagination is a faculty 'linked to the senses' (70) that can stimulate strong responses in actors and audiences. Orthodox in describing a relationship between sense perception, emotional experience and material reality, Dresner advises actors that, 'to be real and believable you will need a strong enough imagination to convince yourself, and therefore the viewer, that these imaginary circumstances are real. If you do not then the story has no context, truth or drama' (70).

Picking up a common theme of the utility of the imagination to actor, Dresner writes, 'your [the actor's] imagination draws you into the reality and immediacy of a scene and keeps you in it' (71). Reiterating commonplace assumptions about acting and the imagination, he continues, 'your imagination will affect your behaviour' and 'the power of the imagination must be controlled of course' (71). Dresner follows convention, establishing 'imagination' in context of acting theory and the concept of 'sense memory' from 'Stanislavski [to] Meisner, Strasberg, Stella Adler et al' (112).

Dresner's account is also typical of the broadly accessible, practical 'how-to' literature in the catalogue for applying a common-language definition of 'imagination', which is expansive and largely uninterrogated.

By contrast, Nicola Shaughnessy and Philip Barnard's edited collection, *Performing Psychologies: Imagination, Creativity and Dramas of the Mind* (2019) contains a range of neuroscientific classifications of 'imagination', especially with regards neuroatypicality, that encompass a carefully-defined and sub-categorized conceptual domain for 'imagination'. (An expected requirement for a book that is *about* 'imagination'!) This domain includes, for example, 'social imagination' – a faculty, linked to empathy, for making assumptions and arriving at conclusions about the motivation and meaning of the behaviour of others. Ilona Roth's contribution to this collection disambiguates different components of imagination, including the social, 'pretend play' (or mimetic play in which the meanings and usages of objects and the subjectivity and identities of people are exchanged, substituted and reconstituted), pattern-finding and pattern-making.

Reflecting Kromholz's observation, Roth notes that the absence of a coherent 'picture of imaginative capacity in autism' relates to a 'wider lack of theoretical consensus about imagination and its relationship to creativity' (71). Roth adopts a 'broad definition' of imagination as encompassing, 'the capacity to imagine what other people are thinking and feeling' and 'the capacity to generate novel, original ideas and outputs' (71–2). This broad definition aligns well with the highest frequency use-case of 'imagination' in the catalogue, which can be found expressed in Dresner's account.

The variation in the meanings of 'imagination' across the sources of the catalogue can also be historicized, with David Hume's significant impact on definitions and interpretations of the imagination from the eighteenth century onwards giving way to Merleau-Ponty's impact on a twentieth-century phenomenological turn in acting theory.

Hume established 'imagination' in the Western philosophical canon as concerned with how individuals form abstract thoughts, reason causality, understand effects, sympathize and empathize and how and why we generate fictions that we commit to as fact.[1] Hume's definitions abide in common-language definitions of 'imagination' and the more self-consciously down-to-earth guides to acting technique in the catalogue.

In Merleau-Ponty, embodied sense perception becomes the foreground of 'imagination' and the clearer contrast between 'fiction' and 'reality' in Hume becomes blurred in what he refers to as *the imaginary texture of the real*.[2] This less clear-cut critique of 'imagination' is more commonly found in the catalogue's late twentieth- and early twenty-first-century academic books investigating the phenomenon of 'postdramatic subjectivity' (Garner Jnr in Boyle, Cornish and Woolf [eds] 2019: 201) after the influential work of Hans-Thies Lehmann (2006).

The broad sweep of philosophical thought on 'imagination' from Hume to Merleau-Ponty is discernible in the changing depictions of actors and audiences' imaginations across the catalogue and perhaps most notable in the changing conceptualization of imagination as a 'mind's eye' through the twentieth century. In commentary by and about Michael Chekhov, a straightforward mind's eye metaphor is evident (for example, Sinéad Rushe's 2013 book, *Michael Chekhov's Acting Technique: A Practitioner's Guide*) and it is also to be found quite prominently in Stanislavski's own writings. In *An Actor's Work*, Stanislavski writes, 'to imagine … means above all to see the things it is thinking about with the mind's eye … we call these mental images, the inner eye' (1936 [2009]: 73).

Despite a notable ocular fetish[3] in Stanislavski's writings on theatre generally – and specifically with regards his commentary on the imagination as an 'inner eye' seeing 'mental images' – there are very diverse recapitulations of the 'Stanislavskian' sense of imagination to be found in practices around the globe.

Pitches and Aquilina's edited collected, *Stanislavsky in the World: The System and its Transformation Across Continents* (2017) is a storehouse of these, with each National example recasting 'imagination' in a National-ideological context and within specific cultural cosmology. This book notes a well-identified 'American bias' (Aquilina, 2017: 4) in the transmission of Stanislavski's practices and ideas and challenges the 'competitive' thinking that measures the influence and ownership of practice by proxies of volume and cultural penetration. Reacting against Carnicke's transactional conclusion that New York has a 'unique place on the map of ["Stanislavskian"] migration, second only to Moscow' (Carnicke, 2009: 10), Aquilina argues that, 'twenty-first-century Stanislavsky studies are concerned with displacing these two images' (2017: 8) – the American and the Soviet myth of Stanislavski. Critiquing the reductionism of these two myths, Pitches and Aquilina collect global perspectives on the transmission, adoption and adaptation of 'Stanislavskian' practice to produce 'a more open-ended picture' (10) of his legacy.

This project notwithstanding, the scopophilia latent in Stanislavski's own writings appears to have been accentuated and exported by the American traditions which, via the acting students of 'Stanislavskian' teachers such as Adler, Meisner and Strasberg, plugged practice directly into the mainframe of a global and globalizing Hollywood narrative-drama film industry that was trading in acting performances of highly emotive and affecting visual imagery.

Stanislavksi's writings in the catalogue can be read many ways but, across translations, they do appear to be marked by a classical opti-centricism that frames the experience of acting on the *skene* and from the theatron.[4] Stanislavski writes, 'feelings and experience are elusive' and 'cannot be pinned down' whereas 'sight is more amendable. The things we see are … more deeply engraved in our visual memory and are resurrected anew in our representations of them' (76). Despite his evolving thesis on the usefulness of memory to acting, the dominant visual aspect of Stanislavksi's early interest in 'mental images' that 'help us to revive and pin down … innermost feelings' (76) carries through to his final experiments with 'active analysis', where the visual appearance of things is summated in the activity of the drama, recreated in rehearsals as an improvised dumbshow.

Carnicke's 2023 book, *Dynamic Acting Through Active Analysis: Konstantin Stanislavski, Maria Knebel and their Legacy* describes 'active analysis' as an 'innovative approach' that 'invites actors to explore the interactive dynamics in plays by enacting them before memorizing lines or setting blocking' (xiii). 'The heart of the technique is the etude – a purposeful, improvisatory study of a scene that uncovers the motives, desires, and subtexts that prompt characters to speak and act as they do in the play' (xiii–xiv). These etudes constitute a series of provisional and contingent improvisations of scenes that require actors to embody imagined physical scenarios taken from a playtext. Through successive etudes actors are taken 'deeper and deeper into the text' and 'the cast drafts and perfects their performance' (xiv) in a 'process of rehearsal [that] taps actors' minds, bodies, and spirits simultaneously' (xiii).

In the 'pyscho-physical' trend that emerged in Anglophone acting discourse during the late twentieth and early twenty-first centuries, the 'mind's eye' metaphor received a Pontian inflection. Ocular imagery was prominent in this trend, typified by Phillip Zarrilli's 'inner eye' imagery:

> when we *actively* utilize our 'inner eye' ('mind's eye' or active imagination) *we are no longer bound by the constraints of the visual field of sight per se*. Visualization as a way of working with the active imagination can be described as a voluntary psychophysical act.
>
> (Zarrilli, 2020: 123; emphasis in original)

In *Psychophysical Acting* (2009), yoking visuality, imagination and sensorial awareness together, Zarrilli valorized an idealized state-of-being for performers, which he described as

> *Meyyu kannakuka*: literally "the body becomes all eyes". A Malayalam folk expression encapsulating the ideal state of embodiment and accomplishment of the actor and the *kalarippayattu* practitioner. When one's "body is all eyes" … one is like an animal – able to see, hear and respond immediately to any stimulus in the immediate environment.
>
> (2009: 1)

In commentary on Zarrilli, in *Performer Training for Actors and Athletes* (2023), Frank Camilleri observes that, in relation to the imagination, the 'inner eye' concept has an uncertain position on the conceptual continuum between a visual 'mental representation' and a 'quasi-perceptual phenomenological experience' (59–60). Whether one sees things with the imagination in any truly visual sense is moot but, for a pithy philosophical assertion on the matter, Denis Diderot's comment that, 'the field of imagination is inversely proportional to that of the eye' (*Diderot on Art*, [1767] 1995: 202) can't really be bettered.

The psycho-physical trend in acting theory adopted a conceptualization of the imagination conducive to prevailing post-structuralist phenomenology and moved attention to the senses and away from the emotions. Across the historical trends and mores of conceptualizing 'imagination' in the catalogue, though, there remains what Krumolz observes as a 'strong connection between imagination and emotion' (155). In

Paul Elsam's writing, the relationship is a juxtaposition wherein, 'actors use emotion and imagination to varying degrees depending on their preferred style of acting' (2011: 123).

With and without a visual metaphor, 'imagination' is a recurrent preoccupation throughout Stanislavski's life and practice, dating from his earliest explorations of an acting 'system' to these final experiments with 'active analysis', or its more Soviet name, the 'Method of Physical Actions'. Several authors in the catalogue, for example, John Gillett (*Acting Stanislavski,* 2014), emphasize Stanislavski's influence in placing 'imagination' at the centre of the actor's work through a focus of self-identification of an actor with a role via various propositional techniques, such as 'given circumstances', emotion or sense memory.

In *My Life in Art* ([1924] 1948), Stanislavski valorizes the imaginative function of 'if' (mostly adopted and adapted by twentieth-century proponents as 'the magic if' or 'the magic what-if') in acting. This is an activity associated most closely with the category of 'pretend' or mimetic play but also related to 'social imagination' and one by which an actor initiates and sustains an imaginary self-identification with a character by undertaking a role-playing that is guided not by representing how a fictive character might behave in a given situation but a role-playing that is guided by an actor exploring how *they themselves* would behave 'if' they were in the character's situation.[5]

Gillett is careful to not overstate the novelty of Stanislavski's contribution to this conceptual approach. Stanislavski's fixation with an actor's imagination as a gateway to transformational experience (for actors and audiences) was no doubt formed by the Realist literary movement in nineteenth-century Russian literature and theatre from Gogol and Pushkin to Ostrovsky and Anton Chekhov and the reverberating image of the Maly Theatre's former-serf actor, Mikhail Shchepkin (1788–1863), whose death coincided with Stanislavski's birth.

Norris Houghton, the leading contemporaneous anglophone commentator on Stanislavski with first-hand knowledge of the Moscow Art Theatre rehearsal room, commented with somewhat ambiguous intent, 'the Stanislavski systems is really only a conscious codification of ideas about acting which have always been the property of most good actors of all countries whether they knew it or not' (*Moscow Rehearsals,* 1936: 57).

Generally a celebrant of Stanislavski and Russian theatre in his native America, Houghton's analysis was almost certainly not as derisive as this quote may read when taken out of context. Multiple sources attest to mutual respect between Stanislavski and Houghton, including a 1991 *New York Times* article (John Russell, 18 August) that records the legend that Stanislavski gifted Houghton a copy of *My Life in Art* with the personal inscription, 'To Charles Norris Houghton, my dear comrade in art, with this friendly advice: love the art in yourself and not yourself in art.' Whether this was a pointed or merely witty dedication, it can also be read as underscoring Houghton's observation about the common property of acting ideas and the counter tendency to over-state the significance of individual contributions to artistic techniques.

Irrespective of the originality or otherwise of Stanislavski's personal contribution to acting ideas, Houghton, Gillett and countless others point to his significance in codifying and popularizing several techniques-of-the-imagination that have become definitive of an 'organic' approach to acting characters, and to championing the aesthetics associated with this approach over a so-called 'representational' style (Gillett, 2014: xvi). Gillett binarizes 'organic acting' and 'representational acting', drawing many (philosophically questionable) juxtapositions. Gillett exemplifies a clear ideological preference for the former which is evident across the 'how-to' sources in the catalogue, framing the latter as characterized by a host of tacitly negative qualities from 'faked feeling', 'left brain dominance' and 'individualism' to 'fashion' and pretence. He contrasts this with representational acting's 'sketch of a real person, described from a distance' (Gillett, 2014: xvi).

According to Gillett:

> 'organic acting' uses the actor's 'full mind and body, senses, feelings, imagination, will, intellect, memory and experience as the raw material for transforming into a character. The human experiences of ourselves and others are recreated in rehearsal and performance through observation, imagination and memory'.
>
> (xvi)

Reinforcing the dominant discourse in the catalogue on the connection between 'imagination' and 'emotion' in acting, Gillett defines the ('Stanislavskian') 'organic' tradition as typified 'by a process involving the imagination' by which 'the actor passes from the plane of actual reality into the plane of another life, created and imagined by himself' (Stanislavski [1924] 1948: 466).

'Emotion' is arguably *the* central organizing principle of an aesthetic of 'organic' acting, or what Peta Tait calls 'twentieth-century realist acting' (in Pitches and Aquilina, 2017: 347) tradition, irrespective of a foundational debate in this tradition around the philosophical and practical consistency of 'beliefs about whether the actor's emotional feelings rather than the dramatic circumstances should be the basis' of acting (Tait in Pitches and Aquilina, 2017: 347). In this regard, the (largely) American post-Stanislavskian lineage is framed in the catalogue as a competition between (Strasberg's) fealty to an 'early' doctrine triangulating privately-felt emotions, imaginations and memories and (Adler and Meisner's) other alternative 'outward-focused' approaches that, to varying degrees, open each of these three categories to external stimuli (see Tait, 2017: 352–4).

For Meisner, an actor's imagination can deliver 'emotional aliveness' because, despite his fixation on the 'reality of doing' – the material circumstances and not fictive facts of a drama or character – he acknowledges that, as fuel for the imagination, personal experience is limited (Meisner and Longwell, 1987: 78). Meisner's USP is generally taken as formulated in his encouragement of an 'actor's "reactions" in performance' to others rather than their own internal purpose or 'self-will' (Stinespring, 2000: 98).

To this end, several commentators in the catalogue have organized the practitioners of this 'organic' tradition based on material accounts of the techniques and exercises that they have employed (rather than the concepts they mobilize) to achieve the emotional transformation that is central to this 'organic' aesthetic. Carnicke (1998) and Merlin (2003), for example, have generated genealogical commentary on post-Stanislavskian approaches on this basis and in line with a popular historical narrative of Stanislavski's increasing interest in physical action rather than emotion towards the end of his life and career.

In compiling this entry I have been struck that, positing 'imagination' as a basis of acting – as an example of the 'property of all actors', to use Houghton's metaphor – intellectually disrupts the emotion-centric epistemology of 'twentieth-century realist acting'. It recasts the binarization of 'organic' and 'representational' acting as properly aesthetic rather than ontological. Reflecting on the different uses of 'imagination' in the catalogue provides a refreshing inflection of the discourse on an 'organic acting' by quieting the noise in debates around the status and relevance of 'emotion' to acting practice and elevating the significance of other related concepts, such as 'observation'.

For Ewan and Green, 'imagination' is on a continuum with 'observation' and the 'transformation' that actors undertake requires a 'balancing' of the 'equation' between the two (2015: 129). Ewan and Green's use of the word is typical of a quasi-Kantian definition of imagination that pertains to both non-being (things that don't exist, haven't happened or in the most minimal sense have not been personally witnessed, understood or felt) and to pure potentiality, and the sublime (put crudely, those things which one might take to be real but which are beyond concrete comprehension).

The neo-Kantian sense of 'imagination' in relation to the sublime emerges in Karen Quigley's *Performing the Unstageable: Success, Imagination and Failure* (2020). Here, 'imagination' is one of 'theatre's ongoing paradoxes' alongside, 'pretence, visuality, mimesis and escape' (2020: 210). Quigley reviews Kantian 'imagination' through the prism of the post-modern philosophizing of Lyotard and Ranciére, connecting the human facility of 'imagination' with phenomena that cannot be adequately represented (15–18). The unrepresentable here is not the sublime but the practicably unfeasible on stage, such as some of Artaud's more lurid stage images, or the morally incomprehensible, such as genocide.

Contrasting the 'Stanislavskian' literature, which looks at imagination largely from the actor's perspective on stage, much of Quigley's analysis is formulated from the spectator's position in the auditorium. However, she provides an interesting set of meditations on the unstageable stage direction, and the intellectual provocation that these provide to actor and theatre-makers (2020: 39–82).

There are examples across the catalogue of the assertion that the imagination is trainable, and a tacit premise that, while this might be so for everybody – actors and audiences – it is *especially* so in the case of actors. Indeed, this seems to be an axiomatic tenet of actor training discourse and (like most axioms) is expressed in rather simple and self-justifying terms: 'the imagination functions like a muscle', writes Sinéad Rushe, 'if unused, it will atrophy and weaken, but if exercised regularly, it will become "fit" and responsive' (2019: 177). Rushe's simile typifies late twentieth- and early twenty-first-century embodiment discourses on actors by conceiving of the imagination as so fundamentally embodied that it should be understood in strictly corporeal terms.

Acting

There is a prominent conception in the catalogue of the actor's imagination as akin to but exceeding the senses and located in but not constrained by cognition. Clive Barker (1977), for example, writes about the imperative for actors' work to 'by-pass' 'intellectual' and 'reflective' 'mind mechanisms' (26–49). Barker's iconic but perhaps somewhat outmoded 1977 title, *Theatre Games,* contains the assertion that acting is quintessentially a process of transformation and, 'at the core is the actor's act of creative imagination' (111).

The seemingly tautological phrasing – the actor's act – indicates a specific phenomenological conception of the 'creative imagination' as an event as well as a facility. For Baker, the *creative imagination* (special to actors) seems to be a sub-genus of *the imagination* (a common human facility). This is not only an imagistic cognitive capability but a productive force that would need to be defined as exceeding the social scope of categories such as 'pretend play'.

In the varied, differentiated and occasionally competing definitions of 'imagination' across the catalogue there is a strong consensus that it is quintessential to theatre. 'Imagination' prescribes a space and a sympathetic bond between actors and audiences where mutual un-knowing connects to feeling and understanding and this is evocatively discussed in Kathleen Gough's *Theatre and the Threshold of Death: Lectures on the Dying Arts* (2024). Here, 'imagination' is asserted as transcendent and central to the mysteries of acting, theatre and life itself. She writes about the 'rebirth of theatre' in the Middle Ages, contending that an historical resurgence of the cultural significance of the theatre occurs in the 'middle of the Easter Mass', in (perhaps the first) mystery play – *Quem quaeritis,* Latin for, 'whom do you seek?' (2). This drama, which would have been enacted mid-Mass, stages the three Marys' hunt for Jesus after their discovery of the disappearance of His body from the tomb, after crucifixion. Gough, an end-of-life doula and hospice volunteer, uses *Quem quaeritis* as a synecdoche of Christian spirituality which frames Faith as a narrative mystery to be decoded by the believer – 'the [Christian] story of a man who is in the middle of death and a new life also puts us squarely in the middle, where death is not an ending, but appears as a threshold, a doorway', she states (1–2). She then frames dramaturgical hermeneutics as essential to this Mystery, describing the Christian narrative as something:

> that requires our curiosity, something that we cannot actually know with any certainty, something that asks us to engage our imagination, something that sounds remarkably like theatre.
>
> (Gough, 2024: 2)

Gough provides the most esoteric account of 'imagination' and acting in the catalogue and the one which most strongly contrasts 'imagination' with 'reality' while unifying actors' and spectators' imagination in the apprehending of *deep reality* beyond sense perception.

Gough observes that Stanislavski, in *An Actor Prepares* (1936), 'returns again and again to the relationship between the hands and the imagination' (Gough, 2024: 61).

In a series of poetic interpretations of the story of Christ, Gough proceeds to draw a distinction between the material reality that we can touch (with our hands) and the immateriality of *the real* that we can't touch but which touches us, and which is so central to the Christian mystery. Drawing on Caravaggio's image of an incredulous St Thomas inserting his fingers in the wounds of a resurrected Christ, literally probing physical reality in search of metaphysical truth, she reminds her reader that most of what is real in the world you can't actually touch. Or at least, can't touch with your hands. Gough recalls Jacob Levi's commentary on the 'epistemological limitations' (2021: 32) of physical touch and re-values the touching that 'imagination' can do in allowing actors and audiences to sense that which eludes the physical senses. Reunifying with Quigley's meditations on the unstageable sublime, Gough's imaginative touch, just as Barker's 'actor's-act' characterizes a strong strand of theorizing in the catalogue on the relationship between 'imagination' and *deep truth*. The accessibility to actors and audiences of profound personal and social insights, moving experiences, and spiritual and metaphysical depth via an imaginative premise underlies key definitions and use-cases of 'Truth' (see Chapter 7).

Notes

1. Hume, *A Treatise of Human Nature*, 2007a; Hume, *An Enquiry Concerning Human Understanding*, 1998; Hume, *A Dissertation on the Passions; The Natural History of Religion*, 2007b).
2. Merleau-Ponty, 1964, 'Eye and Mind,' in *The Primacy of Perception*, 1964: 159–90.
3. Music and musicality feature prominently too, with Sharon Marie Carnicke noting that, 'a great deal of evidence proves that Stanislavsky compared written plays to musical scores' (2023: 93).
4. *Skene*: the antique Greek term for the stage or performing area. *Theatron*: the auditorium but also sometimes the entire theatre architecture including stage.
5. This is perhaps a contentiously simplistic definition: Carnicke tells a story of 'three English-speaking teachers from the Meisner, Strasberg, and Adler schools … arguing over the use of "if," "as if," and "what if" in the development of character', with each presumably imputing a slightly different inflection of meaning. In the story, Natalya Zvereva difuses the disagreement, saying, 'in Russian there is only one word, and so your argument is all yours and not ours' (in Carnicke 2023: xv). This contention might be considered in light of the commentary in this section on the cultural transmission of 'Stanislavski'.

References

Aquilina, S. (2017), 'Introduction: Context 1: Well-trodden Paths: US, UK, Russian and Soviet Perspectives on Stanislavsky's Transmission', in J. Pitches and S. Aquilina (eds), *Stanislavsky in the World: The System and its Transformations Across Continents*, 1–11, London: Methuen Drama.

Barker, C. (1977) *Theatre Games: A New Approach to Drama Training*, 26–49, London: Methuen Drama.

Acting

Boyle, M. S., M. Cornish and B. Woolf (2019), *Postdramatic Theatre and Form*, London: Methuen Drama.

Carnicke, S. M. (1998), *Stanislavsky in Focus*, Amsterdam: Harwood Academic Publishers.

Carnicke, S. M. (2009), *Stanislavsky in Focus*, Abingdon: Routledge.

Carnicke, S.M. (2023), *Dynamic Acting through Active Analysis: Konstantin Stanislavsky, Maria Knebel, and Their Legacy*, London: Methuen Drama.

Diderot on Art: Volume II, The Salon of 1767 (1995), translated by John Goodman, New Haven and London: Yale University Press.

Dresner, D. (2018), *A Life Coaching Approach to Screen Acting*, London: Methuen Drama.

Elsam, P. (2011), *Acting Characters: 20 Essential Steps from Rehearsal to Performance*, London: Methuen Drama.

Ewan, V. and D. Green (2015), *Actor Movement*, London: Bloomsbury.

Gillett, J. (2014), *Acting Stanislavski: A Practical Guide to Stanislavski's Approach and Legacy*, London: Methuen Drama.

Gough, K.M. (2024), *Theatre and the Threshold of Death: Lectures on the Dying Arts*, London: Methuen Drama.

Hume, D. (1998), *An Enquiry Concerning Human Understanding*, Oxford: Clarendon Press.

Hume, D. (2007a), *A Treatise of Human Nature, Vol. 1: The Text*, Oxford: Clarendon Press.

Hume, D. (2007b), *A Dissertation on the Passions; The Natural History of Religion*, Oxford: Clarendon Press.

Krumholz, B. (2023). *Why Do Actors Train?: Embodiment for Theatre Makers and Thinkers*, London: Methuen Drama.

Lehmann, H.-T. (2006), *Postdramatic Theatre*, London and New York: Routledge.

Levi, J. (2021), '"Es wird Leib, es empfindet": Auto-Affection, Doubt, and the Philosopher's Hands,' in Rachel Aumiller (ed.), *A Touch of Doubt: On Haptic Scepticism*, 31–56. Berlin: De Gruyter.

Meisner, S. and D. Longwell (1987), *Sanford Meisner on Acting*, New York: Vintage Books.

Merleau-Ponty, M. (1964), *The Primacy of Perception*, Evanston, IL: Northwestern University Press.

Merlin, B. (2003), *Konstantin Stanislavsky*, London: Routledge.

Quigley, K. (2020), *Performing the Unstageable: Success, Imagination and Failure*, London: Bloomsbury.

Rushe, S. (2013) *Michael Chekhov's Acting Technique: A Practitioner's Guide*, London: Bloomsbury.

Rushe, S. (2019), *Michael Chekhov's Acting Technique: A Practitioner's Guide*, London: Methuen Drama.

Shaughnessy, N. and P. Barnard, eds (2019), *Performing Psychologies: Imagination, Creativity and Dramas of the Mind*, London: Bloomsbury.

Stanislavski, K. ([1924] 1948) *My Life in Art*, Boston, MA: Little, Brown & Company.

Stanislavski, K. ([1936] 2009), *An Actor's Work*, London: Routledge.

Stinespring, L. M. (2000), 'Just Be Yourself: Derrida, Difference and the Meisner Technique', in D. Krasner (ed.), *Method Acting Reconsidered*, New York: St Martin's Press.

Tait, P. (2017), 'Acting Idealism and Emotions: Hayes Gordon, The Ensemble Theatre and Acting Studios in Australia', in J. Pitches and S. Aquilina (eds), *Stanislavsky in the World: The System and its Transformations Across Continents*, 347–66, London: Methuen Drama.

Zarrilli, P. B. (2009), *Psychophysical Acting*, London: Routledge.

Zarrilli, P. B. (2020), *(Toward) A Phenomenology of Acting*, London: Routledge.

CHAPTER 11
STATUS

(stay-tuss)
noun
- An interpretative concept used by and with actors in play analysis, character analysis and development, and in improvisation games and exercises
- An index of power, where power can be understood in several different forms in relation to, for example, social and political capital, physical or intellectual strength
- A measure of power expressed and identifiable in the behaviour of a character
- A measure of power expressed and identifiable in the responses of characters to the behaviour of others
- A subjective description of a character's power in a relational dynamic with another character
- A measure of a character's self-awareness of their power with regards the above
- A descriptor for the level of power assumed by a character irrespective of their actual social standing, physical or political power but respective only to their ability to exert influence on others
- A concept for interpreting power dynamics between characters and which is usually but not necessarily impactful on the events within a narrative
- An interpretative paradigm by which all human interactions are understood as reducible to – and therefore all acting choices reducible to – an essential relationship dynamic of dominance and subservience underlying all contexts and situations.

'Status' is a leading explanatory concept in acting. It has prominent use-cases in treatises on character development and rehearsal techniques. 'Status' is also a prominent explanatory concept in dramatic text analysis for actors and features prominently in accounts of rehearsal and training 'games', which adopt the concept of 'status' as a key feature in what Chirico and Younger refer to as 'active learning techniques' (2020: 7).

Suzanne Maynard Miller's use of a '[rehearsal] card game to help students understand status and power dynamics' (in Chirico and Younger, 2020: 281) exemplifies this trend. Here, in working on the text *Topdog/Underdog*, a deck of cards is used as an index of power, with number cards to royal cards symbolizing a sliding scale of power and 'status' value. These cards are then given to actors in structured improvisational games in which the card values determine characters' status value, and shape relational-dynamics between characters.

Prominent not only in character-development and play-analysis, Maynard Miller's account also indicates another significant sub-field in which the concept of 'status' is central: improvisation. Several authors attribute the predominance of the concept to Keith Johnstone's work on improvisation and specifically to his book *Impro: Improvisation and the Theatre* (1981). Kenneth Rea, in his book *The Outstanding Actor: Seven Keys to Success,* suggests that Keith Johnstone, 'developed the very useful concept of status' (2021: 29). Tom Salinsky and Deborah Frances-Wight also muse in their *Improv Handbook*, that 'Keith Johnstone's work on status alone should ensure his position in the theatre hall of fame' (2017: 82) and Theresa Robbins Dudeck (2013) further emphasizes Johnstone's impact on the currency of the concept in acting practice and discourse.

Several of the writers emphasizing Johnstone's influence on the use of 'status' as an acting concept had personal or indirect contact with Johnstone and all work within an improvisation-focused lineage of acting and actor training. Within this specific lineage, Johnstone's book and teachings appears to have been influential in popularizing the concept.

From within the improvisation sub-field of acting, the use-cases for 'status' have a bias towards behavioural description. Often juxtaposed with other indicators of 'status' – such as dress/costume or the social standing of a character in a drama – behaviour is the most frequently discussed and closely considered signifier of status in this sub-field. In fact, some authors such as Kenneth Rea, juxtapose the significance of everyday indicators of 'status' – *having* possession of things: property, money, weapons, roles of office, etc. – with the self-possession of *doing*:

> whether on or off stage our behaviour can be seen as predominantly high status, low status or somewhere in between. Status shouldn't be confused with your role or social level: it's about the way you *do* things. By adjusting your status you can influence the other person.
>
> (Rea, 2015: 37; emphasis in original)

It ain't what you do it's the way that you do it might be understood as the Newtonian logic tacitly underpinning much of acting theory but, in this sub-field that eminently practical ideology of causality receives an inflection: not directly concerned with the cause-and-effect between actors and audiences, improvisation focused accounts of 'status' fixate on the causative relationship between actors and between characters.

Johnstone's influence on the meaning and use of 'status' outside of this improvisation-focused tradition is moot and an alternative origin story of 'status' as a concept in acting can be found in the catalogue via the iconic figures of Antonin Artaud and Bertolt Brecht, expressed in their concepts of the *Hieroglyph* and the *gestus*.

Erwin Jans (2020) approaches these two concepts via two 'ghost scenes' that 'haunt the later (postmodern and postdramatic) theatre' (151): One ghost scene: Artaud's fantasy image of an actor burning at the stake in his infamous and infamously impenetrable essay, *The Theatre and its Double* (1935). The second, Brecht's fictious 'street scene' in which multiple by-standers re-enact a car accident from the various perspectives of their witnessing from Brecht's 1938 essay, 'a basic model for an epic theatre'. Characteristically cryptic, Artaud writes, 'when we say the word *life*, we understand this is not life recognized by externals, by facts, but the kind of frail moving source forms never attain' (Artaud [1931–7] 1989: 145). If there is 'one truly infernal and damned thing left today' he decries, 'it is our artistic dallying with forms, instead of being like those tortured at the stake, signalling through the flames' (145).

The Theatre and its Double is about as far from a how-to manual as it is possible to be while remaining a didactic treatise on acting. Jans observes that Artaud connects this 'signalling' with his repeated motif of the Hieroglyph, which draws together various representational styles and actions that captivate him – the codified movements of Balinese dance, the language of dreams, the grammar of silent films, and the palsy and paroxysm of plague victims. 'Artaud invests the Hieroglyphs with a knowledge that is neither rational nor discursive and with an intensity that has an immediate effect on our consciousness without any verbal or intellectual intervention' (Jans, 2020: 152) because, for Artaud, there is a 'crisis in representation' (152) meaning that language – and all 'our other artistic dallying with forms' – cannot represent Life. For Artaud, the gesturing of the victim, burning to death at the stake, signalling, gives the sign of Life and thereby gestures in a way that reveals their own and our own 'status' as (implicitly) wretched human creatures.

This is a quite different use of the word 'status'. Not defining transient or socially-confected power but something more like innate humanity stripped of all these things. This image of 'status' has an enduring influence in acting, most notably in the European Laboratory Theatre traditions coalescing around Jerzy Grotowski's *via negativa* (stripping away) and his para-theatrical experiments that begat what Kaynar (2014) has described as the 'performance-oriented aesthetics, distinguished by plot-less, character-less, deconstructed and fragmentary theatrical texts' (86) of the late twentieth century (see Chapter 7).

Despite the clear ongoing influence of Artaud's writing on theatre, that broad historical sketch may be a little reductive and the extent to which the Hieroglyph is a practical or explanatory acting concept beyond the realm of Artaud's thinking is unclear in the catalogue.

Despite appearing only around 200 times in the catalogue, Brecht's concept of *gestus* is significantly more applicable and well-referenced across multiple acting contexts, including Shakespearean acting and play adaptation. Tom Hoenselaars, for example, defines the quintessance of *gestus* as an acting concept via what he calls the 'intersemiotic potential' (2012: 12) of gestic imagery. In other words, the capacity for one semiotic 'system' – writing, here – to have the meanings it generates modulated by another – acting – when these are combined in staged performance, and especially so in the context of *gestus* which works to simplify signation and expose a clearly isolated meaning.

Unlike Artaud, for Brecht, the concept of 'status' refers to the political rather than the metaphysical. As in Artaud, 'status' represents something like a *true* state of being – as humans and within a polis. In *gestus* and the Hieroglyph, this state of being can be the subject and the object of representational acts that disclose it but, in Brecht's *gestus*, the representational act is more easily described and pragmatically understood.

Acting

Although 'one of the most difficult terms in the Brechtian vocabulary' (Unwin, 2005: 61), *gestus* might be a simple as 'the pointed finger, the shrugged shoulder, the turned back' (62).

Déprats provides a more accessible definition of *gestus* as including 'the speaker's [actor's] physical deportment and behaviour toward a [scene] partner, but also the way the speaker considers speech and the theatrical situation' (Déprats, cited in Hoenselaars, 2012: 140). Its defining feature, though, is 'something deeper: a physical embodiment of the relationships between people in society' (140). In *gestus*, is captured a 'particular set of interlocking attitudes and the sum total of these provides the audience with a chart of the society that is portrayed' (Unwin, 2005: 62). In this sense, as an actorly behaviour, *gestus* is much closer than Artaud's Hieroglyph to the everyday body language that preoccupies the improvisation-focused definition and usages of 'status' in the catalogue.

Although an over-simplification, it might help to sort through the differing definitions and use-cases for 'status' discussed thus far in the context of meaning. 'Status' exists *for* acting in the improvisational tradition – as a structuring concept that can be employed technically to exert some control over meaning for actors. In *gestus* and the Brechtian tradition, acting exists *for* 'status' – acting is the structuring concept that reveals the 'true' meaning of things (their 'status') being represented by actors. In the former, 'status' is deployed as a concept that can motivate and structure acting games and performances. In the latter, acting is deployed as a practice that can expose and scrutinize 'status'. As Barnett puts it:

> observing a person's *Gestus* connects actions to (social) context; it asks the actor to look beyond the surface and ask why such actions might be taking place. Observation is no longer an activity of merely registering difference, but one in which difference is the starting point for further observation and inquiry.
> (Barnett, 2014: 116–7)

Both Brecht and Artaud are profoundly aporetic about verisimilitude as a representational mode but where Artaud rails against everyday actions as meaningful or edifying artistic modes of accessing and understanding our status Brecht co-opts the everyday into a highly metonymic modality of actorly representation. Almost as slippery as Artaud's Hieroglyph, *gestus* is perhaps most easily understood as a representational abstraction by intensification of the everyday. Artaud's writing favours the not-everyday: both highly culturally codified (e.g. Balinese dance) and culturally un-codifiable actions (e.g. writhing in agony) as a means of exposing (metaphysical) status by representational means. Brecht's *gestus* also uses representation to expose or disclose (political) status, but by a de-culturing of enculturated action. In contrast to Artaud, his *gestus* aesthetic is hyper-banal and hyper-quotidian.

Although synthesized from a mimetic vision of the everyday, '*gestus* is anything but superficial imitation of reality; rather it delves into a hidden social and political truth', according to Jans (2020: 152).

Related to but distinct from both the improvisation and Brechtian discourses on 'status' as an acting concept is Applied Theatre's culturally-material understanding of the concept as pivotal in both conflict and conflict resolution:

> power exists in many forms—it can exist at the individual level (beauty, money, education, strength, knowledge, positional rank, networks, etc.); at the structural level (organizational, governmental, military); and at the societal systemic level (race, gender, class). These differing forms of power inform and impact each other in extremely complex ways. All conflicts will have issues of power at play.
>
> (Tint, 2018: 209)

In the Applied Theatre context of conflict resolution, 'typically, it will be the parties with smaller amounts of power who are more aware of the power differentials' (Tint, 2018: 209, citing Baker Miller 1995). As Barabara Tint explains, 'conflict resolution work must always include some sort of assessment of the power dynamics among the parties and attempt to address or balance them in some way for the good of the parties and the overall goals of the conflict process' (Tint, 2018).

Applied Theatre for conflict resolution combines Cultural Materialism's worldview with a transactional understanding of human relations, focusing 'status' very firmly in the exchanges *between* people. Accounts such as Tint's valorize 'balance' or harmonization between 'status' positions as a mutually preferable and rewarding situation that provides conditions to deescalate and disincentivize conflict. In conflict resolution, the exchange between people is metaphoricalized as a physical asymmetry between the powerful and powerless and Applied techniques insert themselves to 'rebalance' this exchange.

Drawing a direct parallel between the leading dramaturgical ideal of conflict (between characters) and real-world conflicts, Tint binarizes the equation between parties and conflict, arguing that power 'comes in the form of status dynamics, that is, interactional, visible, and audible behavior related to dominance and submission' (2018: 210). 'Understanding status behavior', she writes, 'can't change systemic power influences such as race or gender' but, 'we can explore status interactions as they relate to these systemic issues' through Applied techniques (209):

> For example, women often feel silenced in organizational contexts with male superiors. The physical and verbal choices for both men and women in this dance reflect longtime conditioning in "status appropriate" behavior across gender. Increased awareness of and training around these dynamics can provide more flexibility and choice in relational behavior.
>
> (2018: 209)

Blurring the dramaturgical and real-word premises, Tint writes that 'being able to shift interactional status dynamics is critical to changing relationships, scenes, and stories' (Tint, 2018: 210). The explicit interchangeability of the ideology of the dramaturgical and the real-world in Applied contexts points towards the fact that, common across the catalogue with regards definitions and use-cases is the sense of the pliability, impermanence and contingency of given 'status' positions and values.

References

Artaud, A., ([1931–7] 1989), 'The Theatre and its Double', in C. Schumacher and B. Singleton (eds), *Artaud on Theatre*, 95–156, London: Methuen Drama.

Baker Miller, J. (1995), 'Domination and Subordination', in P. A. Rothenberg (ed.), *Race, Class & Gender in the United States: An Integrated Study*, 57–64, New York: St. Martin's Press.

Barnett, D. (2014), *Brecht in Practice: Theatre, Theory and Performance*, London: Methuen Drama.

Chirico, M. M. and K. Younger, ed. (2020), *How to Teach a Play: Essential Exercises for Popular Plays*, London: Methuen Drama.

Dudeck, T. R. (2013), *Keith Johnstone: A Critical Biography*, London: Methuen Drama.

Hoenselaars, T. (2012), 'Introduction', in T. Hoenselaars (ed.), *Shakespeare and the Language of Translation*, rev. edn, 1–28, London: Methuen Drama.

Jans, E. (2020), 'Bernadetje, Catastrophes and Gestures', in C. Stalpaert, G. Cools and H.D. Vuyst (eds), *The Choreopolitics of Alain Platel's les ballets C de la B: Emotions, Gestures, Politics*, 145–54, London: Methuen Drama.

Johnstone, K. (1981), *Impro: Improvisation and the Theatre*, London: Methuen Drama.

Kaynar, G. (2014), 'Textual Dramaturgy and Dramaturg-as-Text: Traditional versus New Dramaturgy in the Era of German Post-Dramatic Theatre', in A. Citron, S. Aronson-Lehavi and D. Zerbib (eds), *Performance Studies in Motion: International Perspectives and Practices in the Twenty-First Century*, London: Methuen Drama.

Rea, K. (2015), 'Generosity', in *The Outstanding Actor: Seven Keys to Success*, London: Methuen Drama.

Rea, K. (2021), *The Outstanding Actor: Seven Keys to Success*, 2nd edn, London: Methuen Drama.

Salinsky, T. and D. Frances-White (2017), *The Improv Handbook: The Ultimate Guide to Improvising in Comedy, Theatre, and Beyond*, London: Methuen Drama.

Tint, B. (2018), 'From Hell, No to Yes, And: Applied Improvisation for Training in Conflict Resolution, Mediation, and Law', in T. R. Dudeck and C. McClure (eds), *Applied Improvisation: Leading, Collaborating, and Creating Beyond the Theatre*, 199–220, London: Methuen Drama.

Unwin, S. (2005), 'Key Concepts of Brecht's Theatrical Theory', in *A Guide to the Plays of Bertolt Brecht*, London: Methuen Drama.

CHAPTER 12
BELIEVEABLE

(bee-lee-va-bul)
- A credible fiction
- An obvious but credible fiction
- An aesthetic value correlated with verisimilitude
- A threshold point at which an audience may 'suspend disbelief'
- Foundational to the exchange between actors and audiences
- A proposition of surface vs depth
- A proposition unstably related to truth and reality.

Although used only just over 200 times in the catalogue in the forms 'believable' or 'unbelievable' the concept of 'believability' in relation to acting is deployed well over 2,000 times in the catalogue even after adjusting out the common language usages of 'believe', 'unbelieve' or 'disbelief'. Some few authors are quite prolific users of the term. For example, Lorna Marshall (2001) uses it upwards of thirty times, Daniel Dresner over eighty times (2018) but John Gillett is the heaviest user of the concept in the catalogue, deploying it nearly 200 times (2014, 2021). 'Believable' features disproportionately in 'practical guides', such as Gillett's or Daniel Dresner's *Wrapping it Up: A Life Coaching Approach to Screen Acting* as well as in titles offering *100 Acting Exercises for 8–18 Year Olds* (Marsden, 2019), *Exploring Television Acting* (Paget, 2018) and in multiple 'guides' to auditioning (Bishop, 2015, 2022), crafting and performing (Homan and Rhinehart, 2017) or simply succeeding in given fields of acting (Rea, 2015).

This use-volume may be a result of the vocabulary and style employed in these titles rather than the prominence of the concept in the thinking of these authors, necessarily. Indeed, 'believability' has only ten specific uses but at least one of these – Nancy Bishop's – appears to state something quite explicitly about the meaning of the concept of 'believable' across the catalogue: she writes that, if an acting 'performance is not grounded in truth and believability' then, 'this is poor acting in both film and theatre' (2015: 46). The direct association that Bishop makes between 'believable' acting and 'good' acting is non-contentious across the how-to guides and manual of the catalogue as well as much commentary on TV and Film acting. Indeed, there is a very small but potentially statistically relevant inclination towards use of 'believability' in discourse on acting in screen-based media as opposed to on stage. This may make some logical sense in the context of a predominant narrative cinema style represented in the catalogue but this also carries through into titles on acting for motion capture in games. Dower and Langdale, for example, write that 'motion capture (mocap) is simply a new and unique acting medium' and that their guide – *Performing for Motion Capture* (2022) – 'is going to give you the tools to create compelling and believable characters in the volume [the studio in which motion capture is recorded]' (1). Dower and Langdale use 'believability' as a concept in upwards of 20 specific instances, linking 'believability' to characterization (see Chapter 2), entertainment value and audience enjoyment. In fact, they argue that 'this brand-new medium is reminding us of the ancient one of complete acting skills that require the body and mind working in harmony to create truthful, believable and entertaining performances' (22) and contend that one of mocap's primary uses is to allow acting performances to 'be more life-like' and 'believable' (18).

In most instances where 'believable' or 'believability' is used in the catalogue it is used to mean that a given performance or performative act convincingly depicts that which it intends to depict, and/or that it persuades an audience to accept an intended interpretation of that depiction. Most uses are strongly governed by this sense of a relationship between either intention and affect or between affect and interpretation, with many uses blurring out affect and connecting intention and interpretation directly.

In the specifically theatrical context of the source material, deceit has mostly positive connotations even if it remains a troubling prospect: Lorna Marshall writes that, 'this is one of the central paradoxes of performance. We enact a lie, which is somehow believable to us and to the audience. We pretend we live in a world that has no actual existence ... and yet the lie must ring true' (Marshall, 2001: 233).

When the concept of believability is mobilized in acting theory, practice and the interpretation of performance what is most often being mobilized is an aesthetic preference for verisimilitude in representation. This preference is most strongly associated with realism and Naturalism as genres or styles but, in the context of acting, 'believable' is not synonymous with 'truth' (see Chapter 7) although, as Lorna Marshall indicates, they may in practice be used interchangeably in teaching, rehearsal and criticism. Marshall's statement is a restatement of the folk wisdom that a lie must be believable in order to ring true and a recapitulation of the audience's commission to *suspend their disbelief.*

While 'believability' is strongly connected to the intentions of the actor, as a phenomenon, it resides in the audience. The performer may be believable or act believably, but this can only be said to be so because an interpreter of their action chooses to believe it, or merely acknowledges it to be believable. Fiona Banks quotes the actor, Paul Chahidi, reflecting on their performance as Maria in *Twelfth Night,* as saying, 'if you haven't rooted the character in something truthful then you will struggle when you want the audience to believe in the emotional heart of the character' (Banks, 2019: 227). Chahidi's contemplation on a compact between actors and audiences where 'truth' for the former may translate to 'belief' for the latter is quite typical of reflections on 'believability' across the catalogue.

Salinsky and Frances-White (2017) provide a similar meditation that helps to exemplify the foundational nature of this accepted tenet of acting when they claim that, 'once we have a space with a stage and basic lights, whatever we tell the audience is in that space they will believe is there' (22).

The prevailing usage of the term in acting discourse closely resembles common language usage of the word. In the specifically theatrical and in the common language, 'believable' connotes both sincerity and deceit: that which is believable is not necessarily to be believed.

In fact, one might be encouraged to be suspicious of that which is wholly plausible. In this sense, 'believability' even more so than the related and even slipperier concepts of 'truth' and 'authenticity' (see Chapters 7 and 13), is about *appearance* and not *substance*. Where that which is authentic must in one sense *be* authentic and that which is true must at least at some level *be* true, that which is believable needs only to *appear* to be what it purports to be. It can in fact and in essence be something entirely different.

David Barnett (2014) reminds that, even in realist traditions of acting that place high stock in figurative representation and verisimilitude, being 'believable' in a role is nothing to do with the 'truth' of a situation or its 'reality'; 'believability' is a labour of acting. 'Stanislavsky strove to achieve believability on stage', Barnett writes, 'but he did not simply say "be believable!" to his actors; rather, he spent much of his creative life experimenting with many approaches to achieve this end' (14).

'Believability' is one currency of theatre as a representational realm and while this might predominantly refer to a sense of verisimilitude in acts and objects of representation it is not entirely bounded within the realist frame; one might *believe* in an abstracted representation just as much as one might believe in a figurative one, although this is a more niche interpretation of the term. Trish Reid, in a commentary on *The Theatre of Anthony Neilson* (2017) alludes to a non-figurative form of believability when she asks, 'what do characters need to do, and how do they need to explain what they do, in order to be believable in dramatic terms?' (2017: 127).

In all cases where 'believability' is applied in the catalogue, though, it is concerned with *appearance*. It is certainly related to 'reality' – do I *believe* this is *real*? – but is perhaps more helpfully understood in the context of acting with regards to perception and a sense of the relationship between surface and depth.

'Superficial' has mostly negative connotations in the catalogue and in acting more broadly. It is used over 200 times across the catalogue and almost exclusively with a negative implication. Michael Chekhov, for example, uses 'superficial' antipathetically and antithetically with 'good' or 'correct' (see Rushe, 2019: 15–32, 78–89, 136–46, 205–19).

That which is superficial lacks depth; that which is superficial is all appearance and no substance; the value of things – materially, morally, artistically, etc. – lies *under* the surface. Surface and depth are always already in a representational pairing where the former represents the latter and in which the latter cannot appear of itself. The former is in service of the latter and the latter relies on the former to represent it *properly*. The former is nothing – almost literally no-thing – without the latter. The latter is indivisibly itself irrespective of the former. Of course, what the representational realm of theatre draws our attention to most compellingly is the faultiness of this set of assumptions. We live in a world of appearance and theatre is an intensification of this appearing world; a synecdoche of it, in fact. In theatre as in life more generally the commerce of meaning happens only at the surface. In the context of representation and meaning-making, rather than a cipher for depth, the superficial is the first and only grounds for the meaning of depth. Without depth, surface, obtains meaning. Without surface, depth has no meaning at all.

References

Banks, F., ed. (2019), *Shakespeare: Actors and Audiences*, London: The Arden Shakespeare.
Barnett, D. (2014), *Brecht in Practice: Theatre, Theory and Performance*, London: Methuen Drama.
Bishop, N. (2015), *Auditioning for Film and Television: Secrets from a Casting Director*, London: Methuen Drama.
Bishop, N. (2022), *Intimacy Coordinators. In Auditioning for Film and Television: A Post #MeToo Guide*, London: Methuen Drama.
Dower, J. and P. Langdale, eds (2022), *Performing for Motion Capture: A Guide for Practitioners*, London: Methuen Drama.
Dresner, D. (2018), *A Life-coaching Approach to Screen Acting*, London: Methuen Drama.
Homan, S. and B. Rhinehart (2017), *Comedy Acting for Theatre: The Art and Craft of Performing in Comedies*, London: Methuen Drama.
Marsden, S. (2019), *100 Acting Exercises for 8–18 Year Olds*, London: Methuen Drama.
Marshall, L. (2001), *The Body Speaks*, London: Methuen Drama.
Paget, D. (2018), 'Truth and "Truthiness" in Acting the Real', in T. Cantrell and C. Hogg (eds), *Exploring Television Acting*, London: Bloomsbury Publishing.
Rea, K. (2015), 'Generosity', in K. Rea (ed.), *The Outstanding Actor: Seven Keys to Success*, 29–70, London: Methuen Drama.
Reid, T. (2017), *The Theatre of Anthony Neilson*, London: Methuen Drama.
Rushe, S. (2019), *Michael Chekhov's Acting Technique: A Practitioner's Guide*, London: Methuen Drama.
Salinsky, T. and D. Frances-White (2017), *The Improv Handbook: The Ultimate Guide to Improvising in Comedy, Theatre, and Beyond*, London: Methuen Drama.

CHAPTER 13
AUTHENTICITY

(aww-then-tis-iti)
noun
- the quality of something real or genuine about an actor's performance
- the appearance of something real or genuine about an actor's performance
- a personally-felt experience for actors
- a personally (and perhaps collectively)-felt experience for audience members.

The 'authentic' is, as Daniel Schulze has written in *Authenticity in Contemporary Theatre and Performance* (2017), a 'much-desired something' (1). Used just under 400 times across the catalogue in at least one of its forms (e.g. 'authentic' or 'inauthentic'), 'authenticity' is much desired but comparatively little talked-about.

The term 'authenticity' is latent rather than explicit in much of the catalogue in discussions of 'truth', 'believability', 'character' and 'emotion' (see chapters) and few authors seek to define its meaning in acting discourse. Schulze is a very notable exception, who provides a book-length dissection of the concept, but a few others offer faster and looser descriptions of meaning that aim to define the term in operationally useful ways more directly attuned to use-case. Lorna Marshall, for example, boldly takes on the task of defining 'authenticity', stating:

> Authenticity is the direct, simple expression of feeling. From the heart, with no cover-up or apology. It can be very small, or it can become huge, but it remains a direct and honest manifestation of the moment. And authentic feelings can be very large, odd and extreme in expression. If the inner reality and the demands of the dramatic situation are extreme, then the authentic release of emotion must be equally extreme. Otherwise, it looks false.
>
> (2001: 237)

Marshall notes that:

> sometimes issues of falseness, bad acting, overacting and empty technique get muddled with questions of style. For example, young actors often associate 'small' personal styles of acting with authenticity of feeling, while anything larger in style is associated with falseness and overacting. This leads them to resist working in a larger style, since they fear becoming bad actors. In reality, there are three quite separate factors: authenticity, scale of work and style of work.
>
> (2001: 235)

Acting

Practical and pragmatic in its use and understanding of 'authenticity' as an acting concept, Marshall provides a definition by negation: 'authentic' *doesn't* mean 'small' and it *doesn't* mean 'naturalistic' because, to perform Greek Tragedy, for example, 'too naturalistically (on the scale of ordinary social interaction) is inappropriate' (238) and not 'authentic'.

The habit of defining meaning by negation is quite common in certain schools of thought and practice in the catalogue. Cass Fleming, in an account of Michael Chekhov's acting practices, joins a group of nearly fifty authors in the catalogue by using the term 'non-naturalistic' (2020: 33–35) to describe texts and performing styles. Sara Grochala (2017: 18), Sharon Marie Carnicke (2023: 155) and Louise Owen (2014: 174) all use 'non-realist' while, in context of 'post-human' theorization, 'non-human' appears thousands of times in relation to multiple genres and styles including the 'theatre of the absurd' (Finburgh, 2015) and also quite prominently in titles about Shakespeare, such as Charlotte Scott's edited collection *Shakespeare / Nature: Contemporary Reading in the Human and Non-Human* (2024) or Raber and Edwards' *Shakespeare and Animals: A Dictionary* (2022).

Perhaps no more satisfying or complete than defining a flower as a 'non-tree' and almost as problematic as defining a woman as a 'non-man', negatory definitions abound in the catalogue and in acting. The fact of their existence gives the proof to Raymond William's observation that *keywords* are often words that are used to present 'problems of meaning' ([1976] 1985: 15) and, in context of 'authenticity', meaning is problematized but also with some significant points of consensus.

Ulrike Meg and Garde Mumford take a tautologizing rather than negatory approach, defining 'authenticity' in acting by using 'authentic' as 'a synonym for "truthful", "genuine" and "immediate"' (2013: 149). Focusing more directly on audience perception and experience in their treatise on 'authenticity' in *Theatre of Real People* (2016), Meg and Mumford discuss the capacity of theatre to produce 'Authenticity-Effects', which they describe as 'theatre techniques and modes of representation, as well as the resulting perceptual experiences' (70). These effects have:

> the capacity to generate one or more of the following sensations: that of the sincere and genuine and therefore credible, in the sense of honest and free from pretence or counterfeit, or really originating from its reputed maker or source; that of referential truthfulness and veracity, a sense that the theatrical event accurately refers to the world beyond the staged cosmos and/or is factual; and that of unmediated and intimate contact with people who actually exist or have existed.
>
> (2016: 71)

Meg and Mumford recall a juxtaposition very familiar to late twentieth-century theatre discourse by characterizing and contrasting two different approaches to produce these effects: 'the idealizing' and 'the sceptical (or destabilizing) approach' (69).

Marshall and other authors drawing a naturalistic/non-naturalistic distinction are probably referring to the 'idealizing' category in their definition of 'authenticity':

> In theatre typified by the *idealizing* approach to authenticity, makers or spectators often operate under the assumption that performance can offer direct access to truthful, sincere or unmediated speech, selves or bodies.
>
> (2001: 73)

Meg and Mumford's analysis points out that, despite the apparent obviousness and first-principles-based justifications for 'real people' (i.e. non-actors) in performance generating 'authenticity' effects, this justification does not hold up very well in practice. 'Recent socially engaged Western theatre has shown an intense fascination with Theatre of Real People', they write, describing this as 'a mode of performance that presents contemporary people, who tend not to be trained theatre performers [and] … who often appear live in person, or via an audio and/or visual recording' (3). Considering 'real people' as definitively 'authentic' in one sense or another is a philosophical starting point of Meg and Mumford's approach and yet they also find that twenty-first-century audiences struggle to always accept such 'real people' as *really real* in the sense of their being 'honest and free from pretence or counterfeit'.

In acting performances where 'authenticity' relates less to the ontological status of *real people* and more to 'that of referential truthfulness and veracity' – such as, for Marshall in context of non-naturalistic Greek Tragedy – whether performers are *real* or not is largely immaterial. In fact, counter-intuitively, their non-realness is central to their ability to generate 'authenticity effects' because of what Daniel Schulze calls the 'intrinsic ontological connection between lying and acting' (2017: 7).

Appositely, in context of this book, the 'central claim' of Schulze's book is that 'authenticity' 'is an expression of *a structure of feeling*, such as was defined by Raymond Williams (see 'How and Why to Write *Keywords in Acting*'). Easily the most thorough-going and philosophically informed treatise on 'authenticity' in the catalogue, Schulze's book provides a unifying if incomplete definition of 'authenticity' as 'a reconstructive ascription made by an individual' (37). In other words, something is 'authentic' if an individual accepts it as such. While that might sound like a banal description of meaning, it holds firmly across the 400-odd instances where the concept is explicitly discussed.

In this sense, Schulze considers 'authenticity' as 'performative', in connection with Williams's notion of a Structure of Feeling which produces 'very tangible social reality and influences all kinds of cultural practices' (2017: 7).

Shulze also makes three distinct claims which seem well supported by the evidence and opinions about 'authenticity' across the catalogue. These claims are evidence rather than wholly reason-based and these make them practically useful for actors.

First, he historicizes, arguing that a contemporary (twenty-first century) fixation with 'authenticity' both in the form of 'real people' but also actors *being real* (to paraphrase Marshall, 2001: 55–71) should be understood as a 'backlash against postmodern rationality and doubt' albeit one 'sensitive to postmodern style and structure' (Schulze, 2017: 37).

Acting

Secondly, he dehistoricizes and goes full-ontological, contending that irrespective of contemporary interests, 'authenticity is often consciously created, specifically in the performing arts, as an aesthetic tool; it is both a strategy of creation and reception' (2017: 37).

Finally, he argues against Funk ('there can be no such thing as unmediated experience, no conscious existence before or beyond representation' [Funk, 2015: 16]) that 'authenticity', 'is indeed unmediated … however, for obvious reasons, it evades verbal description' (Schulze, 2017: 37). Uniting much (probably the majority) of the commentary on 'authenticity' in the catalogue, Schulze contends that 'authenticity' – 'the thing itself' – 'cannot be named with words, lest it loses its immediacy' (37). Risking solipsism, Schulze's account of 'authenticity' records clearly the 'you know it when you see it' logic applied to 'authenticity' in acting.

References

Carnicke, S. M. (2023), *Dynamic Acting through Active Analysis: Konstantin Stanislavsky, Maria Knebel, and Their Legacy*, London: Methuen Drama.

Finburgh, C. (2015), 'Nettles in the Rose Garden: Ecocentrism in Jean Genet's Theatre', in C. Lavery and C. Finburgh (eds), *Rethinking the Theatre of the Absurd: Ecology, the Environment and the Greening of the Modern Stage*, 191–217, London: Methuen Drama.

Fleming, C. (2020), '"Theatre of the Future": Chekhov Technique for Devised Theatre and Catalyst Direction', in C. Fleming and T. Cornford (eds), *Michael Chekhov Technique in the Twenty-First Century: New Pathways*, London: Methuen Drama.

Funk, W. (2015), *The Literature of Reconstruction: Authentic Fiction in the New Millennium*, London: Bloomsbury.

Grochala, S. (2017), *The Contemporary Political Play: Rethinking Dramaturgical Structure*, London: Methuen Drama.

Marshall, L. (2001), *The Body Speaks*, London: Methuen Drama.

Meg, U. and G. Mumford (2013), 'Postdramatic Reality Theatre and Productive Insecurity: Destabilising Encounters with the Unfamiliar in Theatre from Sydney and Berlin', in K. Jürs-Munby, J. Carroll and S. Giles (eds), *Postdramatic Theatre and the Political: International Perspectives on Contemporary Performance*, London: Methuen Drama.

Owen, L. (2014), 'The Witness and the Replay: London Bubble', in C. McAvinchey (ed.), *Performance and Community: Commentary and Case Studies*, London: Methuen Drama.

Raber, K. and K. L. Edwards (2022), *Shakespeare and Animals: A Dictionary*, London: The Arden Shakespeare.

Schulze, D. (2017), *Authenticity in Contemporary Theatre and Performance*, London: Bloomsbury.

Scott, C. ed. (2024), *Shakespeare / Nature: Contemporary Readings in the Human and Non-human*, London: The Arden Shakespeare.

Williams, R. ([1976] 1985), *Keywords: A Vocabulary of Culture and Society*, Oxford: Oxford University Press.

CHAPTER 14
A STATISTICALLY IRRELEVANT KEYWORD

(*mim-ey-sis*)
noun
- imitation
- production
- acting.

mīmēsis, as 'mimesis', appears fewer than 100 times and yet is, philosophically at least, a, if not *the*, keyword in acting. Mimesis emerges at the mythic 'first site' of Western theatre in ancient Greece where, appropriately enough, 'actors' first appear alongside hypocrites, in the mostly unsubstantiated myth of Thespis (see 'Preface: What is Acting?'). The Greek word for actor being *hypokrites* means 'answerer' (McLeish, 2011). Transmogrifying out of the Dionysian festivals and rituals, the hypocrite – I mean, 'actor'! – answers the chorus but also answers for society and the Gods when, as Kenneth McLeish has it, he puts 'words directly in the mouths of such individuals as Agamemnon, Athene, Circe or Polyphemos' (3). In the orthodox history of Western theatre the actor appears as singular creature whose singular occupation is mimetic acts: pretending to be other than that which they are – and this, for Plato, was a big problem.

In the *Republic*, Plato aims a stark philosophical critique at the dangers of such an occupation and kicks-off a centuries-long prejudice (Armelle Sabatier charts this across the centuries in her entry on 'imitate' in *Shakespeare and Visual Culture: A Dictionary*, 2017). Pretending to be someone that you're not – 'theatrical mimesis' – is, according to Plato, 'the tip of the iceberg; is setting a bad example; is the thin end of the wedge' (Matthews, 2014: 16). If the 70-year-old Polus[1] can play the young Princess Electra so convincingly, how will we tell the difference between old men and young women? As Aulus Gellius tells it:

> Polus put on a mourning habit and took the urn from the tomb of his son, and as though he were grasping the bones of Orestes, he choked up not with representations and imitation, but with real grief and truly breathing lamentation. And so, though it seemed that everyone was watching a play, it was a performance of real grief.
>
> (*Attic Nights* 6.5)

If Polus and everyone watching him can get 'choked up' on representations and imitations how will the Republic maintain a stable reality in which people and things have a *real* material and immutable place?

In a passage that reads somewhat oddly from a contemporary vantage, Plato heaps praise on actors for their abilities to imitate convincingly while, in the same breath, advising that they will simply have to be banished from an ideal society: 'if a man were to arrive in the city' able to 'become everything and to mimic all things', he writes, then the citizenry 'would worship him as someone holy and wonderful and pleasant' but, nonetheless, they would have to 'tell him there is no man like him in our city, nor by our traditional law can come to be here' and so they would 'send him off to another city' but not before 'pouring myrrh on his head and crowning him with wool' (Book X). I wrote in *The Life of Training* (Matthews, 2021) that most actors would consider this something of a mixed message.

Plato's ambivalent regard for mimesis comes from his insight in the *Meno* that acting, even more so than thinking, is accountable for the formation of our moral character. Despite being one of history's top-most-famous thinkers, Plato concedes that thinking alone would never produce 'good' because virtue cannot be taught. Doing and being 'good' must be learned by the teaching of habits and customs. Morals result from the customs and habits that individuals and groups adopt. Plato recognized that by imitating habits we are adopting them into our character.

Centuries later, 'the Method' made the same recognition. This approach, usually associated with late twentieth-century Hollywood cinema and trainers and directors, such as Lee Strasberg and Elia Kazan, draws mostly from twentieth-century behavioural psychology but rests philosophically on this Platonic sense of the power of mimesis. It appears that Stanislavski's overt interest in the behavioural experiments of Theodule Ribot introduced psychology into Western theories of acting and drove Method Acting's recognizably Pavlovian habit-forming approach to character-building (Autant-Mathieu, 2017: 69–71; Jacono, 2016).

Most commentaries on this Method-based habit-forming approach focus on aesthetic results or psychological risks and neither Stanislavski nor his American followers – Strasberg, Adler and Meisner – appear to have expressed much concern about the moral implications of mimesis, imitation, habit and self-identity. Alan Read, though, in *Theatre in the Expanded Field* notes that acting's capacity to dissemble 'the self-contained identity' represented Plato's 'greatest fear' (2013: 35). Taking Plato's famous cave analogy as a starting point, Read observes that Plato has Socrates describe the cave as 'a particular *kind* of theatre' – a defined space with spectators in it. This is relevant because, while the more modern fear and prejudice against acting might be fixated with personal psychology, Plato's concern was not for the actor's wellbeing but society's order and morality secured on a stable sense of reality: it's the cave-dwellers, apt to accept shadows as reality that one should be worried about.

Within the catalogue we also have mimesis's philosophical saviour (to simplify and dramatize the history of Western philosophy). Aristotle took a much more lenient stance on mimesis than Plato because, writes Daniel Schulze, 'it was evident that art did not imitate but conveyed truths. It did not just play on affect, as Plato had supposed, but spoke to the rational mind by conveying experiences of truth' (2017: 44). Shulze brings in yet more philosophical Big Guns, replaying the modern belief, expressed by Kant, that imitation and genius are opposites. According to Schulze, historiographically speaking, theatre began to lose its 'status as genuine or real' altogether with the emergence of written forms of drama from the fifth-century BC (7).

Coeval with the history of aesthetics that Schulze offers, and foundationally important to some of the key theories of acting expressed in the catalogue, is Aristotle's conceptualization of mimesis as imitative not of *what is already* but productive of *what is yet to be*.

Adrian Kear, following Lacoue-Labarthe, describes mimesis in this sense as *pure potentiality* (2011). This is imitation that reproduces nothing but supplements deficiencies in nature's ability to *do everything*. This 'productive mimesis' is, in fact, imitative of the creative energy of nature, as Aristotle sees it. Crucially, it is even superior to it because it can complete the work of natural production and *do* that which nature *cannot do*.

This ferocious and difficult-to-understand power of mimesis is commonplace in the catalogue, although it is seldom discussed in these philosophical terms. This is both in the sense of actor's transformations into other people and things, including things and people who never existed but also in the oft-politicized power of performance to prefigure new ways of being. Examples of this can be found in manifold commentaries on 'political theatre', such as Don Watson's *Theatre with a Purpose* (2024), which detects and records theatrical experiments concerned with prefiguring social change, or Goran Petrović Lotina and Théo Aiolfi's mandate to 'progressive actors' to 'envision a more hopeful future' (2023: 21) so that it might come into being.

More directly grounded in theories of acting in the catalogue, this might also be framed in context of Brecht's well-noted political agenda for theatre. He defines acting in his 'epic' theatre as a practice whose mimetic affects both auger and produce very real social effects because it can, 'put reality in the hands of people in such a way that it can be mastered' (Barnett, 2014: 210). David Barnett, in *Brecht in Practice: Theatre, Theory and Performance,* connects this 1938 comment from Brecht to the much-disputed acting technique of *Verfremdung* (usually, to 'alienate' or 'alienation' in English): 'it presents the familiar in such a way that it is rendered strange and worthy of curiosity', writes Barnett, and this 'questions whether values and behaviours are universal, and invites audiences to compare the way things were with the way things are in order to tease out differences and to account for them' (2014: 209). This orthodox interpretation of Brecht's view on *Verfremdung* and acting – a technique associated with the rational and not emotional aspects of the audience's being – minimizes Brecht's clear commitment to an emphatic audience experience: commenting on surrealism in painting, Brecht wrote that surrealists were pursuing a 'primitive' version of the so called *v-effekt* because they were seeking to 'shock their observers by hampering, confusing and disappointing their associations'; his own more evolved use of alienating shock wants to exceed the 'amusement' that 'you end up with' in surrealism after the 'aforementioned shock' (Brecht, 1953: 110). Brecht wanted and expected shock, no doubt, and dormant in this expectation is productive mimesis; most potent because it is not *imitative*. Or, perhaps, most shockingly productive of something new when it is least imitative of anything old or familiar.

Acting

Interpretations of Brecht's theories on acting in the catalogue tend towards an 'inventive' rather than 'imitative' interpretation of mimesis. This appears to be at least partially produced by his well-documented antipathy towards Naturalism and an overdetermination in discourse of the salience of imitation to Naturalism. In *Brecht on Performance: Messingkauf and Modelbooks,* he states, 'I've never been a Naturalist, I've never really liked Naturalism, but I can see that, despite its flaws, it has enabled the breakthrough of realism into modern literature and modern theatre' (1953: 265).

Although Brecht's interpretation of realism might differ from some contemporary interpretations of the term, his distinction between realism that 'contain[s] raw material' and Naturalism where this raw material has been 'idealized to saturation point' (265) is seemingly quite current. As John Willett points out in *Brecht in Context* (1998), Brecht 'distrusted the Stanislavsky method' and, although he never 'overtly rejected it, his remarks on the theatre of Stanislavsky denied it by implication' and his own announcement in 1936 of the 'alienation' effect 'represents a degree of heresy that can hardly have been unconscious' (95).

In commentary on Brecht and acting, there is a risk of philosophical confusion about the power and potential of mimesis. Mimesis can't do everything – can't bring anything into being. However, it can *represent* anything and bring that representation into being from anything (and that is pretty nifty). Take, for example, as Karen Marselak does, a prop skull in a production of *Hamlet*. The skull *becomes* Yorick's head; becomes 'a character rather than a prop' (2018: 183). Although Marselak is primarily talking dramaturgically it is clear that, in even the mostly lowly production of *Hamlet*, a very 'unconvincing' prop skull still very perfectly becomes the character of Yorick both on and off the stage precisely because of the pervasive power of mimesis and the ubiquity of representations of the *alas poor Yorick* moment. Taking the consideration of the productive power of mimesis another step, *anything*, convincing or otherwise can serve as Yorick's skull, and thus Yorick. In fact, nothing can serve as Yorick – if you want to test this premise, stand up in a public place with your empty hand and arm outstretched and recite, 'alas, Poor Yorick! I knew him, Horatio'. When the applause dies down, ask your fellows what they think you were doing and revel in their confirmation of the awesome power of mimesis.

This awesome power is often (and mostly unhelpfully) misattributed to the concept of 'suspension of disbelief', which, as Raphael Falco explains, derives from Samuel Taylor Coleridge's comment about poetic faith. Recalling again the cave wall shadows, Coleridge writes about a 'transfer from our inward nature a human interest and a semblance of truth sufficient to procure for these shadows of imagination that willing suspension of disbelief for the moment' (Coleridge [1817] 1997: 47).

Interpreting the cave analogy regarding the concept of mimesis, what is going on here is nothing to do with the will. It is not the rational, willed rejection of disbelief but the precisely unwilled quality of belief in the representations produced by mimesis that renders them so dangerously powerful. That is Plato's story of the cave anyway.

The power of mimesis is also reflected in the catalogue's testimonies to 'performativity'. These are most closely associated with the theorization of Judith Butler, and her central assertion that subjectivities and their characteristics (for example, identity characteristics) were essentially performative rather than innately essential, and could therefore be both performed and constituted differently. Fragkou (2019), for example, takes up this line of thinking from Judith Butler, and her theorization of the performativity of gender, in the context of twenty-first-century politics.

In this strand of theorization, mimesis' power to produce and not only imitate is fully accommodated into theories of acting because this is no longer, as it was for Coleridge, about a 'willingness' to 'suspend disbelief', this was about imitation's connection to being itself and not only our perceptions of or beliefs about it.

The mass of antagonistic theorization of acting and the multiplicity of schools and approaches vying for prominence in discourse can be organized by categorizing these according to the definition of mimesis adopted by any given source, theory, system, method or approach.

Descending from the thin atmosphere at an altitude of philosophical discourse in the catalogue, Platonic interpretative subtleties dissolve into thin air as they reach the ground of the day to day experience of actors from the most professionally marginalized groups. The intellectual property matter of imitation-rights (not imitation-concepts), for example, pushes into the foreground in Kirsty Johnston's *Disability Theatre and Modern Drama* (2016: 37–58), which provides a pertinent contemporary perspective on the relationship between imitation and verisimilitude in the politics of casting actors. As Johnston wrote, 'over the past decades the pressing need for more innovative, expansive, and diverse casting practices has prompted many to lobby for change' (38). Determining what that change should be, for example in the case of colour, age or gender-blind casting, has drawn the politics of casting and of acting more generally back to this foundational consideration around imitation and the mimetic relationship between the person *doing the representing* and the person *being represented*.

Note

1   I take some license here. It is difficult to date precisely when Polus gave his seminal performance as Electra but it is recorded by Plutarch (Plutarch, *Dem.* p. 859, An seni ger. sit Resp. 3. p. 785b) and Lucian (*Necyom.* vol. i. p. 479, ed. Hemst.) that, aged 70 he acted in eight tragedies on four successive days.

References

Aquilina, S. (2017), 'Introduction: Context 1: Well-trodden Paths: US, UK, Russian and Soviet Perspectives on Stanislavsky's Transmission', in J. Pitches and A. Aquilina, *Stanislavsky in the World: The System and its Transformations Across Continents*, London: Methuen Drama.

Aulus Gellius ([1927] 1946) *Attic Nights*, Loeb Classical Library, Cambridge, MA: Harvard University Press.

Acting

Autant-Mathieu, M.-C. (2017), *Stanislavsky in the World: The System and its Transformations Across Continents*, London: Methuen Drama.

Barnett, D. (2014), *Brecht in Practice: Theatre, Theory and Performance*, London: Methuen Drama.

Brecht, B. (1953), 'Katzgraben Notes 1953', in *Brecht on Performance: Messingkauf and Modelbooks*, translated by Charlotte Ryland, London: Methuen Drama, 2017, 251–76.

Brecht. B. (2014), *Brecht on Performance: Messingkauf and Modelbooks*, London: Methuen Drama.

Coleridge, S. T. ([1817] 1997), *Biographia Literaria*, edited by Nigel Leask, London: J. M. Dent.

Falco, R. (2018), 'Suspense Revisited: The Shared Experience of Time', in L. Shohet (ed.), *Temporality, Genre and Experience in the Age of Shakespeare: Forms of Time*, 43–56, London: The Arden Shakespeare.

Fragkou, M. (2019), *Ecologies of Precarity in Twenty-First Century Theatre: Politics, Affect, Responsibility*, London: Methuen Drama.

Jacono, V. (2016), 'Introduction: Complexity, Cognition, and the Actor's Pedagogy,' in C. Falletti et al. (eds), *Theatre and Cognitive Neuroscience*, 103–16, London: Methuen Drama.

Johnston, K. (2016), *Disability Theatre and Modern Drama: Recasting Modernism*, London: Methuen Drama.

Kear, A. C. (2011), 'Troublesome Amateurs: Theatre, Ethics and the Labour of Performance', in J. Matthews and D. Torevell (eds), *A Life of Ethics and Performance*, 1st edn, 87–114, Cambridge: Cambridge Scholars Publishing.

Lotina, G. P. and T. Aiolfi, eds (2023), *Performing Left Populism: Performance, Politics and the People*, London: Methuen Drama.

Matthews, J. (2014), *Anatomy of Performance Training*, London: Methuen Drama.

McLeish, K. (2011), *A Guide to Greek Theatre and Drama*, London: Methuen Drama.

Sabatier, A. (2017), *Shakespeare and Visual Culture: A Dictionary*, London: The Arden Shakespeare.

Schulze, D. (2017), *Authenticity in Contemporary Theatre and Performance: Make it Real*, London: Methuen Drama.

Watson, D. (2024), *Theatre with a Purpose: Amateur Drama in Britain 1919–1949*, London: Methuen Drama.

Willett, J. (1998), *Brecht in Context: Comparative Approaches*, London: Methuen Drama.

HOW AND WHY TO WRITE *ACTING: KEYWORDS AND CONCEPTS*

I can't know for sure (despite much research and analysis for this book) but I suspect that more has been written about 'acting' than about any other aspect of performing or production, playwriting included. Many of these accounts of 'acting' have been produced by practitioners, theorists or commentators who really know an awful lot about it and so producing yet another book on 'acting' wouldn't add much to collective understanding. Why, then, write one?

It seemed to me that a valuable and novel contribution to the field, and pertinent to a series on *readings* in Theatre Practice would be a book on 'acting' that provided an account-of-the-accounts as opposed to yet-another-account. However, a meta-analysis of the largest sub-field of literature in performance and production sounded like a daunting endeavour and certainly prompted the next question: *how* to write a novel and useful book on acting? In this chapter, I have answered the questions 'how' and 'why' to write this book in the sub-headings that follow.

Thinking about the sheer scale of the undertaking of handling that volume of literature focused the challenge of *reading* that it would entail. It was clearly beyond human capability to read everything ever written about acting but, today, with the advent of Large Language Model Artificial Intelligence, it was perhaps not completely beyond the bounds of all possibility. In fact, the reading associated with a comprehensive meta-analytical account of acting might be crystallizing as a theoretically surmountable problem of computer logistics. The writing of such an account, though, still looked like a very sharp hermeneutic challenge.

Readings in Theatre Practice don't need to be exhaustive to be valuable, of course, but with 'acting' they would need to be extensive and reasonably comprehensive to justify a place in the series as something other than another-book-about-acting.

Rather than being *what I think about acting*, this book is concerned with what *we say* about acting, 'we' being very many of those informed practitioners, theorists and commentators I mentioned earlier. Corrupting a phrase from the American poet and short-story writer, Raymond Carver, this book is about *what we talk about when we talk about acting*. Or, if you prefer a different point of reference, borrowing from the German philosopher, Martin Heidegger, this book is about, *what is called 'acting'*.

Not an account of 'acting' directly as such, this book is an account of accounts of acting that identifies the key things that 'we' consider to be constitutive of acting. This approach is inspired by some key observations in the later work of the Austrian philosopher, Ludwig Wittgenstein, and the philosophical approach of the Welsh social theorist, Raymond Williams.

FOR PHILOSOPHICAL REASONS

Wittgenstein's *Philosophical Investigations* (1953) contains the central and much-quoted premise that the meaning of a word can only be understood as constituted in and by its use in language. Contrary to preceding Platonic theories of the meaning of words which posited that meaning was concerned with references to the independence of objects, ideas or phenomenon denoted in language, Wittgenstein asserted that meaning was formed by the purpose for which a word was used.

I have adopted this insight here in context of acting and been led in my readings by acceptance of the assertion that 'acting' is not a *thing* independent of what is said or written about it. Rather, the meaning of 'acting' can be read in the uses to which this word is put. Indeed, the meaning of 'acting' *is* the uses to which the word is put.

Raymond Williams's *Keywords: A Vocabulary of Culture and Society* (1975) is interrelated to his earlier seminal book, *Culture and Society* (1958), which examined the meaning and development of these two phenomena in Britain from the eighteenth to the twentieth century. *Keywords*, as it is invariably known, acknowledges that the meaning of 'culture' and 'society' must be understood with regards to not only the meaning of these two words but also the meanings of multiple other *keywords* that scaffold these two concepts. Such scaffolding words could be thought of as 'keywords'.

The meaning of keywords are contingent and somewhat fugacious and in the spirit of this insight, The Raymond Williams Society (established by Williams's estate the year after his death) has been continually updating them with each issue of its journal – *Key Words: A Journal of Cultural Materialism* – featuring a new entry providing a 'deliberately brief account of a socially significant or problematic term in our contemporary language'.

Theatre and Performance Studies from Williams's time to the present has recognized that fundamental things about the meaning of 'acting' are to be grasped by taking a cultural materialist approach, and by considering where and how 'acting' is used in language. Understanding anything about the meaning of 'acting' will require an understanding of related *keywords* that support its meaning and use-cases.

As Marie Moran noted in 2021, 'within the recent renewal of attention to the work of Raymond Williams, there has been a revival of interest in the "keywords" form of analysis he initiated' (1021) with four new books published in a single twenty-first century year (2017–18). Despite the initial impact of *Keywords* in the late stages of the twentieth century, the twenty-first century may well have seen the steadiest stream of interest in the work, methodologically speaking, with 'keywords' books by Tony Bennet, Bruce Burgett and Glenn Hendler, Andrew Levine, Rodney Smith and Juliam Wolfreys all appearing on library shelves before the first decade of this century was done (Moran, 2021).

'Culture' and 'society' are more hotly contested than ever now, as concepts, but my use of a similar methodological approach to Williams is not driven by the urgent culture wars of what he would have called 'C21' but by the potential for the new twenty-first-century digital tools to tell us more about what we are talking about when we are talking about acting, now.

BY METHODOLOGICAL MEANS

Methodologically, *Keywords* was, as Williams wrote in the introduction, 'not a neutral review of meanings' but 'an exploration of the vocabulary of a crucial area of social and cultural discussion, which has been inherited within precise historical and social conditions and which has to be made at once conscious and critical' (1975: 'introduction'). The method was etymological but also semantic in the linguistic and philosophical sense. Not mere glossary but deep analysis of the cultural materiality of terms and their ideological basis, and in this book on acting, I pursue a similar method.

Perhaps because the original compendium of *Keywords* resulted from the field notes of the earlier *Culture and Society* rather than as a summary of a discrete research project, Williams did not appear to have any specific method in selecting the keywords, nor any unambiguous criteria by which to judge whether or why words were *key*. A prodigious bibliophile, Williams no doubt conducted a one-man analysis of the breadth of his source material and noted, perhaps quite intuitively, the crude fact of the frequency of certain words. However, his selection is quite clearly motivated not only by the ubiquity of words but also their significance in given discourses. Several of his selections, for example 'bureaucracy' and 'masses' are comparatively scarce in noun-form in most of the literary sources for *Culture and Society* and yet they are sub-textually omnipresent as concepts, just as Williams must have noticed that they were firmly embedded in the phenomena of culture and society.

Williams's *Keywords* can be described as many things but certainly not as an encyclopaedia. Indeed, the most refreshing thing about *Keywords*, for me as for many readers, it seems, is its succinct wit, and this makes it stylistically quite unlike the encyclopaedia, whose methodology, intention and, quite often, execution are altogether staider and more pedantic. Flaubert, whom Williams described as a 'radical innovator' in his famous 'When Was Modernism?' March 1987 Lewis Fry Memorial Lecture, derided the encyclopaedist's method – 'laugh at it pityingly for being quaint and old fashioned, or else thunder against it' (Flaubert [1880] 1976: 303). Flaubert satirized it in *Bouvard and Pécuchet*'s 'Dictionary of Received Ideas': an incomplete anthology of erroneous and omissive intention. *Keywords* is no *Dictionary of Received Ideas* and, though polemical, Williams certainly meant it to be genuinely didactic and its enduring positive reception and republication testifies to his success in this endeavour.

Williams certainly didn't intend the compendium to conclude or to be exhaustive. I suspect he would have joined with Flaubert in scoffing at this totalizing imperative of the encyclopaedia. Neither did he intend to say everything about any given keyword. Some entries are expansive and many are concise, and there is in this polarity evidence both of Williams's gift for brevity but also his desire to dismiss or at least diminish the totemic value of certain keywords; to reduce their political power just as the young child does when they call out in front of the obsequious adult crowd, 'the Emperor has no clothes!'

Williams's selectiveness was a rigorous act of radical scepticism that produced a potent methodological template for uncovering the a priori grounds of human relations within the constructs and complications of social and cultural life via the language used in and about these. The words that he chose mattered before his intervention – therefore he chose them – but they mattered differently afterwards and, of course, they must have mattered *to him*. This auto-selective criterion is distinct from the totalizing desire of the encyclopaedia and necessarily rooted within culture and society rather than aspiring to any kind of objectivity or totality.

FOR PERFORMANCE SCHOLARSHIP, NOW

From within the field of Theatre and Performance Studies, Ric Allsopp and David Williams made their own apology for a similar approach in an editorial for *Performance Research*'s 'A Lexicon' (2006) edition. They noted the 'eclectic and thematic approaches to publishing' of the *Performance Research* journal as well as, 'our continuing interest in the languages and vocabularies' (iii–v) of the performing arts. They cite the 'Fragments of The Intersubjective Encyclopaedia of Contemporary Theatre' which appeared in *Theaterschrift* journal, which were suggested by Hans-Thies Lehmann's support for a 'sort of open encyclopaedia' which can always be added to and in which the terms, notions and components of 'new theatre' and 'new dramaturgy' might be explained.

Allsopp and David Williams also refer to Forced Entertainment's performative and durational 'essay-cum-lecture' *Marathon Lexicon* (Mousonturm, 2003; LIFT, 2004) and Patrice Pavis's 1996 *Dictionary of the Theatre: Terms, Concepts and Analysis* as discipline-specific descendants of Raymond Williams's seminal work. For Allsopp and David Williams, the selective criteria for keywords were even more idiosyncratic than Raymond Williams's – the editors simply 'invited contributors to write on one or more key terms or concepts that were of particular interest to them' and which would 'signify a key term or concept that the author deemed to be making an impact on performance in its broadest sense, and would reflect aspects of the current state of ideas and practices in the field of contemporary performance research' (Allsopp and Williams, 2006: iv).

My selection of the 'keywords' in this book owes much to Raymond Williams as well as to Lehmann and Pavis, Allsopp and David Williams. There is no satirical or eclectic intent in my selection but with Lehmann, Pavis and Williams (both, but principally, Raymond) I have sought to identify and understand not just key-words but *key ideas* embedded in and integral to the philosophical category of 'acting'.

Some of the entries in this book are, as the entries attest, 'high frequency' words in the literature in the field but others are more often heard than read; more apt to be spoken in the studio or rehearsal room and notably less-likely to feature in *serious academic writing*. As Raymond Williams observed across his *oeuvre*, the unspoken convention is usually the most powerfully influential rule in socio-cultural life just as, in acting, we know that what is not-said often carries more meaning than what is shouted.

A few of the terms I have selected are seldom uttered although, as the entries explain, some of them used to be and, even though they may have fallen out of fashion in usage the concepts that they connote have continued to influence, shape, motivate, interpret and delimit acting practices.

How and Why to Write *Acting: Keywords and Concepts*

Although I never intended, as Raymond Williams did, to annex a glossary to any of my previous books, some of the impetus for selecting the entries for this book comes from re-reading my field notes for *Training for Performance, Anatomy of Performance Training* and *The Life of Training*. The research for those three books spanned the period 2004–2019 and entailed participatory research in theatres, rehearsal rooms, monasteries, dance studios and rehabilitation wards as well as observational analysis and expert sampling with Olympic athletes and coaches, yoga teachers, choreographers, acting coaches and trainers. The research for this book began with a review and analysis of these notes. That analysis prompted the realization that, over this period in which I was doing research for the three earlier books, the tools of research were changing and enabling new modalities and methodologies for keyword analysis that were not hitherto available to Williams, Pavis, Lehmann, Allsopp, David Williams, or me.

That is why, in researching this book, I have employed what could be called a 'syncretic' methodology. *Synkrētismos*, meaning 'federation of Cretan cities' is a compound (of syn, 'together', and Krēt, 'Cretan') and the word 'syncretic' has its root in an ancient alliance between Cretan cities who decided that they were stronger together.

The concept of the syncretic in the English language has been used to denote a coming together and combination of things, or phenomena that are by their nature composite. The syncretic research methods I employed to generate this book bring together the linguistic, semantic, etymological and philosophical methods of analogue technology – reading and thinking about stuff, getting a feel for it and looking for patterns, omissions and commonalities – and the digital tools of massive cross-sectional data set analysis – compressing complex sources into binary values and processing these through scripts of computer code with bespoke-designed rules for sorting and categorization.

As Vassilis Lambropoulos writes, 'In a vague sense, of course, syncretization is the process of culture itself. Some might also argue that we live in peculiarly syncretic times' (2001: 225) and, here, in this account of the research methodology used to generate the findings in this book, I contend that syncretic times call for syncretic measures.

Syncretism, as distinct from the concept of the syncretic, has specific definitions in religious studies, anthropology, linguistics, psychology, theology and political theory, which, as Lambropoulos explains, refer 'to the alliance of incompatible movements and positions in opposition to a hostile one' (2001: 226).

Or, as Chinitz (1990) has it, 'a syncretic situation' is one in which 'two or more forces declare a truce and agree to disagree against another force whose opposition allows for no agreement' (in Lambropoulos, 2001: 226). Lambropoulos has proposed in an article for the *Journal of Modern Greek Studies*, that we might see Syncretism as 'Mixture and Method': as a descriptor of our smooshed-together societies, and their smooshed-together phenomena, but also as a method for looking at these smooshy societies and their smooshed-up phenomena, such as, for example, 'acting'.

The term 'syncretism' refers to the cultural mixture of diverse beliefs and practices within a specific socio-historical frame; to the congruity of dissent within such a frame, despite differences of opinion; to the non-organic solidarity of heterodoxy which constitutes a collective worldview; to the forging together of disparate, often incompatible, elements from different systems; and to their intermingling and blending. Syncretism connotes not juxtaposition (the early postmodern idea of comparison) or fusion (the late postmodern idea of comparison) but mixing and mingling. It is by definition a cultural term that presents operations as inter-cultural and intra-cultural ones (since there is a possibility of syncretism within a culture and not only through contact among cultures).

(Lambropoulos, 2001: 225)

The field demarcated by this book is syncretic in this sense, described by Lambropoulos, as a tight but heterogeneous constituency of people, places, practices, ideas and ideals all contributing to the cultural value of the practice and profession of acting. Recognizing and representing the superabundance and diversity of such a conceptual whole is more straightforward than designing research methods by which to investigate it. In designing the research methodology for this book I attended to the fact that, syncretic times notwithstanding, syncretic approaches might be needed to interrogate syncretic phenomena.

BY SHRINKING THE LARGEST TOPIC IN THE FIELD TO THE SIZE OF MERELY THE LARGEST DIGITIZED DATABASE OF LITERATURE ON THAT TOPIC (USING COMPUTERS)

Ric Allsopp and David Williams took a crowd-sourcing approach to generating their lexicon, inviting a (small and exclusive) crowd to define the source-base for their taxonomy. Today, amid an intensifying wave of Artificially Intelligent approaches to research, such a methodology felt outmoded. Given the massively increased capabilities for compiling and analysing 'big data' since the publication of Raymond Williams's *Keywords,* or even the *Performance Research* 'lexicon', I recognized the need to locate a big and heterogenous – and necessarily digitized or digitizable – source base for the research of this project.

I scoped multiple sources for this, including digitized academic journal holdings and 'scrapable' open-access web content. The term 'scraping' is used for an automated harvesting of (usually) web-based data. In the context of Intellectual Property, scraping raises ethical and legal concerns, especially in context of training algorithms and AI models but, this very significant consideration bracketed for now, it became clear that both subscription-protected academic holdings and open-access data sets had notable limitations as source-bases for analysis. The former was comparatively limited in this field and expert to the point of bordering insularity while the latter was excessive and amateur to the point of an unstable accuracy. The former would be relatively easy to handle digitally but, ideologically it was quite homogeneous, generated by authors almost exclusively with academic affiliations. The latter data are potentially massive and very hard to handle, and heterogeneous to the point of obfuscation with regards content-authors identities, ideological values or even the integrity of material as human-generated content.

As a meeting point between these two poles – the academic and the lay – I explored the digital holdings of global publishing houses publishing the work of academics, theorists and practitioners of acting. By far the largest and most inclusive publisher on acting in this regard is Bloomsbury, who have developed and acquired a global portfolio of key imprints spanning this field including Methuen Drama, Arden Shakespeare, and Oberon as well as the academic end of the market too, with imprints including Continuum, Berg and Bloomsbury Academic. Described by Nick Hern books (since acquired by Bloomsbury) as 'the Netflix of Theatre' (Nick Hern Blog), Bloomsbury's web-based subscription service 'Drama Online' gives access to a very considerable portfolio of material from these imprints, as well as archival resources from the Victoria and Albert Museum and The American Shakespeare Centre. Holding multiple text-based sources ranging from books and bibliographic guides to interview transcripts, diaries and reviews but, accounting only for 'titles', to use the publishing parlance, there are over 6,000 books in the Drama Online database by over 2,000 authors making it the largest digitized archive of literature in the field of drama, theatre and performance studies.

Supported by the series editor, Professor Simon Shepherd (FBA), I worked with the Senior Publisher at Bloomsbury, Mark Dudgeon, to develop a non-disclosure agreement giving exclusive access to the digital files of Drama Online's holdings. This gave me the 'primary data set' needed to begin the project.

As an artefact of culture, this data set can be decoded as representative of culture and also marked by it. This is true of all archives just as it is true that all archives are bias. Extensive as the Drama Online holding may be, and composite as it is of multiple smaller holdings that have been accumulated by the publisher over time, it will be marked by the ideological preferences of the publishers; by the hegemonic viewpoints of publishing editors associated with commissioning and copy-editing the titles and holdings. Furthermore, the primary data set has a very strong anglophone bias with comparatively few texts in translation or by non-anglophone authors. Despite the counter-bias design elements of my methodology these limitations of the primary source data cannot be wholly mitigated. Nor, in context of Williams's depictions of *keywords*, should they be, seeing as the project here is to understand the concepts germane to a prescribed set of acting traditions. However, I make this qualification to acknowledge that this book is produced both from and about a specific cultural and historical vantage point. The vantage on 'acting' does not perceive the whole historical and cultural domain of 'acting' nor does it claim to account for a meta-critical or ahistorio-cultural domain for acting. Rather, by accounting for the largely seventeenth- to twenty-first-century anglophone traditions of acting this book makes a useful account of a part of that larger domain.

This limitation of the archive notwithstanding, it is an extensive – the most extensive available – if not fully comprehensive store house of ideas about acting, and this makes the findings that I have wrought from it informative and representative if not completely exhaustive or definitive. Further, given the digitized nature of the archive, these findings are verifiable, cross-referenceable and explorable by Drama Online users. Users will be able to use the search tool in the Drama Online interface to zone in and out on findings in this book to pin down reference content quickly and easily and open up wider reading about these keywords for themselves, using the entries in this book as a starting point. With that capability in mind, I have provided focused 'selected' bibliographies for each entry so that readers can readily access indicative source material exemplifying the meanings and use-cases defined in each entry.

Having secured this access, one of the primary methodological challenges of this book now was, how to identify that corpus of writings-on-acting within these extensive holdings so that it could be analysed? Even if only considering book-length files, and even excluding playtexts, there remain over 2,000 books on a range of theatre-related topics and, conceptually, somewhere within that corpus is a smaller corpus about 'acting'. A subset of titles and a subcategory of content within those titles could be considered as *about* acting.

As an academic, I am quite used to reading a lot but reading and analysing 2,000 books would take me a long time! More to the point, although I might like to think that I have been academically well-trained to bring a level of critical objectivity to literary analysis I am not sure that publishing an account of key terms in discourse derived from such a solo endeavour would amount to much more than publishing the personal views about discourse of a single academic who reads-a-fair-bit-and-is-probably-reasonably-objective-about-what-he-reads. Discourse analysis of a corpus on this scale that seeks to analyse the contested meanings of concepts and ideas central to the practice of acting was clearly going to require a more robust methodology than reading-a-fair-bit and having a pretty-good-think.

The size of the corpus is one thing but to the great advantage of this research project was the fact that it was digitized. The digitization of the titles that would need analysing enabled a computational approach that could work with 'big data'. While, in the context of 'big data', even Drama Online's extensive and incomparable holding is pretty small, analysing a few thousand book-length data sources still requires meaningful computational power, especially when considering that I couldn't know at the outset what the corpus I was searching for even looked like.

Using computational power to access the corpus required me to categorize what the corpus looks like. It also required me to do that categorization without overdetermining the analysis outcomes in ways that would mean that these only reflected to me what I already knew and felt (or, thought I knew and felt) about acting.

Computational power is excellent for handling data too big for human processing power but even machine learning algorithms can only operate from the parameters set for them by their human programmers, and this human programmer has some competency limitations when it comes to designing programmes to operate without considerable shortcoming biases. (I have evidently spent too much time thinking about acting and not enough time learning coding). In designing a computational analysis methodology to deploy on the Drama Online database I was presented with the challenge of in-building methods to counteract my own bias alongside an even more foundational problem around how to define what I was even looking for in the first place – what *is* the corpus and what *even are* 'key words'?

To begin to answer this question I would need to determine which titles in the database were about acting or contained relevant commentary on acting. One way to identify titles about 'acting' would be to use Drama Online's web taxonomy – the structure of terms used to organize and make searchable the digitized content. (Indeed, that is the approach I tried first!) Technically, it should be relatively straightforward to use a website's API (application programming interface) to generate sub-catalogues and search digital content by using the taxonomy of 'key terms' assigned to each title. Aside from some technical issues with this due to the organizing structure of the database, this approach is very exposed to bias. This is because the assigning of 'key terms' is done by authors and editors with their own individual interpretations and understandings of what titles are *about*. Further, the taxonomical structuring of web databases such as the Drama Online collections is underpinned by business principles designed to direct consumers to products and central to these principles is a concept of 'low friction': taking consumers to products in the fewest steps possible. These factors mean that the web taxonomy was largely redundant in accessing and analysing the philosophical and ideological structures of thought within and across the titles of a web-based data-access subscription service.

User search information would be another data source for analysing themes of intellectual curiosity and relevance in the field. Which terms users search for and in what combinations and sequences could reveal interesting insights about the intellectual preoccupations of stakeholders in a community of interest in 'acting', albeit that these might be best understood as primarily 'consumers' rather than 'producers' of the discourses on 'acting'. All limitations and opportunities of user search data analysis considered, though, I have excluded this data from this analysis because, quite simply, I am legally required to do so. User search data is covered by Article 4.1 of the General Data Protection Regulation and so Drama Online operates within legal boundaries of how it can collect, use or share user search data. Search data cannot straightforwardly be anonymized for analysis, especially from a subscription service such as Drama Online which is required to securely hold 'personal data' about its paying users. It would be possible to work within these legal parameters and to design and recruit participants to an ethical and legal user-search data analysis but, for the findings of that enquiry to be of any value to analysis of the meaning of 'key words' in acting it would be necessary to know what those 'key words' are as well as their meanings and uses first. The 'reader-focus' of a search data analysis could reveal interesting insights about the words and terms that shape reader curiosity about acting and it would be fascinating to assess how these terms may be being shaped by the consumption of literature about acting in the database in a process of intellectual feedback. That could be a great project ... for the future, but before a researcher could undertake that comparative analysis of 'key words' in the database and 'key words' used to navigate the database it would be necessary to have defined the corpus and exposed at least some 'key words'.

At the limits of my programming competency and recognizing that I was going to need some expert help with the computational part of the analysis, I reached out to Professor of Informatics at the University of Music and Performing Arts Vienna, Georgios Sioros. Professor Sioros's research is in computational analysis of 'groove' – the structure of sound that is felt and perceivable as a pattern. His research has developed multiple tools for analysing the complex and largely ineffable phenomenon of groove by using creative computing programming to extract and codify patterns of sound in music.

The structuring of the music that Professor Sioros analyses can be understood as a rules-based systems of grammar and applying that logic to his analysis he has been able to decode 'rules' – conventions or, principles – using computing power. The sympathy between the grammatology of language and groove in music allowed some of Professor Sioros's insights and methods to be applied to the Drama Online database to expose and decode structures and patterns within it, and with his support I developed a methodology for this project that I refer to here as Syncretic Aspect Based Meaning Analysis (SABMA).

BY DEVELOPING NEW TOOLS AND METHODS

My methodology – Syncretic Aspect Based Meaning Analysis – is evolved from the recognized computational methodology of Aspect Based Sentiment Analysis (ABSA). This is an established computational approach to analysing language data sets that decodes 'sentiments' expressed within data sets. In ABSA 'aspects' might be understood as subjects or topics and 'sentiments' are the feelings expressed in language about these aspects by the individual or groups that have generated the data sets.

ABSA computer programmes have multiple uses. Product and services companies can ABS-analyse internet reviews to extract information about individuals' feeling for a given product or service and use this information to tailor and develop new lines. Intelligence services use ABSA too (I am told), on the private messaging of surveilled groups and 'cells', to calibrate threat and response levels in accordance with the changing feelings of its members. ABSA works not only with words but with short word sequences, analysing not only the frequency but also their occurrence in combinations and patterns. ABSA assigns positivity values, known as a 'polarity', to each individual instance of a word or word sequence, usually to produce a visualization of the sentiments being expressed about that word or sequence within a data set. In the case of surveillance monitoring, this is done with machine learning altohyrtins in real-time but in most other cases this is done on a fixed data set – for example, a download of customer product reviews for a given period – with a less sophisticated computer program. Language data sets are indexed against a positivity matrix which, in simple analyses, might have a polarity from 1–5, with 1 being most positive and 5 being least positive. Polarities are usually scored numerically to allow for statistical analysis of the results of ABSA. For example, a user review that contains words and statements such as, 'great', 'excellent', 'changed my life', 'most innvoative book about acting I have ever read' will receive high positivity scores for each of these comments (for example, 1s and 2s) and the scores of all product reviews can be aggregated and analysed mathematically to inform publishers about how much readers like their products.

ABSA has manifold uses and, working with Professor Sioros it was becoming apparent that an ABSA-type approach could have considerable utility in my project. However, ABSA doesn't produce information about *meaning*; it produces information about *feeling*. While it would be fascinating to use ABSA to conjecture and contend what authors feel about key concepts in acting this wouldn't help greatly in analysing the meaning of those concepts. It also wouldn't help in identifying what those concepts even are in the first place, and so I developed SABMA to address this specific challenge.

BY MAKING A 'CATALOGUE'

Before you can SABMA you need a digital data set so, having secured access to the xml files constituting Drama Online's holdings, I received these as a set of (very large) data files. As these files have considerable commercial value and sensitivity they required a robust data storage system and approach. As I would be working with commercial assets and intellectual property with considerable financial value and sensitivity, my access to these for the purpose of researching this book is within a non-disclosure agreement with Bloomsbury Publishing, the owners of the database. This agreement interacts with the individual author agreements between all authors and the publisher, conserving author rights and enabling me to conduct the research within a strictly enforced ethical protocol that protects intellectual property. These protections limit the publication of various research 'assets' generated during production of this book, including full 'word-count records' for each title, 'library' and 'sub-library', libraries and sub-libraries themselves, as well as 'ABMA' files and other files and graphs generated during the research. The non-disclosure agreement does allow me to publish selected data from the research, including indicative approximate word counts for titles, indicative data about groups of titles and the full list of the 'catalogue' generated during the computational research phase. This enables me to disclose all the information about the database and its titles that is relevant to my findings and the purpose of this book, as well as information relevant to the explanation of the methodology.

Operating under the non-disclosure agreement, I received xml files of the selected sub-database of nearly 2,000 scholarly book titles. These were parsed – computationally analysed and organized – using a bespoke programming script developed with Professor Sioros. This programme parsed the catalogue several times into progressively more focused 'sub-libraries' of titles that contained at least one of the below words at least once.

Act
Acts
Acted

How and Why to Write *Acting: Keywords and Concepts*

Acting
Actress
Actresses
Actor
Actors
Player
Players
Playing
Playacting

This first parse reduced the starting data source by nearly half, excluding all books that did not feature any of these terms. This gave the first sub-library of 'titles about acting'.

A second parsing of this sub-library undertook to word count the frequency of any of these terms within each individual title, to produce a number value for each title representing the number of times any of these words feature in the text of the book. These number values were then used to plot all the number of occurrences of terms (y axis) in each book (x axis) on the graph below, showing the relative and comparative frequency of these terms in each book in the first sub-library.

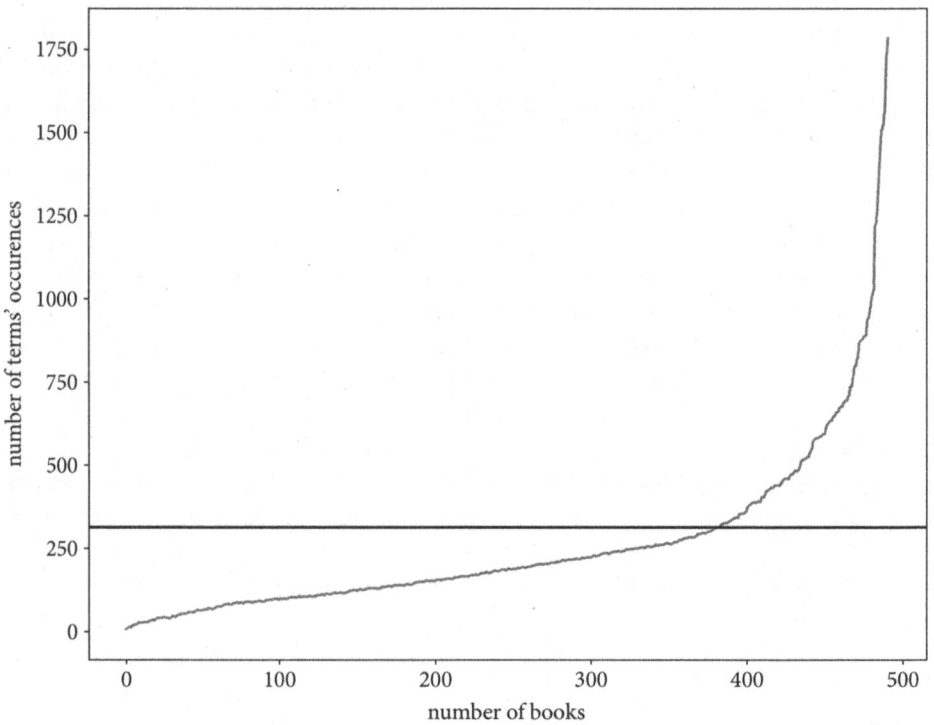

Generating a further and more focused sub-library now required drawing an exclusionary line (straight line) across the sub-library. This was not straightforward mathematically or graphically, and this is a limitation in the analysis. However, there is a point in the graph where the occurrence of terms becomes significantly more important from one book to the next (where you see the graph line pitching steeply upwards). The new sub-library (sub-sub-library, for accuracy) was formed of all books that are beyond that point as shown above. Mathematically, this is the point at which a single title contains 308 or more occurrences of any of the terms used in the first parse. All the titles above this threshold point – 109 titles in total – were parsed into a new sub-library that is referred to throughout this book as the 'catalogue'.

Generating the catalogue was an important step towards identifying a corpus of writing on acting, and excluding some titles which were not 'about' acting brought the corpus into focus. Through successive parsing into sub libraries the catalogue is produced and somewhere in the catalogue are the keywords. This is not to say that the research would then be constrained to the catalogue only. Having access to the full Drama Online holding, the catalogue might be thought of as something like a targeted bore sample in the wider terrain in which the analysis would take place.

The next phase of SABMA is about extracting the keywords from the catalogue and the first part of this phase is also computational.

BY TURNING THE CATALOGUE INTO A LIST AND TUNING OUT NOISE

Next, a further phase of computational analysis is undertaken with the catalogue whereby each title is word-counted. This is a process by which a computer program counts the number of times any word is used in each title to produce a (very, very long) list of all the words used in the catalogue and a record of the number of times that they are used. This process is commonly used to generate the 'word clouds' that may be familiar to readers of this book and, in this methodology, this was used to obtain a list of the frequency of all words in the catalogue.

To make this list manageable in size it needs harmonizing; there is a fair bit of 'noise' to tune out in the list. 'Noise' is information in a data set that is extraneous or misleading to the interpretation and understanding of the data set. Commonly used words, such as 'one', 'way', 'well', 'go', 'end', 'day' and 'keep' are noisy and need to be quietened down. This quietening is a two-step process. First, some noise is silenced by a computational eliminatory comparison between this list and readily available lists of high frequency words that have been generated from massive data sets of language.

This reduces the massive scale of the lists but, this approach is relatively insensitive to the polysemy factor; the fact that some words (in fact quite a few words when it comes to acting parlance) have multiple meanings and therefore are used in both generic and discipline specific ways in the catalogue. 'Act' may be the definitive example in this case but other polysemous words, such as 'breath', 'play' and 'set', all create noise that needs tuning out in this phase of the hunt for keywords.

In the next methodological phase, the human elements of the syncretic methodology are more dominant as the list of eliminated words is manually processed. I read through the elimination list and manually reinput some words deleted from the main list which may be being used in an acting-specific meaning-sense. This step of SABMA is both more informed by expert knowledge and more exposed to bias. The relevance and value of my personal subject knowledge is evident: for example, the eliminatory comparison deletes 'action', as a common-language word, but I reinstate it to the list because I know that 'action' has a specific meaning and use-case in several theories and practices of acting. I cancel the deletion for this and other common-language words, including 'play', 'part', 'idea', 'feel' and 'game'. My prior knowledge of the field tells me that these words shouldn't be discounted as keywords just yet, and that I will need a method to check their specific usage in titles in the catalogue before I could be confident that they shouldn't remain in a list of potential keywords.

By this point in the methodological process I have isolated a list of titles which might contain entries that could be considered key to discourses in the catalogue by dint of the straightforward fact of their relative levels of occurrence. I've also generated a list of words within those titles that are candidates for keyword status but their potential key-ness thus far rests largely on their numerical frequency with only a limited level of knowledge-based inference. To select from within this list the terms that are *key* to discourses on acting and not just present or frequent within discourse it becomes necessary to consider in more detail their meanings and use-cases.

The linguistic philosophical principle that advances the analysis here is, that a *key*word would be a word that could not be eliminated from discourse without undermining the discourse of which it is a part. Semiotically speaking, these words would denote or connote concepts fundamental to discourses and analysing the meaning and use of these words would reveal something about the philosophical and ideological foundations of discourses. A useful taxonomy of these keywords would need to establish the singularity and consistency of each of their meanings (because they may, of course, have several meanings) and these would be situated in their use-cases – the use to which a word is put in discourse. Referring to Raymond Williams's introduction to the first edition of his *Keywords* (1976), this could be understood as their 'binding' quality in discourse; certain uses binding together certain ways of seeing a phenomenon. Acting, in this case.

Keywords, according to Williams, might also be words that 'open up issues or problems' and might be part of an 'active vocabulary – a way of recording, investigating and presenting problems of meaning' ([1975] 1985: 15) that have formed in a discourse. Williams describes keywords as 'a shared body of words and meanings', and notes that a keyword might also be characterized by 'problems of its meanings … inextricably bound up with the problems it was being used to discuss' ([1976] 1985: 15). In this book, keywords therefore are definable by their centrality to 'formations' of meanings 'implicit in the connections which people were making' and as 'ways not only of discussing but at another level of seeing', 'central experiences' ([1976] 1985: 15) of acting.

BY RETURNING HUMAN INTELLECT TO THE METHODOLOGY

Methodologically speaking, at this point the usefulness of computational methods starts to give out to the capability of the human intellect as a superior and more flexible judge of meaning and use. Moving from the realm of frequency to the realm of meaning becomes a central concern of the methodology, hence its syncretic nature, but there is still something to preserve in the next phase from the computational and mathematical ABSA approach. At this point, an ABSA approach might look to reduce the list further by repeating earlier parses and then assigning polarities before reprocessing a reduced list with polarity index back through the catalogue to capture and score the words and phrases used in conjunction and proximity to the entries in the list.

It doesn't seem possible to produce a polarity of meaning in the same way that one can produce a polarity of sentiment. Even if there was some merit in 'scoring' potential meanings using a polarity index it would first be necessary to know what those meanings are, and thus far the methodology has done very little on this, except for the 'elimination remediation' step. The only way to establish the meaning of the words in the list and ascertain which are keywords will be to read all or part of the titles in the catalogue with a critical focus on how the words in the list are used in each title, and then to collate the meanings assigned to these and consider these relative to Williams's definition. Using the metaphor of Professor Sioros's groove analysis, while keywords – like musical notes or beats – are individual entities their meanings would be constructed in grammar and interdependent upon the context in which they were used, secured in and also securing the structural whole of which they are a part.

So, while I had shrunk the catalogue to a more readable scale (107 book-length titles), I was still facing the challenges of reading *a lot* in order to advance the taxonomy of keywords in acting. However, evolving an insight for the polarity indexing approach of ABSA I noticed that most content about the use-case of the words in the list would be located in sentences directly before and after the appearance of a word from the list in each title. Although keywords might also be latent in statements not including these keywords and although their meaning may be obliquely referenced or implicit in statements not including these keywords, most content in titles about keywords would be located in the text, or more accurately, 'copy', in which these words were embedded. Put even more simply, all those sentences in titles containing the words in the lists would contain information about how these words were being used in the description, mobilization, construction and contestation of ideas and concepts these words were being used to define. These sentences containing the words in the lists would therefore contain most if not all of the information about the meaning of these words, and this insight allows for an additional parsing of the catalogue.

Using the xml files for titles in the catalogue and reducing these to the sentences within these files that use the words from the initial parse drastically scaled down the catalogue to a large but readable-within-my-lifetime size. This scaling-down produced 'SABMA files' for each title – xml files of all sentences in each title containing at least one word from the initial parsing list. I was able to read the SABMA files for each title over the course of a matter of months and, by a human process, reduce and refine again the list by eliminating all content that was not germane to acting, which might, for example, be potentially using keywords in common-language use cases despite the eliminations.

Developing the human side of the syncretic method through a further phase, I was now able to use the SABMA files alongside the whole text xml files for each title. Using a simple search program, I could quickly navigate the whole text files to enable me to read SABMA file insights in more expansive context, and thereby do a further elimination of words from the list.

I was now able to proceed with the human analytical aspects of SABMA in earnest having provided myself with a focused and manageable data set of xml files that could be read expansively and intensively, targeting and cross-referencing content using search tool file navigation. During this later stage of the research methodology I was now able to identify and collate use-cases across titles in the catalogue and interpret these use-cases in context to reveal the meanings being assigned to words.

Contextualizing use-cases frequently required me to reference outside of the 'catalogue'. During this phase it became clear that use-cases which appear in the catalogue also appear in sources in the earlier sub-libraries. In response to this finding I have provided something of a 'parsed' bibliography for the reader. In the back matter of this book readers will find a list of sources including the mathematically generated 'catalogue' as well as a full bibliography of all sources cited in the text, enabling a reader to explore and verify the findings of the book for themselves. I have also provided a succinct 'selected bibliography' with each chapter to enable readers to easily identify and access the specific material that I have cited to contextualize the use-cases in each entry.

During the later methodological phase, *keywords* came finally into focus as words that were being used not only to 'discuss' but to 'see' acting, phenomenologically speaking. Words that opened up 'issues or problems' with these ways of seeing the phenomena of acting. Words that formed an 'active vocabulary', 'a way of recording, investigating and presenting problems' of the meaning of acting.

In this phase I collated all use-cases for these keywords and I have recorded these in a succinct glossary at the top of each entry in this book. Collating these use-cases and interpreting the meaning of words from them confirmed that sheer frequency (of words and uses) was a pertinent but not necessarily defining measure of key-ness.

Given the pertinence of this measure, though, and the insights that might be wrought for readers by sharing information about it, I have sequenced the book entries in a descending order of frequency from 'high' to 'mid' to 'low frequency' keywords. I have not drawn a graph line to divide the list of entries into thirds, but use the terms 'high', 'mid' and 'low' only when a comparative frequency factor bears relevance to the keyword discourses. I have also provided some commentary in most entries on the absolute or relative numerical value of frequency of each word in the catalogue.

I would invite readers to view the descending sequence of the contents page, and the notional 'high', 'mid' and 'low' descriptor as primarily an organizing feature of a book and caution against over-interpreting the significance of terms to acting discourses based on this measure alone. Indeed, you will observe in the commentary on some entries that some low frequency keywords are more *key* to acting discourse than other high frequency ones.

Some of the more surprising findings of the research undertaken for this book (at least to me anyway) are that words I would have considered to be key to acting discourses before I even began to think about this book barely feature in discourse at all. This finding might say something about the weakness of the methodology or it might say something about my ideological prejudices. Perhaps it says something about both, in which case at least one person will learn something from this book, but I think it may also relate to what Williams and others have said about keywords as components of an 'active vocabulary'. To paraphrase and restate, keywords are problematic words bound up with the problems they are being used to discuss. For the reader, I hope that this book lays out some of these problems – aesthetic, ideological, political – and makes these keywords useful and useable with some confidence and clarity despite the contingency of their active meanings.

WITH SOME WRITING-UP STRATEGIES

Channelling Williams stylistically as well as methodologically, I have worked hard to make my commentaries on the problems of each *keyword* succinct and impactful. I have imposed a strict limit of 5,000 words on each entry with most entries being 2,000–3,000 words in total with an intention to make this book easily accessible, easy to reference and cross-reference and, hopefully, pleasurable to read.

I have challenged myself to write about the *keywords* that you will find here in ways that explode the problems. My writing mantra has been, 'not entries; incendiaries' and I have sought to craft each entry into a small explosive device to insert into discourse, not for wanton destruction but to break apart, expose and isolate some of the problems that *keywords* grapple with. Each entry, and some in particular, take a provocative stance towards some of these problems and I hope that it will be clear that this is not because I assume a moral or intellectual superiority over these problems or the authors who speak about them. Writing provocatively is a stylistic choice that I have adopted from Williams, and others, but provocativeness and pugnaciousness are not, of course, the same thing. These entries are built on the foundation of a rigorous research methodology committed to attaining as much objectivity about my sources as is practicable but do not intend to produce neutral accounts of the meanings of *keywords*. These are problematic words grappling with quite real problems for actors and for acting. My entries and this book don't look to resolve these problems but to present them in the sharpest relief possible.

Whether the Aspect Based Syncretic Meaning Analysis should be thought of as a discourse analysis approach, a text linguistics approach, a sociolinguistic, semiotic or even applied ethnomethodological model is moot but, of the various methodological schema by which words and meaning are analysed, Raymond Williams might have defined keywords as a 'sub-language', to use the mathematical and computational term (see Lambek, 1958, 1961; Curry, 1961; Sørensen and Urzyczyn, 2006). While Williams was assembling a 'Vocabulary of Culture and Society' (1976) this book has taken a more circumscribed focus on what one of Williams's contemporaries, Kenneth Hudson, called, 'the jargon of a profession' (1978). Baden Eunson of Monash University and the author of *Communication in the Twenty First Century* wrote in an article in *The Conversation* (2015) that professional jargon transforms through three stages. It 'starts out as a simple technical sublanguage' that 'helps reinforce group solidarity in that it becomes a semi-private language, but with clarity its main aim' (2015) but progressively 'become less transparent' and 'unable to communicate' until it can become 'an object of ridicule' (ibid). Eunson is most interested in acronyms and 'buzzwords' used in businesses but some of his insights pertain to keywords in acting too; Robert Gordon has written on the 'myths' of acting discourse: seemingly neutral language-expressions about acting that come to justify the principles they purport to merely express (2006: 2–5). Gordon argues that 'acting is a practice at the core of all cultural expression, articulating social values "invisibly" as well as being overtly the medium in which dramatic writing is communicated' (2). 'As with any discourse of culture', he writes, 'these "myths" are themselves the product of ideology' (5) even though they might ostensibly comment objectively on phenomena.

For all these methodological and philosophical reasons, this book gives a thorough but not-neutral account of acting by describing in close and systematic detail the meanings of the words used to define it and in this sense this book contributes to the discourse it ostensibly describes.

References

Allsopp, R. and D. Williams (2006), 'Editorial', *Performance Research* 11 (3): iii–v.
Chinitz, J. (1990), 'If Synthesis is Impossible, Let's Try Syncretism', *Midstream* 44 (5): 21.
Curry, H. B. (1961), 'Some Logical Aspects of Grammatical Structure', in R. Jacobson (ed.), *Structure of Language and its Mathematical Aspects, Proceedings of the Symposia in Applied Mathematics* (Volume XII), 56–68, American Mathematical Society.
Eunson, B. (2006) *Communication in the Twenty First Century*, New York: John Wiley and Sons.
Eunson, B. (2015) 'A Call to Arms: Let's Get Rid of All the Jargon!', in *The Conversation,* available at: https://theconversation.com/a-call-to-arms-lets-get-rid-of-all-the-jargon-37165
Hudson, K. (1978), *The Jargon of the Professions*, London and Basingstoke: Macmillan.
Lambek, J. (1958), 'The Mathematics of Sentence Structure', *American Mathematical Monthly*, 65: 154–70.
Lambek, J. (1961), 'On the Calculus of Syntactic Types', in R. Jacobson (ed.), *Structure of Language and its Mathematical Aspects, Proceedings of the Symposia in Applied Mathematics* (Volume XII), 166–78, American Mathematical Society.
Lambropoulos, V. (2001), 'Syncretism as Mixture and as Method', *Journal of Modern Greek Studies,* 19(2): 221–35.

Moran, M. (2021), 'Keywords as Method', *European Journal of Cultural Studies*, 24(4): 1021–9.
'Nick Hern Blog', October 2, 2015, available at@ https://nickhernbooksblog.com/2015/10/02/drama-online-the-netflix-of-theatre/ accessed on January 17, 2025.
Sørensen, M. H. and P. Urzyczyn (2006), *Lectures on the Curry-Howard Isomorphism, Studies in Logic and the Foundations of Mathematics* (Volume 149), Amsterdam: Elsevier.
Williams, R. ([1975] 1985), *Keywords: A Vocabulary of Culture and Society*, London: Fontana.

THE CATALOGUE

Ainsworth, A., O. Double and L. Peacock, eds. (2015), *Popular Performance*, London: Bloomsbury Academic.
Banks, F. (2014), *Creative Shakespeare: The Globe Education Guide to Practical Shakespeare*, London: The Arden Shakespeare.
Banks, F., ed. (2019), *Shakespeare: Actors and Audiences*, London: The Arden Shakespeare.
Barker, C. (1977), *Theatre Games: A New Approach to Drama Training*, London: Methuen Drama.
Barker, H.G., C. Chambers and R. Nelson, eds. (2017), *Granville Barker on Theatre: Selected Essays*, London: Methuen Drama.
Barnett, D., E. Brater and M. Taylor-Batty, trans. (2014), *Brecht in Practice: Theatre, Theory and Performance,* London: Methuen Drama.
Barton, J. (1984), *Playing Shakespeare*, London: Methuen Drama.
Bessell, J. (2019), *Shakespeare in Action: 30 Theatre Makers on Their Practice*, London: The Arden Shakespeare.
Bishop, N. (2015), *Auditioning for Film and Television: Secrets from a Casting Director,* London: Methuen Drama.
Blair, R. and A. Cook, eds (2016), *Theatre, Performance and Cognition: Languages, Bodies and Ecologies*, London: Methuen Drama.
Bleeker, M., A. Kear, J. Kelleher and H. Roms, eds. (2019), *Thinking Through Theatre and Performance*, London: Methuen Drama.
Braun, E. (1982), *The Director and the Stage: From Naturalism to Grotowski,* London: Methuen Drama.
Braun, E. (2016), *Meyerhold on Theatre*, London: Methuen Drama.
Braun, E., trans. (2016), *Meyerhold on Theatre,* London: Methuen Drama.
Brecht, B. (2015), *Brecht on Theatre*, London: Methuen Drama.
Britten, B. (2014), *From Stage to Screen: A Theatre Actor's Guide to Working on Camera*, London: Methuen Drama.
Britton, J., ed. (2013), *Encountering Ensemble*, London: Methuen Drama.
Brody, J.D. (2015), *The Actor's Business Plan: A Career Guide for the Acting Life,* London: Methuen Drama.
Brook, P. (2018), *The Shifting Point: Forty Years of Theatrical Exploration, 1946–87*, London: Bloomsbury Academic.
Cantrell, T. and C. Hogg, eds. (2018), *Exploring Television Acting,* London: Bloomsbury Publishing.
Charry, B. (2017), *The Arden Guide to Renaissance Drama: An Introduction with Primary Sources*, London: The Arden Shakespeare.
Citron, A., S. Aronson-Lehavi, and D. Zerbib, eds. (2014), *Performance Studies in Motion: International Perspectives and Practices in the Twenty-First Century,* London: Methuen Drama.
Clifton, A. (2016), *The Actor's Workbook: A Practical Guide to Training, Rehearsing and Devising*, London: Methuen Drama.
Cockin, K. (2017), *Edith Craig and The Theatres of Art,* London: Methuen Drama.
Cohen, R.A. (2018), *ShakesFear and How to Cure it: The Complete Handbook for Teaching Shakespeare,* London: Arden Shakespeare.

Corcoran, N. (2018), *Reading Shakespeare's Soliloquies: Text, Theatre, Film*, London: The Arden Shakespeare.
Croall, J. (2011), *John Gielgud: Matinee Idol to Movie Star*, London: Methuen Drama.
Croall, J. (2015), *Performing King Lear: Gielgud to Russell Beale*, London: The Arden Shakespeare.
Croall, J. (2018), *Performing Hamlet: Actors in the Modern Age*, London: Methuen Drama.
D'Monté, R. (2015), *British Theatre and Performance 1900–1950*, London: Bloomsbury Academic.
Double, O. (2014), *Getting the Joke: The Inner Workings of Stand-up Comedy*, London: Methuen Drama.
Dresner, D. (2018), *A Life-coaching Approach to Screen Acting*, London: Methuen Drama.
Dunmore, S. (2012), *An Actor's Guide to Getting Work*, London: Methuen Drama.
Dustagheer, S. and G. Woods, eds. (2017), *Stage Directions and Shakespearean Theatre*, London: The Arden Shakespeare.
DuVal, C. (2016), *Stage Combat Arts: An Integrated Approach to Acting, Voice and Text Work*, London: Methuen Drama.
Eisen, K. (2018), *The Theatre of Eugene O'Neill: American Modernism on the World Stage*, London: Methuen Drama.
Elsam, P. (2011), *Acting Characters: 20 Essential Steps From Rehearsal to Performance*, London: Methuen Drama.
Elsam, P. (2014), *Stephen Joseph: Theatre Pioneer and Provocateur*, London: Methuen Drama.
Ewan, V. and D. Green (2015), *Actor Movement: Expression of the Physical Being: A Movement Handbook for Actors*, London: Methuen Drama.
Ewan, V. and K. Sagovsky (2019), *Laban's Efforts in Action: A Movement Handbook for Actors with Online Video Resources*, London: Methuen Drama.
Falletti, C., G. Sofia and V. Jacono, eds. (2016), *Theatre and Cognitive Neuroscience*, London: Methuen Drama.
Findlay, A. (2014), *Women in Shakespeare: A Dictionary*, London: The Arden Shakespeare.
Flacks, N. (2015), *Acting With Passion: A Performer's Guide to Emotions on Cue*, London: Methuen Drama.
Gillett, J. (2014), *Acting Stanislavski: A Practical Guide to Stanislavski's Approach and Legacy*, London: Methuen Drama.
Gobert, R.D. (2014), *The Theatre of Caryl Churchill*, London: Methuen Drama.
Goy-Blanquet, D. (2018), *Shakespeare in the Theatre: Patrice Chéreau*, London: The Arden Shakespeare.
Griffiths, T.R. (2003), *The Theatre Guide: A Comprehensive A-Z of the World's Best Plays and Playwrights*, London: Methuen Drama.
Gutekunst, C. and J. Gillett (2021), *Voice into Acting: Integrating Voice and the Stanislavski Approach*, London: Methuen Drama.
Harrison, J. (2016), *Actor-Musicianship*, London: Methuen Drama.
Holland, P. (2010), *Garrick, Kemble, Siddons, Kean: Great Shakespeareans*, London: The Arden Shakespeare.
Homan, S. and B. Rhinehart (2017), *Comedy Acting for Theatre: The Art and Craft of Performing in Comedies*, London: Methuen Drama.
Johnston, C. (2017), *Disobedient Theatre: Alternative Ways to Inspire, Animate and Play*, London: Methuen Drama.
Johnston, K. (2016), *Disability Theatre and Modern Drama: Recasting Modernism*, London: Methuen Drama.
Johnstone, K. (1981), *Impro: Improvisation and the Theatre*, London: Methuen Drama.
Karim-Cooper, F. and T. Stern, eds. (2014), *The Arden Shakespeare Library: Shakespeare's Theatres and the Effects of Performance*, London: The Arden Shakespeare.

The Catalogue

Keenan, S. (2014), *Acting Companies and their Plays in Shakespeare's London*, London: The Arden Shakespeare.

Kenrick, J. (2017), *Musical Theatre: A History*, London: A Giniger Book, published in association with Bloomsbury Methuen Drama.

Knopf, R. (2017), *Script Analysis for Theatre: Tools for Interpretation, Collaboration and Production*, London: Bloomsbury Methuen Drama.

Kumiega, J. (1985), 'Paratheatrical Research 1970–1975', in *The Theatre of Grotowski*, London: Methuen.

Manfull, H. (1999), *Taking Stage: Women Directors on Directing*, Birkenhead: Methuen Drama.

Marsden, R. (2022), *Inside the Rehearsal Room: Process, Collaboration and Decision-Making*, London: Methuen Drama.

Marsden, S. (2019), *100 Acting Exercises for 8–18 Year Olds*, London: Methuen Drama.

Marty, P. (2019), *Contemporary Women Stage Directors: Conversations on Craft*, London: Methuen Drama.

Matthews, J. (2019), *The Life of Training*, London: Methuen Drama.

Mayer, J. (2016), *Steppenwolf Theatre Company of Chicago: In Their Own Words*, London: Methuen Drama.

Mazer, C.M., ed. (2013), *Poel, Granville Barker, Guthrie, Wanamaker: Great Shakespeareans Volume XV*, London: The Arden Shakespeare.

McCaw, D. (2017), *Training the Actor's Body: A Guide*, London: Methuen Drama.

McMullan, G., L.C. Orlin and V.M. Vaughan, eds. (2014), *Women Making Shakespeare: Text, Reception, Performance*, London: Bloomsbury Arden.

Menzer, P. (2015), *Anecdotal Shakespeare: A New Performance History*, London: Bloomsbury Arden Shakespeare.

Menzer, P. (2017), *Shakespeare in the Theatre: The American Shakespeare Center*, London: The Arden Shakespeare.

Monday, M. (2017), *Directing with the Michael Chekhov Technique: A Workbook with Video for Directors, Teachers and Actors*, London: Methuen Drama.

Morris, E. (2017), *Rhythm in Acting and Performance: Embodied Approaches and Understandings*, London: Methuen Drama.

Murray, B. (2007), *The Worst it Can Be is a Disaster: The Life Story of Braham Murray and the Royal Exchange Theatre*, London: Methuen Drama

Nadel, I. (2002), *Double Act: A Life of Tom Stoppard*, London: Methuen Drama.

Ney, C. (2016), 'Adding the Audience', in *Directing Shakespeare in America: Current Practices*, London: The Arden Shakespeare.

Ney, C. (2016), *Directing Shakespeare in America: Current Practices*, London: The Arden Shakespeare.

Ostlere, R. (2019), *The Actor's Career Bible: Auditioning, Networking, Survival and Success*, London: Methuen Drama.

Palfrey, S. (2011), *Doing Shakespeare*, London: The Arden Shakespeare.

Pitches, J. and S. Aquilina, eds. (2017), *Stanislavsky in the World: The System and its Transformations Across Continents*, London: Methuen Drama.

Piven, J. and S. Applebaum (2012), *In the Studio with Joyce Piven: Theatre Games, Story Theatre and Text Work for Actors*, London: Bloomsbury Publishing.

Purcell, S. (2017), *Shakespeare in the Theatre: Mark Rylance at the Globe*, London: The Arden Shakespeare.

Rea, K. (2021), *The Outstanding Actor: Seven Keys to Success*, 2nd edn, London: Methuen Drama.

Reynolds, J. and A.W. Smith (2015), *Howard Barker's Theatre: Wrestling with Catastrophe*, London: Methuen Drama.

Reynolds, P.M. (2019), *Performing Shakespeare's Women: Playing Dead*, London: The Arden Shakespeare.

Robbins, J.S. (2019), *The Actor's Survival Guide: How to Make Your Way in Hollywood,* London: Methuen Drama.
Roche, A. (2015), *The Irish Dramatic Revival 1899–1939*, London: Methuen Drama.
Rodenburg, P. (2019), *The Actor Speaks: Voice and the Performer,* London: Methuen Drama.
Rushe, S. (2019), *Michael Chekhov's Acting Technique: A Practitioner's Guide,* London: Methuen Drama.
Ryland, C., trans. (2017), *Brecht on Performance: Messingkauf and Modelbooks*, London: Methuen Drama.
Salinsky, T. and D. Frances-White (2017), *The Improv Handbook: The Ultimate Guide to Improvising in Comedy, Theatre, and Beyond*, London: Methuen Drama.
Salt, C. (2001), *Make Acting Work*, London: Methuen Drama A & C Black Publishers Limited.
Shaughnessy, N., ed. (2013), *Affective Performance and Cognitive Science: Body, Brain and Being,* London: Bloomsbury Methuen Drama.
Skinner, A., (ed. (2019) *Russian Theatre in Practice: The Director's Guide,* London: Methuen Drama.
Snow, J. (2012), *Movement Training for Actors,* London: Methuen Drama.
Soto-Morettini, D. (2022), *My Character Wouldn't Do That: Acting, Cognitive Science and the Optimal Performance Brain*, London: Methuen Drama.
Stephens, S. (2016), *Simon Stephens: A Working Diary,* London: Methuen Drama.
Thomas, J. (2016), *A Director's Guide to Stanislavsky's Active Analysis: Including the Formative Essay on Active Analysis by Maria Knebel*, London: Methuen Drama.
Thompson, K. (2019), *Directing Professionally: A Practical Guide to Developing a Successful Career in Today's Theatre,* London: Methuen Drama.
Trencsényi, K. (2015), *Dramaturgy in the Making: A User's Guide for Theatre Practitioners,* London: Methuen Drama.
Tribble, E. (2017), *Early Modern Actors and Shakespeare's Theatre: Thinking with the Body*, London: The Arden Shakespeare.
Voltz, J. (2007), *Working in American Theatre: A Brief History, Career Guide and Resource Book for Over 1,000 Theatres,* London: Methuen Drama.
Walton, J.M., ed. (1983), *Craig on Theatre,* London: Methuen Drama.
Wetmore Jr., K.J., S. Liu and E.B. Mee (2014), *Modern Asian Theatre and Performance 1900–2000*, London: Methuen Drama.
White, M. (2019), *Staging Musicals: An Essential Guide,* London: Methuen Drama.
Wooster, R. (2016), *Theatre in Education in Britain: Origins, Development and Influence*, London: Methuen Drama.

BIBLIOGRAPHY

Allain, P. and J. Harvie (2014), *The Routledge Companion to Theatre and Performance*, 2nd edn, London: Routledge.
Allsopp, R. and D. Williams (2006), 'Editorial', *Performance Research*, 11 (3): iii–v.
Aquilina, S. (2017) 'Introduction: Context 1: Well-trodden Paths: US, UK, Russian and Soviet Perspectives on Stanislavsky's Transmission', in J. Pitches and S. Aquilina (eds), *Stanislavsky in the World: The System and its Transformations Across Continents*, 1–11, London: Methuen Drama.
Artaud, A. (1989), 'The Theatre and its Double (1931–7)', in C. Schumacher and B. Singleton (eds), *Artaud on Theatre*, 95–156, London: Methuen Drama.
Autant-Mathieu, M. (2017), 'Stanislavsky and French Theatre: Selected Affinities', in J. Pitches and S. Aquilina (eds), *Stanislavsky in the World: The System and its Transformations Across Continents*, 63–86, London: Methuen Drama.
Autant-Mathieu, M. (2017). Stanislavsky and French Theatre: Selected Affinities. In J. Pitches & S. Aquilina (Ed.). *Stanislavsky in the World: The System and its Transformations Across Continents*, 63–86, London: Bloomsbury Methuen Drama.
Baker Miller, J. (1995), 'Domination and Subordination', in P. S. Rothenberg (ed.), *Race, Class & Gender in the United States: An Integrated Study*, 57–64, New York: St. Martin's Press.
Banks, F., ed. (2019), *Shakespeare: Actors and Audiences*, London: The Arden Shakespeare.
Barker, C. (1977), 'Thought and Action', in *Theatre Games: A New Approach to Drama Training*, London: Methuen Drama.
Barnett, D. (2014), *Brecht in Practice: Theatre, Theory and Performance*, London: Methuen Drama.
Berlin, I. (1969), *Four Essays on Liberty*, Oxford: Oxford University Press.
Bishop, N. (2015), *Auditioning for Film and Television: Secrets from a Casting Director*, London: Methuen Drama.
Bishop, N. (2022), 'Intimacy Coordinators', in *Auditioning for Film and Television: A Post #MeToo Guide*, London: Methuen Drama.
Black, M. (1954–55), 'Metaphor', in *Proceedings of the Aristotelean Society*, 273–94, N.S., London: Harrison & Son Ltd.
Black, M. (1977), 'More About Metaphor', *Dialectica*, 31 (3–4): 431–57.
Blattès, S. (2007), 'Is the Concept of "Character" Still Relevant in Contemporary Drama?', *Contemporary Drama in English* 14: 69–81.
Boyle, M. S., M. Cornish, and B. Woolf (2019), *Postdramatic Theatre and Form*, London: Methuen Drama.
Brecht, B. (1953), 'Katzgraben Notes 1953', in C. Ryland (trans), *Brecht on Performance: Messingkauf and Modelbooks*, London: Methuen Drama.
Britten, B. (2014), *From Stage to Screen: A Theatre Actor's Guide to Working on Camera*, London: Methuen Drama.
Britten, B. (2014). *From Stage to Screen: A Theatre Actor's Guide to Working on Camera*. London: Bloomsbury Methuen Drama
Buckley T., M. T. Burnett, S. Datta, and R. García-Periago, eds (2022), *Women and Indian Shakespeares*, London: The Arden Shakespeare.

Bibliography

Cahill, A. J. and C. Hamel (2021), *Sounding Bodies: Identity, Injustice, and the Voice,* London: Methuen Drama.

Camilleri, F. (2019), *Performer Training Reconfigured: Post-Psychophysical Perspectives for the Twenty-First Century*, London: Methuen Drama.

Camilleri, F. (2023), *Performer Training for Actors and Athletes*, London: Methuen Drama.

Carnicke, S. M. (2023), *Dynamic Acting Through Active Analysis: Konstantin Stanislavsky, Maria Knebel, and Their Legacy*, London: Methuen Drama.

Chirico, M. M. and K. Younger, eds. *How to Teach a Play: Essential Exercises for Popular Plays,* London: Methuen Drama.

Chothia, J. (1991), *André Antoine*, Cambridge and New York: Cambridge University Press.

Chow, B. (2019), 'How Does the Trained Body Think', in M. Bleeker, A. Kear, J. Kelleher, and H. Roms (eds), *Thinking Through Theatre and Performance*, 145–157, London: Methuen Drama.

Clifton, A. (2016), *The Actor's Workbook: A Practical Guide to Training, Rehearsing and Devising,* London: Methuen Drama.

Cohen, L., ed. (2010), *The Lee Strasberg Notes*, London and New York: Routledge.

Coodin, S. (2010), 'What's Virtue Ethics Got to Do With It? Shakespearean Character as Moral Character', in M. D. Bristol (ed.), *Shakespeare and Moral Agency*, 184–199, London: Bloomsbury Academic.

Cook, H. C. (1915), *The Play Way*, London: Heinemann.

Cook, R. (2012), *Voice and the Young Actor: A Workbook and Video,* London: Bloomsbury Methuen Drama.

Counsel, C. (1996), *Signs of Performance: An Introduction to Twentieth Century Theatre*, London: Routledge.

De Marinis, M. ([1988] 2008), *Capire il teatro. Lineamenti di una nuova teatrologia*, Roma: Bulzoni Editore.

De Marinis, M. (2011), 'New Theatrology and Performance Studies: Starting Points Towards a Dialogue', *The Drama Review* 55(4): 64–74.

De Marinis, M. (2016), 'Body and Corporeity in the Theatre: From Semiotics to Neuroscience. A Small Multidisciplinary Glossary', in C. Falletti, G. Sofia, and V. Jacono (eds), *Theatre and Cognitive Neuroscience*, 61–74, London: Methuen Drama.

Diderot on Art: Volume II, The Salon of 1767 (1995), translated by John Goodman, New Haven, CT and London: Yale University Press.

Diderot, D. (1991), 'Conversations on *The Natural Son*', in M. J. Sidnell (ed.), *Sources of Dramatic Theory: Volume 2, Voltaire to Hugo*, 35-57, Cambridge: Cambridge University Press.

Diderot, D. (1991), 'Discourse on Dramatic Poetry', in M. J. Sidnell (ed.), *Sources of Dramatic Theory: Volume 2, Voltaire to Hugo*, 36-56, Cambridge: Cambridge University Press.

Diderot, D. ([1758] 1918), 'On Dramatic Poetry', in H. Clark Barrett (ed.), *European Theories of the Drama*, 286–299, Cincinnati, OH: Stewart & Kidd.

Dixon, L. (2003), *Play-acting: A Guide to Theatre Workshops*, London: Methuen Drama.

Dixon, L. (2003) *Playacting*, London: Methuen.

Donnellan, D. (2002), *The Actor and the Target*, London: Nick Hern Books.

Double, O. (2015), '"It Feels Like a Group of Friends Messing Around Onstage": Pappy's and Live Sketch Comedy', in A. Ainsworth, O. Double, and L. Peacock (eds), *Popular Performance*, 247–68. London: Bloomsbury Academic.

Dowd, M. M. and T. Rutter, eds. (2023), *The Arden Handbook of Shakespeare and Early Modern Drama: Perspectives on Culture, Performance and Identity*, London: The Arden Shakespeare.

Dower, J. and P. Langdale (2022), *Performing for Motion Capture: A Guide for Practitioners,* London: Methuen Drama.

Dresner, D. (2018), *A Life-coaching Approach to Screen Acting,* London: Methuen Drama.

Dudeck, T. R. (2013), *Keith Johnstone: A Critical Biography*, London: Methuen Drama.

Bibliography

Dugan, H. (2013), '"To Bark with Judgment": Playing Baboon in Early Modern England', *Shakespeare Studies* 41: 77–93.

Edward, M. and S. Farrier (2020), 'Drag: Applying Foundation and Setting the Scene', in M. Edward and S. Farrier (eds), *Contemporary Drag Practices & Performers: Drag in a Changing Scene: Volume 1*, 1–18, London: Methuen Drama.

Elsam, P. (2011), *Acting Characters: 20 Essential Steps from Rehearsal to Performance*, London: Methuen Drama.

Ewan, V. and D. Green (2015), *Actor Movement: Expression of the Physical Being: A Movement Handbook for Actors*, London: Methuen Drama.

Falco, R. (2018), 'Suspense Revisited: The Shared Experience of Time', in L. Shohet (ed.), *Temporality, Genre and Experience in the Age of Shakespeare: Forms of Time*, 43–56, London: The Arden Shakespeare.

Finburgh, C. (2015), 'Nettles in the Rose Garden: Ecocentrism in Jean Genet's Theatre', in C. Lavery and C. Finburgh (eds), *Rethinking the Theatre of the Absurd: Ecology, the Environment and the Greening of the Modern Stage*, 191–217, London: Methuen Drama.

Findlay, A. (2014), *Women in Shakespeare: A Dictionary*, London: The Arden Shakespeare.

Finlay-Johnson, H. (1911), *The Dramatic Method of Teaching*, London: Nisbet.

Flaubert, G. (1976), *Bouvard and Pécuchet*, Harmondsworth: Penguin.

Fleming, C. (2020), '"Theatre of the Future": Chekhov Technique for Devised Theatre and Catalyst Direction', in C. Fleming and T. Cornford (eds), *Michael Chekhov Technique in the Twenty-First Century: New Pathways*, London: Methuen Drama.

Fletcher, J. (2022), *Classical Greek Tragedy*, London: Methuen Drama.

Fragkou, M. (2019), *Ecologies of Precarity in Twenty-First Century Theatre: Politics, Affect, Responsibility*, London: Methuen Drama.

Funk, W. (2015), *The Literature of Reconstruction: Authentic Fiction in the New Millennium*, London: Bloomsbury.

Gillett, J. (2014), *Acting Stanislavski: A Practical Guide to Stanislavski's Approach and Legacy*, London: Methuen Drama.

Gonsalves, A. and T. Irish (2021), *Shakespeare and Meisner: A Practical Guide for Actors, Directors, Students and Teachers*, London: The Arden Shakespeare.

Grae, J. (2024), "Glitching" of Gender and Temporality in *Lift* (2013)', in C. Chandler and G. Gowland (eds), *Contemporary British Musicals: 'Out of the Darkness'*, 53–62, London: Methuen Drama.

Grochala, S. (2017), *The Contemporary Political Play: Rethinking Dramaturgical Structure*, London: Methuen Drama.

Gutekunst, C. and J. Gillett (2014), *Voice into Acting: Integrating Voice and the Stanislavski Approach*, London: Methuen Drama.

Harriman-Smith, J. (2024), *What Would Garrick Do? Or, Acting Lessons from the Eighteenth Century*, London: Methuen Drama.

Hetzler, E. (2007), 'Actors and Emotion in Performance', *Studies in Theatre and Performance*, 28 (1): 59–78.

Hodge, A., ed. (2000), *Twentieth Century Actor Training*, New York and London: Routledge.

Hoenselaars, T. (2012), 'Introduction', in T. Hoenselaars (ed.), *Shakespeare and the Language of Translation*, rev. edn, 1–28. London: Methuen Drama.

Homan, S. and B. Rhinehart (2017), *Comedy Acting for Theatre: The Art and Craft of Performing in Comedies*, London: Methuen Drama.

Howard, J. E. (1994), *The Stage and Social Struggle in Early Modern England*, New York: Routledge.

Howe, E. (1992), *The First English Actresses: Women and Drama, 1660–1700*, Cambridge: Cambridge University Press.

Hume, D. (1998), *An Enquiry Concerning Human Understanding,* Oxford: Clarendon Press.
Hume, D. (2007), *A Dissertation on the Passions; The Natural History of Religion,* Oxford: Clarendon Press.
Hume, D. (2007), *A Treatise of Human Nature, Vol. 1: The Text,* Oxford: Clarendon Press.
Hurley, E. (2010), *Theatre and Feeling,* Basingstoke: Palgrave Macmillan.
Hutchins, E. (2010), 'Cognitive Ecology', *Topics in Cognitive Science* 2 (4): 705–15.
Jacono, V. (2016), 'Introduction: Complexity, Cognition, and the Actor's Pedagogy', in C. Falletti, G. Sofia and V. Jacono (eds), *Theatre and Cognitive Neuroscience,* 103–116. London: Methuen Drama.
Jans, E. (2020), 'Bernadetje, Catastrophes and Gestures', in C. Stalpaert, G. Cools and H.D. Vuyst (eds), *The Choreopolitics of Alain Platel's les ballets C de la B: Emotions, Gestures, Politics,* 145–54, London: Methuen Drama.
Jardine, L. ([1983] 1989), *Still Harping on Daughters: Women and Drama in the Age of Shakespeare,* 2nd edn, New York: Columbia University Press.
Johnston, K. (2016), *Disability Theatre and Modern Drama: Recasting Modernism,* London: Bloomsbury Methuen Drama.
Johnstone, K. (1981), *Impro: Improvisation and the Theatre,* London: Methuen Drama.
Kaynar, G. (2014), 'Textual Dramaturgy and Dramaturg-as-Text: Traditional versus New Dramaturgy in the Era of German Post-Dramatic Theatre', in A. Citron, S. Aronson-Lehavi and D. Zerbib (eds), *Performance Studies in Motion: International Perspectives and Practices in the Twenty-First Century,* 86-102, London: Methuen Drama.
Konijn, E. (2000), *Acting Emotions: Shaping Emotions on Stage,* Amsterdam: Amsterdam University Press.
Krumholz, B. (2023), *Why Do Actors Train?: Embodiment for Theatre Makers and Thinkers,* London: Methuen Drama.
Kumiega, J. (1985), *The Theatre of Grotowski,* London: Methuen.
Lambropoulos, V. (2001), 'Syncretism as Mixture and as Method', *Journal of Modern Greek Studies,* 19(2): 221–35.
Latour, B. (1990), 'Om aktor-netvaerksteroi. Nogle fa afklaringer og mere end nogle fa forviklinger', *Philosophia,* 25 (3–4): 47–64.
Lavery, C. (2019), 'How Does Theatre Think Through Ecology?', in M. Bleeker, A. Kear, J. Kelleher and H. Roms (eds), *Thinking Through Theatre and Performance,* 257–69, London: Methuen Drama.
Lehmann, H.-T. (2011), 'Wie politisch ist Postdramatisches Theater?', in J. Deck and A. Sieburg (eds), *Politisch Theater Machen. Neue Artikulationen des Politischen in den darstellenden Künsten,* Bielefeld: Transcript.
Lehmann, H.-T. (2006), *Postdramatic Theatre,* Abingdon and London: Routledge.
Levi, J. (2021), '"Es wird Leib, es empfindet": Auto-Affection, Doubt, and the Philosopher's Hands,' in R. Aumiller (ed.), *A Touch of Doubt: On Haptic Scepticism,* 31–56, Berlin: De Gruyter.
Lotina, G. P. and T. Aiolfi, eds (2023). *Performing Left Populism: Performance, Politics and the People,* London: Methuen Drama.
Lovelock, J. (2019), '"What About Love?" Claiming and Reclaiming LGBTQ+ Spaces', in S. Whitfield (ed.), *Reframing the Musical: Race, Culture, and Identity,* 187–211, London: Red Globe Press.
Malaev-Babel, A. (2011), *The Vakhtangov Sourcebook,* Abingdon: Routledge.
Malaev-Babel, A. (2019), 'Yevgeny Vakhtangov: The Future Head of the Russian Theatre', in A. Skinner (ed.), *Russian Theatre in Practice: The Director's Guide,* 61–78, London: Methuen Drama.
Mamet, D. ([1997] 1999) *True and False,* London: Vintage.

Bibliography

Marsalek, K. (2018), '"Whose Head's That Then?": Head-tricks, Bed-tricks and Theatrics in *The Revenger's Tragedy*', in G. E. Minton (ed.), *The Revenger's Tragedy: The State of Play*, 183–204, London: The Arden Shakespeare.

Marsden, S. (2019), *100 Acting Exercises for 8–18 Year Olds*, London: Methuen Drama.

Marshall, L. (2001), *The Body Speaks*, London: Methuen Drama.

Matthews, J. (2011), *Training for Performance*, London: Methuen Drama.

Matthews, J. (2014), *Anatomy of Performance Training*, London: Methuen Drama.

Matthews, J. (2019), *The Life of Training*, London: Methuen Drama.

Matthews, J. and D. Torevell, eds. (2011), *A Life of Ethics and Performance: Liverpool Hope University Studies in Ethics Book 6*, Newcastle Upon Tyne: CSP.

McAllister-Viel, T. (2009), '(Re)considering the Role of Breath in Training Actors' Voices: Insights from Dahnjeon Breathing and the Phenomena of Breath,' *Theatre Topics*, 19 (2): 165–80.

McAllister-Viel, T. (2016), 'The Role of "Presence" in Training Actors' Voices', *Theatre, Dance and Performance Training*, 7 (3): 438–52.

McAllister-Viel, T. (2019), *Training Actors' Voices: Towards an Intercultural/Interdisciplinary Approach*, New York: Routledge.

McCaw, D. (2017), *Training the Actor's Body: A Guide*, London: Methuen Drama.

McCaw, D. (2020), *Rethinking the Actor's Body: Dialogues with Neuroscience*, London: Methuen Drama.

McLeish, K. (2011), *A Guide to Greek Theatre and Drama*, London: Methuen Drama.

McMullan, G., L. C. Orlin and V. M. Vaughan, eds. (2014) *Women Making Shakespeare: Text, Reception, Performance*, London: The Arden Shakespeare.

Meg, U. and G. Mumford (2013), 'Postdramatic Reality Theatre and Productive Insecurity: Destabilising Encounters with the Unfamiliar in Theatre from Sydney and Berlin', in K. Jürs-Munby, J. Carroll and S. Giles (eds), *Postdramatic Theatre and the Political: International Perspectives on Contemporary Performance*, London: Methuen Drama.

Meisner, S. and D. Longwell (1987), *Sanford Meisner on Acting*, New York: Vintage Books.

Merleau-Ponty, M. (1964), *The Primacy of Perception*, Evanston, IL: Northwestern University Press.

Miller, S. M. (2020), 'Topdog/Underdog by Suzan-Lori Parks', in M. M. Chirico and K. Younger (eds), *How to Teach a Play: Essential Exercises for Popular Plays*, 281–3, London: Methuen Drama.

Mons, A. (2024), *Spectatorship and the Real in French Contemporary Theatre*, London: Methuen Drama.

Moran, M. (2021), 'Keywords as Method', *European Journal of Cultural Studies*, 24 (4): 1021–9.

Morris, E. (2017), *Rhythm in Acting and Performance: Embodied Approaches and Understandings*, London: Methuen Drama.

Mouffe, C. (2013), *Agonistics: Thinking the World Politically*, London: Verso.

Murphy, B. (2014), *The Theatre of Tennessee Williams*, Critical Companions, London: Methuen Drama.

Orgel, S. (1997), *Impersonations: The Performance of Gender in Shakespeare's England*, Cambridge: Cambridge University Press.

Owen, L. (2014), 'The Witness and the Replay: London Bubble', in C. McAvinchey (ed.), *Performance and Community: Commentary and Case Studies*, London: Methuen Drama.

Paget, D. (2018), 'Truth and "Truthiness" in Acting the Real', in T. Cantrell and C. Hogg (eds), *Exploring Television Acting*, 110–24, London: Bloomsbury Publishing.

Palfrey, S. (2011), *Doing Shakespeare*, London: The Arden Shakespeare.

Paterson, E. (2015), *The Contemporary American Monologue: Performance and Politics*, London: Methuen Drama.

Pitches, J. and S. Aquilina, eds (2017), *Stanislavsky in the World: The System and its Transformations Across Continents*, London: Methuen Drama.

Primavesi, P. (2011), 'Theater/Politik – Kontexte und Beziehungen', in J. Deck and A. Sieburg (eds), *Politisch Theater Machen. Neue Artikulationen des Politischen in den darstellenden Künsten*, 49, Bielefeld: Transcript.

Quigley, K. (2020), *Performing the Unstageable: Success, Imagination and Failure*, London: Bloomsbury.

Raber, K. (2018), *Shakespeare and Posthumanist Theory*, London: The Arden Shakespeare.

Raber, K. and K. L. Edwards (2022), *Shakespeare and Animals: A Dictionary*, London: The Arden Shakespeare.

Rea, K. (2021), *The Outstanding Actor: Seven Keys to Success*, 2nd edn, London: Methuen Drama.

Read, A. (2013), *Theatre in the Expanded Field: Seven Approaches to Performance*, London: Methuen Drama.

Reid, T. (2017), *The Theatre of Anthony Neilson*, London: Methuen Drama.

Reynolds, P. M. (2019), *Performing Shakespeare's Women: Playing*, London: The Arden Shakespeare.

Roach, J. (1993), *The Player's Passion: Studies in the Science of Acting*, Ann Arbor, MI: University of Michigan Press.

Robbins, H. T. (2024), "Something Precious You Don't Simply Give Away": Intersections of Love and Queer Expression in *Everybody's Talking About Jamie*', in C. Chandler and G. Gowland (eds), *Contemporary British Musicals: 'Out of the Darkness'*, 125–36, London: Methuen Drama.

Robbins, J. S. (2019), *The Actor's Survival Guide: How to Make Your Way in Hollywood*, London: Methuen Drama.

Rodenburg, P. (2015), *The Right to Speak: Working with the Voice*, London: Methuen Drama.

Rodenburg, P. (2018), *The Need for Words: Voice and the Text*, London: Methuen Drama.

Rodenburg, P. (2019), *The Actor Speaks: Voice and the Performer*, London: Methuen Drama.

Rodosthenous, G., ed. (2017), *Contemporary Adaptations of Greek Tragedy: Auteurship and Directorial Visions*, London: Methuen Drama.

Rushe, S. (2019), *Michael Chekhov's Acting Technique: A Practitioner's Guide*, London: Methuen Drama.

Sabatier, A. (2017), *Shakespeare and Visual Culture: A Dictionary*, London: Arden Shakespeare.

Salinsky, T. and D. Frances-White (2017), *The Improv Handbook: The Ultimate Guide to Improvising in Comedy, Theatre, and Beyond*, London: Methuen Drama.

Salter, C. (2020), 'Performance in the Age of the Technosphere', in B. Ferdman and J. Stokic (eds), *The Methuen Drama Companion to Performance Art*, London: Methuen Drama.

Sánchez, J. A. (2022), *The Bodies of Others: Essays on Ethics and Representation*, London: Methuen Drama.

Schneider, R. (1997), 'Review of the Book: The Death of Character: Perspectives on Theater After Modernism', *Theatre Journal*, 49(4): 541–3.

Schulze, D. (2017), *Authenticity in Contemporary Theatre and Performance*, London: Bloomsbury.

Scott, C., ed. (2024), *Shakespeare / Nature: Contemporary Readings in the Human and Non-human*, London: The Arden Shakespeare.

Scruton, R. (2017), *Coleridge and Contemplation*, Oxford: Oxford University Press.

Serrano, R. (2017), 'A Teacher's Perspective: Stanislavsky at the Escuela de Teatro de Buenos Aires in Argentina', in J. Pitches and S. Aquilina (eds), *Stanislavsky in the World: The System and its Transformations Across Continents*, 261–8, London: Methuen Drama.

Shaughnessy, N. (2012), *Applying Performance: Live Art, Socially Engaged Theatre and Effective Practice*, Basingstoke: Palgrave Macmillan.

Shaughnessy, N. and P. Barnard, eds. (2019), *Performing Psychologies: Imagination, Creativity and Dramas of the Mind*, London: Bloomsbury.

Bibliography

Sierz, A. and L. Ghilardi (2021), *The Time Traveller's Guide to British Theatre: The First Four Hundred Years,* London: Methuen Drama.

Skinner, A., ed. (2019), *Russian Theatre in Practice: The Director's Guide,* London: Methuen Drama.

Snow, J. (2012), *Movement Training for Actors,* London: Methuen Drama.

Sofia, G. (2016), 'Introduction: Towards an Embodied Theatrology?', in C. Falletti, G. Sofia and V. Jacono (eds), *Theatre and Cognitive Neuroscience,* London: Methuen Drama.

Spatz, B. (2015), *What a Body Can Do: Technique as Knowledge, Practice as Research*, London: Routledge.

Stafford, M. B. (2017), 'From Communicable Matter to Incommunicable "Stuff": Extreme Combinatorics and the Return of Ineffability', in T. D. Knepper and L. E. Kalmanson (eds), *Ineffability: An Exercise in Comparative Philosophy of Religion*, 9–27, Cham: Springer International.

Staniewski, W. and A. Hodge (2004), *Hidden Territories: The Theatre of Gardzienice*, New York and London: Routledge.

Stanislavski, K. (1980), *An Actor Prepares*, London: Methuen.

Stanislavski, K. ([1936] 2009), *An Actor's Work*, London: Routledge.

Stinespring, L. M. (2000), 'Just Be Yourself: Derrida, Difference and the Meisner Technique', in D. Krasner (ed.), *Method Acting Reconsidered*, New York: St Martin's Press.

Streeton, J. and P. Raymond (2014), *Singing on Stage: An Actor's Guide,* London: Methuen Drama.

Sutton, J. and K. Bicknell, eds (2022), *Collaborative Embodied Performance: Ecologies of Skill,* London: Methuen Drama.

Tait, P. (2021), *Theory for Theatre Studies: Emotion,* London: Methuen Drama.

Thompson, A. (1996), 'Women / "Women" and the Stage', in H. Wilcox (ed.), *Women and Literature in Britain 1500–1700*, 100–16, Cambridge: University of Cambridge Press.

Tint, B. (2018), 'From Hell, No to Yes, And: Applied Improvisation for Training in Conflict Resolution, Mediation, and Law', in T. R. Dudeck and C. McClure (eds), *Applied Improvisation: Leading, Collaborating, and Creating Beyond the Theatre*, 199–220, London: Methuen Drama.

Trencsényi, K. (2015), *Dramaturgy in the Making: A User's Guide for Theatre Practitioners,* London: Methuen Drama.

Tribble, E. B. and J. Sutton (2013), 'Introduction: Interdisciplinarity and Cognitive Approaches to Performance', in N. Shaughnessy (ed.), *Affective Performance and Cognitive Science: Body, Brain and Being*, London: Methuen Drama.

Trivedi, P. (2022), 'The "Woman's Part": Recovering the Contribution of Women to the Circulation of Shakespeare in India', in T. Buckley, M. T. Burnett, S. Datta and R. García-Periago (eds), *Women and Indian Shakespeares,* 21–42. London: The Arden Shakespeare.

Unwin, S. (2005), 'Key Concepts of Brecht's Theatrical Theory', in *A Guide to the Plays of Bertolt Brecht,* London: Methuen Drama.

Watson, D. (2024), *Theatre with a Purpose: Amateur Drama in Britain 1919–1949*, London: Methuen Drama.

Welton, M. (2012), *Feeling Theatre*, Basingstoke: Palgrave Macmillan.

Willett, J. (1998), *Brecht in Context: Comparative Approaches*, London: Methuen Drama.

Williams, R. (1975), *Keywords: A Vocabulary of Culture and Society*, London: Fontana.

Wooster, R. (2016), *Theatre in Education in Britain: Origins, Development and Influence*, London: Methuen Drama.

Zarrilli, P. B. (2009), *Psychophysical Acting*, London: Routledge.

Zarrilli, P. B. (2020), *(Toward) A Phenomenology of Acting*, London: Routledge.